Name of School	Post card sent 9/8	information received
- ~~Barrie School~~	✓	
✓ - FIELD School	✓	* ✓
- ~~Mcdonogh Sch.~~	✓	✓
- ~~Parkmont Sch.~~	✓	✓
- ~~Queen Anne Sch.~~	✓	✓
✓ - St. Anselm's Abbey	✓	more to come.
~~St. Johns College High school~~	✓	✓
~~St. Stephens & St Agnes school.~~	✓ ~~resent~~	✓
r - Sandy Spring Friends	✓	* ✓

WASHINGTON AREA PRIVATE SCHOOLS

A complete guide to independent schools in and around Washington, D.C. including a directory of local Educational Specialists and Counselors.

INDEPENDENT SCHOOL GUIDES CHEVY CHASE, MARYLAND

Lois H. Coerper Shirley W. Mersereau

Additional copies may be obtained @ $12.95 (add $2.00 for mailing) from

Independent School Guides
7315 Brookville Road
Chevy Chase, Maryland 20815
(301) 986-5370
or
652-8635, 986-0698

Published in the United States of America

FOREWORD

With the growing pressures for quality education, independent schools in the Washington area have become of vital interest to an increasing number of parents. Prior to the publication of our first edition of The Independent School Guide in 1971, there was no single source of information about the more than 300 elementary and secondary schools in the area. Now in our ninth printing, we are even more aware of the variety of school choices available to parents at all levels of education.

The guide sets forth a concise, factual and comprehensive listing of non-public schools serving the normal child in grades 1 through 12. It does not include pre-schools with no primary grades nor schools with curriculum directed exclusively towards children with severe handicaps: for assistance in this area contact IPACHI:

Information, Protection & Advocacy Center for Handicapped Individuals
4455 Connecticut Avenue, N. W., Washington, D. C. 20008; phone (202) 966-8081.

This Guide also includes some Catholic Parochial elementary schools which generally welcome non-parish and non-Catholic students; a more complete list of these schools is available from the local Catholic Diocesan Offices (see following page).

The Independent School Guide includes as much information on the student body, faculty, and special programs offered by the various schools as it was possible to secure from interviews, brochures, and our own questionnaire. The facts reported are, of course, subject to yearly change although provision was made for schools to announce planned changes in plant or programs. Also included is useful information on summer programs (recreational and academic), as well as Day Care (Extended Day).

We are most grateful for the enthusiastic support of the school community, including teachers, administrators, and counselors; we also would like to express a special thank you to The Association of Independent Schools of Greater Washington for their ongoing cooperation. We hope that this directory will continue to be a valuable aid to them as well as to parents seeking the best placement for their individual child.

For those parents who are seeking professional advice and counseling, a brief description of some Washington area Educational Specialists can be found immediately following the last school in the back of this book.

Lois H. Coerper

Shirley W. Mersereau

Scholarship Aid is available at most of the larger independent schools and many smaller ones. Some schools have funds specifically designated for scholarships. Many schools allow tuition reductions for more than one family child enrolled. In certain instances when a child has not been able to perform in the public setting state/local jurisdictions may fund part of the private school costs. The Black Student Fund provides extensive counseling for black parents and students seeking scholarship aid; they also provide some funding for scholarships. It is always appropriate to inquire about scholarship aid or some form of financial assistance when contacting an independent school. Most of these schools seek a broad economic and ethnic student body.

Black Student Fund: 3636 16th Street N.W., Suite AG 19, Washington, D.C. 20010. (202- 387-1414).

Catholic Archdiocese Office of Education for D.C. and Maryland:
5001 Eastern Avenue, Hyattsville, MD.; P.O. Box 29260, Washington, D.C. 20017. (301-853-3800).
For Northern Virginia: Diocese of Arlington (703-841-2519)

Montessori Institute: 2119 S Street, N.W., Washington, D.C. 20008 (202-387-8020).

Association of Independent Schools of Greater Washington (AISGW): Executive Director: Ritalou Harris, P.O. Box 9956, Washington, D.C. 20016. (202-537-1114)

National Association of Independent Schools (NAIS): 1620 L Street, N.W., Washington, D.C. 20036. (202-833-4757); Boarding Schools and Summer Program Directories: 1-800-541-5908

Washington Small Schools, 4894 16th Street N.W., Washington, D. C. 20011 or Ron McClain (202) 762-0740.

ABBREVIATIONS

ACE..............Accelerated Christian Education Program
AP............... Advanced Placement
ESL..............English as a Second Language
IPS............. Introductory Physical Science
K............... Kindergarten
N............... Nursery
PG............... Post Graduate
Req............. Required
SAT..............Scholastic Aptitude Test
SRA..............Scientific Research Association
SSAT...........Secondary School Admission Test
LD/ED..........Learning Disability/Emotionally Disturbed

ACADEMIC ENRICHMENT CENTER PREPARATORY SCHOOL..........(202) 829-2429

6119 Georgia Avenue N.W., Washington, D.C. 20011
Founded 1977 **Head**: Ms. C. Lillette Green-Campbell B.A., M.Ed.

Grades: N-8 **Enrollment**: 170 Co-ed **Faculty**: 13 full-, 5 part-time.
Average Class Size: 15.

Special Courses: Spanish Pre K-7. Sign Language PreK-7. Pre-Algebra, Computer. General Science. History Studies include American, European, African, and African American Heritage. Remedial Reading and Math. Art, Music, Chorus, Drum Corps, Majorettes, African Dance Troupe. **Extended Day**: 6:30 a.m.-6:30 p.m.

Athletics: P.E. req. Intramural Soccer; Tennis, Basketball. **Clubs**: Cooking, Sewing, Drama, Crafts, Computer. **Publications**: Yearbook, Newspaper. **Community Involvement**: Inter-generational interaction, students grade 5 and above must perform 6 hours per tri-mester of community service.

Plant: Library 3,500 vol., Language Lab, Science Labs, Art Studio, Playing Fields.

Admission: Entrance exam March-June by appointment; Interview with parent and child; School Day Visit by child.

Tuition: (1993-94) N & K, $3,500; 1-8, $3,850; includes Lunch. Books: Extra
Dress Code: Uniform req. K-7 **Scholarship Aid**: Available .

Future Plans: Plan to build and occupy new building on Quackenbos St N.W. within 5 years.

Summer Program: Academic: SOAR (Summer Opportunities for Advancement and Reinforcement) Reading, Math, & Language; 5 weeks. Summer Camp: Swimming, music, sign language, life skills, study hour, field trips, sports, overnight camping. Similar, slower paced pre-school activities.

ACADEMY OF THE HOLY CROSS........... (301) 942-2100

4920 Strathmore Avenue, Kensington, MD. 20895.
Catholic 1868. **Head**: Sister Katherine Kase, CSC.

Grades: 9-12. **Enrollment**: 416 Girls. **Faculty**: 40 full-, 2 part-time.
Average Class Size: 18.

Special Courses: Latin I-IV, French I-V, Spanish I-V, Math through AP Calculus, Computer Skills-Introd. & Advanced BASIC. Science Physical Science, Biology, Chemistry, Physics, Physiology, Environmental Science, Independent Study Science, Psychology. History- World, Asian and Latin American Studies, U. S. History, American Gov't, World History. Religious Studies req. Art, Music, Speech. Note: Each senior participates in a three week off- campus internship program which is overseen and evaluated (on completion) by a school coordinator. AP.: French, Biology, Chemistry, Calculus, English, American History.

Athletics: Not required. Interscholastic: Field Hockey, Soccer, Lacrosse, Tennis, Basketball, Volleyball, Track, Softball, Swimming, Diving. **Clubs:** French, Spanish, Latin, Amnesty International, SADD, Drama. EARTH, Black Student Assn., Cheerleading, Equestrian, Golf, Archery, National Honor Society, Student Senate. **Publications**: Literary Magazine, Newspaper, Yearbook. **Community Involvement**: Each grade is involved in ongoing Service Projects.

Plant: Library 10,000 vol.; Science Labs, Art Studio, Auditorium, Gym, Playing Fields, Computer Lab, Chapel, Cafeteria.

Admission: Archdiocese Test, Transcript, Recommendations; Transfer students must have Interview; school visit for prospective 9th graders is recommended but not required.

Tuition: (1993-94) $5,700. Books: $200 Activities Fee: $100 *Dress Code* Uniform Req. **Financial Aid**. Some available.

Summer Program: Basketball camp.

ACCOTINK ACADEMY..........(703) 451-8041

8519 Tuttle Road, Springfield, VA. 22152.
Founded 1963. **Head**: Mrs. Elaine McConnell.
Educational Director: Mrs. Julia Warden

Ungraded: Ages 6-20 for LD/ED students. **Enrollment**: 104 Co-ed. **Faculty**: 65 full-time; 4 psychologists, 5 speech pathologists, 2 art therapists, 3 occupational therapists, physical education director. **Average Class Size**: 10 students/3 teachers.

Special Courses: One of the primary goals is the re-establishment of a good self-image. Program is structured but ungraded so each child may progress at own rate without undue pressure. Reading, Math, and Perceptual Skills are developed through individualized programs, while language arts provide group work experience. Oral classrooms provided for Science, Social Studies & History. In addition to regular classroom, school offers intensive services: psychiatric consultation, language, physical and occupational therapy. Art therapy; individual and group counseling.

Athletics: Full-time adaptive program with special emphasis placed on perceptual motor activities.

Plant: Library, Multi-purpose Room, Observation Rooms for Doctors & Educators. Testing Facilities.

Admission: Referral through local area school systems. Generally referred by local agencies.

Tuition: Call for information. Lunch: Bring. **Transportation** & **Financial Aid**: Available.

AIDAN MONTESSORI SCHOOL..........(202) 966-0360

3100 Military Road, N.W., Washington, D.C. 20015
Founded 1961. **Administrator**: Marsha Donnelly

Ungraded: N-age 9. **Enrollment**: 136 Co-ed. **Faculty**: 8 full-, 11 part- time.
Average Class Size: 25.

Special Courses: Association of Montessori Internationale ; Montessori program with integrated curriculum in major subject areas (specialty teachers): Spanish, Art, Music, Computer (elementary level), and Great Books (elementary level). Mixed aged classes, 18-30 months, 3-6 yrs., 6-9+yrs. **Extended Day**: 7:30 a.m.-6:30 p.m.

Athletics: P.E.; Program offered for ages 5-9+

Plant: Library, Playground, Art Room.

Admission: Rolling admissions; follow AISGW guidelines. Interview parent and child required. Class Observation and attendance at Open House recommended.

Tuition: (1993-94) $2,061-$6,670 ; reduced rates for siblings. **Transportation**: Available
Scholarship Aid: Some available after first year of enrollment

Future Plans: To move to own building

Summer Programs: Art Summer- ages 3-10; includes studio art, music, creative dramatics, dance.

ALEPH-BET JEWISH DAY SCHOOL..........(410) 263-9044

1125 Spa Road, Annapolis, MD 21403
1989 Jewish-Community **Head** : Leslie Rosen, M.A.

Grades: K(full day)- grade 5. **Enrollment**: 45 Co-ed **Faculty**: 4 full-, 1 part-time.
Average Class Size: 10

Special Courses: Traditional, rigorous elementary school curriculum enriched by daily prayer, Hebrew and Judaic classes, full Judaic and general curriculum.. Bi-lingual Hebrew.
Extended Day: As needed.

Athletics: Various sports, Israeli Folk Dancing.

Admission: Rolling admission; call school for further information.

Tuition: $4,000 **Financial Aid**: Available

Future Plans: 1995 begin building

Summer Programs: Summer camp on premises.

ALEXANDRIA COUNTRY DAY SCHOOL ....(703) 548-4804

2400 Russell Rd., Alexandria, VA. 22301
Founded 1983 **Head**: Dr. Joan Barton

Grades: K-8 **Enrollment**: 181 Co-ed **Faculty**: 18 full-, 6 part- time.
Average Class Size: 12

Special Programs: Spanish K-8. Algebra, Geometry, Computer. General Science, Biology, Earth and Space. History- U.S., Ancient, Medieval, Virginia. Note: Kingsbury Center tutor for special needs students. Art, Music, Drama & Public Speaking; Band, Chorus. After-school Enrichment Program. **Extended Day**: 7 :30 a.m.- 6 p.m.

Athletics: Req. all grades. Soccer, Basketball, Softball, Field Hockey. **Clubs**: Art, Drama, Student Council. **Publications**: Yearbook, Newspaper. **Community Involvement:** School Chorus performs for Senior Citizen groups and for the town; students participate in fund raising for local charities.

Plant: Library, Computer Lab, Science Lab, Art Studio, Gym, Auditorium. Playing Field.

Admission: School Visit, Interview, Testing.

Tuition: (1993-94) $3,100-$6,700. Lunch: Extra Books: $175 *Dress Code*: Neat, Clean, No "Message" T Shirts, Shirts tucked in, No shorts, K-4; Grades 5-8, Uniform shirts & sweaters **Financial Aid**: Some available.

Future Plans: Possible expansion to 300 students.

Summer Program: Summer activities/camp program

ANNAPOLIS AREA CHRISTIAN SCHOOL............(410) 266-8251

716 Bestgate Road, Annapolis, MD. 21401.
Non-denominational Christian 1971. **Head**: Ron Whipple

Grades: K-12. **Enrollment**: 650 Co-ed. **Faculty**: 40 full-, 3 part time.
Average Class Size: 26.

Special Courses: French and Spanish 8-12. Math through Calculus. Science Gen'l Science, Biology, Chemistry, Physics, Anatomy, Physiology. History-Ancient, World, U.S., Gov't, Maryland, World Geography. Religious Studies req. Typing, Band, Art, Music, Drama. Learning Disability Program. **Extended Day** 7:30 a.m.-5:30 p.m.

Athletics: Req.; Intramural & Interscholastic: Soccer, Softball, Baseball, Basketball, Cheerleading, Wrestling, Golf. Publications: Yearbook, Newspaper. Clubs: Activities vary.

Plant: Library 11,000 vol., Gym, Use of nearby Playing Fields.

Admission: Interview; Testing and/or Transcripts.

Tuition: (1993-94) Half-day K, $2,300; K-12, $3,000- $3,924. **Transportation**: Available from select areas. *Dress Code*: Uniform req. **Financial Aid**: Available.

Future Plans: To build new Gym facility by 1994.

ANNUNCIATION SCHOOL..........(202) 362-1408

3825 Klingle Place, N.W., Washington, D.C. 20016
(Corner of 39th and Massachusetts Avenue, N.W.)
Catholic 1954. **Head**: Sister Joan Rigney, SHCJ

Grades: K-8. **Enrollment**: 200 Co-ed. **Faculty**: 12 full-6 part-time: Aides in Primary Department 2 full-time, 1 part-time. **Average Class Size**: 25

Special Courses: Spanish 7-8. Enrichment Math courses, 4-8; Algebra 8, Computer. English Language Center. Art, Music. Religious Studies req. Science Fair grades 4-8.
Extended Day: 3 p.m.- 6 p.m.

Athletics: P.E. req.; Intramural Basketball. CYO Basketball, Softball, Baseball, Soccer.

Plant: Library, Science Lab, Art Room, Computer Room, Gym, Auditorium, Church.

Admission: Parent Tour/Interview, Child Visits for half day; Transcripts and Recommendations $20 fee; Testing.

Tuition: (1993 -1994) K-$2,550. Grades 1-8, In-Parish $2,050; Out-of-Parish $2,550. Discount for siblings. *Dress Code*: Uniform req. 1-8. Lunch: Bring. Books and Activity Fees: $275 (Discount for siblings).

ANTIOCH CHRISTIAN SCHOOL......(410) 757-5000

1535 Ritchie Highway, Arnold, MD. 21012
Head: Alice Wright.

Grades: age 2 1/2- grade 12 **Enrollment**: 130 Co-ed

Special Programs: **Extended Day**: 7:30 a.m.-5 p.m.

Tuition: (1993-94) $1,600 grade 1-12.

APPLE TREE SCHOOL...........(703) 281-2626 or 281-7747

712 Tapawingo Road, S.E., Vienna, VA 22180
9655 Blake Lane, Fairfax, VA 22031
Head: Mrs. Klaasen

Grades: N3-grade 3. **Enrollment**: 165 Co-ed

Special Programs: **Extended Day**: 7 a.m.-6 p.m.

Tuition: (1993-94) Half-day, $70/wk.; Full day $112/wk.

AQUINAS MONTESSORI SCHOOL ....(703) 780-8484

8334 Mount Vernon Highway, Alexandria, VA. 22309
Founded 1966. **Head**: Mrs. Kathleen Futrell.

Grades: Ungraded age 2 1/2 to 12. **Enrollment**: 175 Co-ed. **Average Class Size**: 25
Faculty : 7 full, 9 part-time.

Special Courses: French K-6, German 1-6, Art, Music. Science, Geography. Great Books Discussion Program. Drama. **Extended Day**: Call for information.

Athletics: Required-grades 1-6.

Plant: Library, Science Lab, Swimming Pool, Playing Fields.

Admission: Evaluation Test for elementary; Interview; $45 Application fee.

Tuition: (1993-1994) K 1/2 day, $3,150; K full day, $3,744; 1-6, $4,257 Lunch: Bring
Extended Day: Extra **Transportation**: round trip $1,215. *Dress Code:* Uniform req.

Summer Program: 8 weeks - ages 2 1/2- 7 (hours 9 a.m.-12:30 p.m.) Transportation available; Swimming instruction, nature study, music, folk singing. Experience with many forms of creative art media. Opportunity to work with Montessori manipulative learning materials; field trips, sports and organized games.

ARCHBISHOP CARROLL HIGH SCHOOL...........(202) 529-0900

4300 Harewood Road, N.E., Washington, D.C. 20017.
Catholic 1951. **Head**: Mrs. Wilma Durham

Grades: 9-12. **Enrollment**: 700 Co-ed. **Faculty**: 45 full-, 3 part-time.
Average Class Size: 20.

Special Courses: Latin 9-10, French 10-12, Spanish 10-12; Science General Science, Biology, Chemistry, Physics, Environmental Science, Ecology, Lab Ass'ts; Math through Calculus; Economics, Accounting; Computer Science. History: U.S. and World, U.S. Government, World Cultures;Psychology; Remedial Reading; Religion req.; Art, Architectural Drawing, Engineering Graphics; Mechanical Drawing; Music, Concert, Band, Orchestra, Typing. Note: Concurrent enrollment with colleges and universities hi/Skip; work study with government agencies. Special education tutoring course with Mamie D. Lee School for students who want to enter the special education field. AP.: English, History, Physics, and Calculus.

Athletics : P.E. Req.; Interscholastic: Football, Basketball, Soccer, Baseball, Wrestling, Tennis. **Clubs**: Swimming, Drama, Cycling, History, Science, Chess, Guitar, Bowling, Film-making, Glee. **Publications**: Yearbook **Community Involvement**: Service at Zacchaeus Community Kitchen, Thanksgiving Food Drive.

Plant: Library 18,000 vol., Science Labs, Art Classroom, Gym, Auditorium, Playing Fields, Computer Lab, Typing Room..

Admission: Non-Catholic elementary school students must register for exams (301-853-3800). Interviews and Recommendation Letter advised.

Tuition: (1993-94) Catholic $3,375; Non-Catholic $3,590. Lunch: Extra Books: Averages $250. **Transportation**: Metro-CUA Station. *Dress Code*: Boys: Shirt, tie, dress pants, & shoes; Girls, Uniform. **Financial Aid** : Available

Summer Program:. Academic Enrichment and repeat credit courses offered. Summer Camp: Band Camp, Football Camp.

ARCHBISHOP SPALDING HIGH SCHOOL..........(410) 969-9105 or (301) 261-2170

8080 New Cut Road, Severn, MD. 21144
Catholic, 1966 **Head**: Mrs. Barbara Schwitzer

Grades 9-12 **Enrollment**: 602 Co-ed **Faculty**: 31 full-, 2 part- time.
Average Class Size: 24

Special Courses: French, Spanish, 9-12, Russian. Math includes Calculus, Computer-Basic Programming, and Programming in Micro-Application and in Micro-Spreadsheets Lotus. Science Biology, Chemistry,Physics, Psychology, Introd. to Life Science, Physical Science, Botany, Zoology, Human Anatomy, & Physiology, Earth Science, Marine Science, and Introd. to Research. History- World, U..S., Introduction to World Geography, Amer. Gov't & Current Issues. Religious Studies required. Remedial Reading & Math, 9-10. Skills courses 9-12. Art- Drawing, Print Making, Ceramics, Art History & Aprreciation, Painting, General Fine Arts. Music- Band, Chorus, Guitar, Music Theory I & II. Home Economics, Childhood Develop. AP: English, Calculus, Biology, U.S.History, Current Events & Gov't., European History. Various Honors Courses; some students may enroll for a course at Anne Arundel Community College.

Athletics: P.E. req.; Interscholastic: Field Hockey, Lacrosse, Ice Hockey, Basketball, Baseball, Softball, Volleyball, Wrestling, Swimming, Golf, Soccer, Football. **Clubs**: Drama, Spanish, French, Health Careers, Black Student Union, Chess, SADD, "Help Our Planet Earth". **Publications**: Yearbook, Literary Magazine. **Community Involvement**: 30 hours of Community Service required during Jr. & Sr. years.

Plant: Library, 11,000 vol.; Science Labs, Art Studio, Gym, Auditorium, Playing Fields, Chapel, Cafeteria, Computer Lab, Home Ec.Labs for Sewing & Cooking.

Admission: Archdiocese Test, Transcript, Teacher Recommendation. $100 Registration fee.

Tuition: (1993-94) $3,800. Lunch, Books, & Transportation: All Extra. *Dress Code*: Uniform req. **Scholarship and Financial Aid**: Available.

Future Plans: Renovation of Outdoor Athletic Facility

Summer Programs: Remedial and Developmental in all disciplines for students grades 10-12; For entering 9th grade students, offerings available in English and Math only.

ARNOLD CHRISTIAN ACADEMY..........(410) 544-1882

804 Windsor Road, Arnold, MD. 21012
Head: Mrs. Joan Harris

Grades: K4-grade 6. **Enrollment**: 50 Co-ed.

Special Courses: ABEKA program. Students work independently at their own pace with a supervisor/teacher in each class to assist as needed. Note: K classes meet only in afternoon; Care provided from 9 a.m.-12:30 p.m. for those K students (if needed). School day ends at 2:30 p.m. on Mondays, 3:30 p.m. other days. **Extended Day**: 7:30 a.m.-Noon

Plant: Library, Math room, Auditorium.

Admission: Interview with Administrator

Tuition: (1993-94) Half-day K, $114/mo; Grades 1-6, $185/mo. *Dress Code*: Uniform req. **Extended Care**: Extra

Future plans: Possible extension of care to 6 p.m.

ASCENSION LUTHERAN SCHOOL..........(301) 577-0500

7420 Ardmore Road, Landover Hills, MD. 20784
Lutheran 1952 **Head**: Jack Bartels

Grades: N-7 **Enrollment**: 200 Co-ed

Special Courses: Music & Art; Religious Studies, req.; P.E. req.; After school programs: Choir, Computer, Drama. **Extended Day Care**: 7 a.m.-6 p.m.

Plant: Library, All- Purpose Room, Playing Fields.
Admission: Interview, Transcript.

Tuition: (1993-94) N3 $75/mo.; N4 $100/mo.; K-7 $2,750. **Extended Day**: Extra

Future Plans: To extend grades through grade 8, 1994.

Summer Camp: Ages 5-12.; 7 a.m.-6 p.m. $70/wk; Summer School: 4 weeks, Remedial & Enrichment Program

ASSUMPTION SCHOOL..........(202) 562-7070

220 High View Place, S. E., Washington, D. C. 20032
Catholic **Head**: Ms. Emma Fleming

Grades: N-8 **Enrollment**: Co-ed

Special Programs: **Extended Day**: 6 a.m.-6 p.m.

Tuition (1993-94) $1,680 **Extended Day**: Extra

ATHOLTON ADVENTIST SCHOOL..........(301) 596-5593

6520 Martin Road, Columbia, MD. 21044
Head: Linda Bates

Grades: PreK-8 **Enrollment**: 80 Co-ed **Extended Day** 7 a.m.-6 p.m.

Tuition: (1993-94) PreK $3,000; K-8, $1,500; K-8 for Non-Adventist, $2,100.

THE BANNER SCHOOL..........(301) 695-9320

1730 N. Market Street, Frederick, MD. 21701
Founded 1982. **Head**: Mr. Michael Mullin

Grades: K-8. **Enrollment**: 130 Co-ed. Faculty: 10 full-, 6 part-time.
Average Class Size: 15.

Special Courses: Spanish K-8, General Science. Music Appreciation, Drama, Photography.
Extended Day: 7:30 a.m.-6 p.m.

Athletics: req. **Clubs**: After school activities-according to interest.

Community Involvement: Annual winter drama based on Frederick 100 years ago as published in newspapers, etc. presented to public. Participation in local charity and historical events.

Plant: Library 1500 vol., Science Labs, Auditorium, Playing Field.
Admission: Interview, Informal Reading Evaluation, grades 1-2. Iowa test of basic skills grades 3-8.

Tuition: (1993-94) Half-day K, $2,108; Full day K, $3,874; 1-3, $4,180; 4-8, $4,396
Extended Day: Extra Books: Extra Lunch: Bring.

Summer Programs: (Age 4-14). Art & Science Day Camp - may include Swimming and Tennis depending on age of child.

BARNESVILLE SCHOOL..........(301) 972-0341

21830 Peach Tree Rd.,(P.O. Box 404) Barnesville, MD. 20838.
Founded 1969. **Head**: Jaralyn L. Hough

Grades: N-6. **Enrollment**: 180 Co-ed. **Faculty** : 13 full-, 9 part-time.
Average Class Size: 15

Special Courses: Strong Basic Skills program, Computers, hands-on Science. Involvement with community service. **Extended Day**: until 6 p.m.

Athletics: Developmental skills program, all grades. **Publications**: Literary magazine.

Plant: Library 6,000 vol., 2 Buildings, 11 acre campus. Playground, Soccer Field.

Admission: $50 Application fee. Transcript; student visits school for one or two days. Preference given to siblings

Tuition: (1993-94) $4,950 includes Books for full day student; **Transportation**: $950 round trip to designated stops. *Dress Code*: Good taste **Financial Aid**: Some available.

Future Plans: Additional of Middle School by 1995

Summer Program: Ages 3-12 - Computers, horseback riding, sports, crafts. 9 a.m.- 4 p.m..

BARRIE SCHOOL..........(301) 871-6200

13500 Layhill Road, Silver Spring, MD 20906
Founded 1932. **Head**: McClain Jeffrey Moredock

Grades: N-12. **Enrollment**: 500 Co-ed. **Faculty**: 45 full-, 11 part-time.
Average Class Size: 16.

Special Courses: French 7-12, Spanish K-12. Math includes Calculus, Computer. General Science, Biology, Chemistry, Physics, Life Sciences. History - Ancient Civilizations, World, U.S., Modern World, World Culture. Humanities, Human Relations, Literature, Government, Creative Writing, Journalism, Journalizing: Integrated Curriculum. Art, Music, Drama, Choral, Note: Extension Day Program, 7-12: once a week, Science/Cultural/ Environmental Activities outside classroom. AP.: Students have opportunity to prepare for AP Exams. **Extended day**: 7 a.m.-6 p.m.

Athletics: (P.E. req.) Intramural and Interscholastic. Basketball, Softball, Movement, Soccer, Track, Horseback Riding, Camping\Outdoor Exploration. **Clubs**: Drama, Keyette, Service, Ski. **Publications**: Student Newspaper, Yearbook **Community Involvement**: Grades 9-12, Internship Program for one semester, grades 11-12; Grades N-12: Food, Clothing, Service Programs-Environmentalism/Wildlife.

Plant: 3 Libraries 16,500 vol., 2 Art Studios, Gym,, Playing Field, 2 Swimming Pools, Stables.

Admission: Open House twice weekly. Application Fee $50. Interview, Classroom Visit, Testing. Recommendations and Transcript.

Tuition: (1993-94)) N half-day $5,000; N full day $6,500; K-3 $7,190; 4-12, $7,400-$8,700. **Transportation**: Available **Extended Day**: $750-$1,125. Books: $250 Other Fees Building & Grounds Assessment $400 per family. **Scholarship Aid**: Some partial Aid

Future Plans: To build new Athletic Facility, Science/Language Center, Arts Studio, Cafe, New Stables by Fall of '96.

Summer Program: Day camp: for age 3 1/2- 14, swimming, riding, camping, canoeing, arts and crafts, nature study, sports, etc. computer camp & drama camp,

BEAUVOIR.........(202) 537-6492

3500 Woodley Road, N.W., Washington, D.C. 20016
(On the grounds of the National Cathedral.)
Episcopal, 1933 **Head** : Paula J. Carreiro

Grades : N-3 **Enrollment** : 357 Co-ed **Faculty** : 40 full-time
Average Class Size : K & 1,-19; 2 &3, 18.

Special Courses: General Science, Art Workshop, Music, Media, Sports, Computers; Learning alternatives provides academic support. Chapel Service in the Cathedral.

Plant : Library 6,200 vol.; Computer Lab. Science Lab, Art Workshop, Gym, Auditorium, Playing Fields, Swimming Pool; Access to 60 acres of Cathedral Close.

Admission : Applications accepted Oct. - Jan. for following year; Children applying are evaluated on an individual and group basis. Application and Testing fee $180

Tuition: (1993-94) $8,038 includes Lunch and Books. **Transportation** : one way, $600, both ways $825. **Scholarship Aid** : Available

Summer Program ; Recreational Junior Program, Half day, Mid June thru July, Ages 3-4. Summer Adventure; ages 4-7; arts & crafts, drama, music movement, science, P.E., and field trips; Academic: for ages 6-10, Enrichment program concentrating on regular skills and learning alternative program; " Computers of Course" Logo, graphics, Bank Street Writer and Problem solving challenges. Note: all programs offer daily swim instruction in Olympic-size outdoor pool. **Extended Day** :3 p.m.-6 p.m.

BEDDOW SCHOOL....(301) 567-0330

8600 Loughran Road, Ft. Washington, MD. 20744
Founded 1972. **Head**: Trudy Beddow.

Grades: Ungraded ages 2-1/2-14. **Enrollment**: 170 Co-ed

Program: Montessori. **Extended Day Care**: 7:30 a.m.-6:00 p.m.

Tuition: (1993-94) $2,900-$4,000 depending on age level. **Extended Day** : Extra

Summer Program: Camp, ages 2 1/2-11

BELTSVILLE SEVENTH DAY ADVENTIST SCHOOL..........(301) 937-2933

4200 Ammendale Road, Beltsville, MD. 20705.
Adventist 1956. **Head**: Wendy Pega

Grades: K-8. **Enrollment**: 215 Co-ed. **Faculty**: 10 full-, 1 part-time.
Average Class Size: 25

Special Courses: Music, Religious Studies req., Gymnastics; 2 Bell Choirs, Treble Choir.
Extended Day: 7:30 a.m.- 6 p.m.

Athletics: Req. 1-8. Publications: "Small Talk."

Plant: Library, Playing Fields, Auditorium/Gym.

Admission: Application, Interview. Registration fee $60.

Tuition: (1993-94) $312/mo. (reduction for church members) **Limited Transportation**: $45- $80/mo., depending on distance *Dress Code*: Neat, modest attire.

BERWYN BAPTIST SCHOOL..........(301) 474-1516

4720 Cherokee Street., College Park, MD. 20740
Baptist, 1967. **Head**: Ann Elizabeth Zibrat

Grades: N3-grade 6. **Enrollment**: 150 Co-ed **Faculty** : 12 full-, 2 part-time.
Average Class Size : 20.

Special Program: Computer in each class; Self-contained classes for each grade. Separate instructors for Library, Music, & P.E.

Athletics: P.E. **Clubs** : Gymnastics, Handbell Choir **Publications** :Yearbook

Admission: Open Enrollment begins March 1

Tuition: (1993-94) N 3, $735; N4, $1,070; K, $1,435; grades 1-6, $2,465.

BETHEL BIBLE CHRISTIAN SCHOOL..........(301) 449-3000

5406 Brinkley Road, Camp Springs, MD. 20748
Founded 1981 I.F.C.A. **Head**: Charles Weinberg

Grades: N3-grade 8. **Enrollment**: 236 Co-ed **Faculty**: 14 full-time, 2 aides.
Average Class Size: 22

Special Programs: Religious Studies required. Music. **Extended Day** : 6 a.m.- 6 p.m.

Athletics: Not required. **Clubs**: Chess, Yearbook. **Publications**: Yearbook.

Plant: Library 4,000 vol.; Gym, 3 Playing Fields

Admission: Pre-Registration Feb.-April: N3-K5, $100; grades 1-8, $125.
Regular Registration, May 1: N3-K5 $150; grades 1-8, $175. Testing, Interview required.

Tuition: (1993-94) N3-K5 $2,030; 1-8 $2,150. **Extended Day**: $1,000/yr. **Transportation**: Limited, $1,000/yr. *Dress Code*: Uniform required.

Summer Programs: Academic for ages 3-12: Remedial Reading and Math. Non-Academic: one week of Basketball camp; Arts & Crafts, Swimming, Field Trips for ages 3-12.

BETHEL CHRISTIAN ACADEMY.......(301) 725-4673

8455 Savage-Guilford Road, Savage, MD. 20763
Head: Rose Marie Cox

Grades: K3-8 **Enrollment**: 200 Co-ed **Faculty** : 12 full-, 6 part-time
Average Class Size 20-24

Special Programs: Academic Night; Bible -Quiz-A-Thon Team; Spelling Quiz-A-Thon Team; Art, Music, P.E. (Private tutoring available for a nominal fee)
Extended Day: 7:15 a.m.-6 p.m.

Athletics : Girls Volleyball, Co-ed Basketball, Boys Soccer

Plant: Facilities with large classrooms; Multi-purpose room, Media Center

Admission: Application fee $100

Tuition: (1993-94) K3- K4, $1,750; K5, $2,100; grades 1-5, $2,200; 6-8, $2,400. Note may be paid in 10-12 equal payments. Reduction for siblings; 4th child Free Books Extra

Future Plans Expand to High School

BETHLEHEM BAPTIST CHRISTIAN ACADEMY..........(703) 631-1467

4601 W. Ox Road, Fairfax, VA. 22030.
Independent Fundamental Baptist 1973. **Head**: Mr. Gene Spurrier

Grades: K3-12 **Enrollment**: 450 Co-ed **Faculty**: 30 full-, 5 part-time
Average Class Size: 20.

Special Courses : Spanish I-IV, Math: Algebra-Calculus; Business Math, Computer. Science Physical Science, Biology, Chemistry, Physics. History- World Geography, World History, US/VA History, U.S./VA Gov't, Political Science/Economics. Religious studies req.; Remedial Reading & Math. Note: Limited LD enrollment. Art, Music, Speech, Typing, Accounting, Choir, Band. **Extended Day:** 7 a.m.-5:30 p.m.

Athletics: Req. to grade 10. Interscholastic: Soccer, Baseball, Basketball, Cheerleading, Track, Volleyball, Softball. Clubs: American Christian ,Honor Society. **Publications:** Yearbook, Newspaper.

Plant: Library, Science Labs, Art Studio, Gym, Auditorium, Playing Fields

Admission : Parent/child Interview, $75 Registration Fee. Nine-week probationary period; satisfactory academics.

Tuition: (1993-94)) $2,810-3,440 Lunch Program Books: $250. **Transportation**: Available, fees vary with distance. Dress Code: Conservative.

Summer Program: Recreational camp, K4-8

BISHOP DENIS J. O'CONNEL HIGH SCHOOL..........(703) 237-1400

6600 Little Falls Road, Arlington, VA. 22213
Catholic, 1957. **Head:** Alward V. Burch.

Grades: 9-12. **Enrollment**: 1300 Co-ed. **Faculty**: 70 lay, 15 religious.
Average Class Size: 19.

Special Courses: Religion; Latin, French, Spanish, German, Russian; Science Biology, Chemistry, Physics; History: World Culture, Mod. European History, U.S. & Va. History, U.S. & Va. Gov't.; Math includes Trig, Functions & Finite Math, Analysis, Calculus; Economics, Practical Law, Accounting, Business & Law Management, Computer Programming; Studio Art, Technical Drawing, Public Speaking, Journalism, Theater Arts, Creative Writing; Music, Typing AP: English, Spanish, Biology, Chemistry, History, Calculus, French, German, Art, Economics, U.S. Government.

Athletics: Intramural & Interscholastic: Football, Basketball, Soccer, Swimming, Tennis, Golf, Wrestling, Cheerleading, Bowling, Track, Cross Country, Softball. **Clubs**: 30, all varieties. **Publications**: Newspaper, Literary Magazine, Yearbook. **Community Involvement**: Key & Keyette Clubs, Red Cross. Parish Activities, Junior Achievement, Charity Drives.

Plant: Library, Science Labs, Art Studio, Gym, Auditorium, Cafeteria,
Playing Fields, Computer Lab; Use of Tennis Courts and Swimming Pool.

Admission: Grade 9-High school Entrance Exam; All grades: Transcripts, Interview, References; Application fee, $100.

Tuition: (1993-94) Parish member $3,850; Non-Parish member $4,300; Non-Catholic, $5,000 (note: reduced tuition for siblings). Lunch: Cafeteria. Books: Extra. *Dress Code*: Uniform req. **Transportation**: Limited-from E. Falls Church Metro, and some areas.
Financial Aid: Available

Summer Program: Sports Camp - basketball for boys. Academic- enrichment program for incoming 9th graders, Study Skills, Typing. Computer Programming. Credit courses in Math and Languages.

BISHOP IRETON HIGH SCHOOL..........(703) 751-7606

201 Cambridge Road, Alexandria, VA. 22314
Catholic 1964. **Head**: Rev. William J. Metzger, OSFS

Grades: 9-12. **Enrollment**: 750 Co-ed. **Faculty**: 40 full-, 6 part-time.
Average Class Size: 19.

Special Courses: French, Spanish, German, Latin, all 9-12; Japanese, Chinese, Russian. Math includes Calculus; Computer-Introd., Pascal, Applications, Programming, Keyboarding; Science: Biology, Chemistry, Physics, Astronomy, Organic Chemistry, Introd. to Psychology.

History- World Cultures, Modern European, U.S.& Virginia Government and History. Economics. Religious Studies req. Remedial Reading & Math Creative Writing, Public Speaking, Journalism, Publishing, Art, Wind Ensemble, Concert Band, Drama, Theatre, Stage Crafts. Honors and AP Program: English, U.S. History, Gov't., Chemistry, Art I & II, Computers, Biology, Calculus, AB, BC. Note: Seton Center for LD; Academic Enrichment, Study Skills.

Athletics: Req. 9-10. Intramural Basketball. Interscholastic: Football, Basketball, Baseball, Tennis, Swimming & Diving, Lacrosse, Soccer, Golf, Cross-Country, Wrestling, Track & Field, Softball, Field Hockey, Cheerleading. **Clubs**: Chorus, Competition Math, Drama, French, German, Spanish, Latin, "It's Academic", Key, Model U.N., National Honor Society, Stage Crew, Student Government. **Publications**: Newspaper, Yearbook. **Community Involvement**: Key Club, Blood Bank, Social Concern, Tutoring in grade schools, Volunteers.

Plant: Library, 12,000 vol., Computer Lab, Science Labs, Art Room, Gym, Fields, Use of Tennis Courts & Pool.

Admission: Placement exam for incoming 9th grade; Interviews upper grades. Transcripts and Recommendation

Tuition: (1993-94) $4,000-$5,600. Books: Extra Lunch: May be purchased. **Transportation**: $800-$1,000 both ways. *Dress Code*: School uniform req. **Financial Aid**: Available.

Summer Program: Academic- Remedial and study skills.

BISHOP McNAMARA HIGH SCHOOL............(301) 735-8401

6800 Marlboro Pike, Forestville, MD. 20747
Catholic 1963. **Head**: Brother John Paige, CSC

Grades: 9-12. **Enrollment**: 565 Co-ed. **Faculty**: 40 **Average Class Size**: 22.

Special Courses: French, Spanish, Latin, all 9-12; Math includes Trig & Calculus; Computer Programming, Literacy, Applications. General Science, Biology, Chemistry, Physics, Anatomy & Physiology, Psychology History: U.S. & World. Sociology. Religious Studies req. Remedial Reading & Math. Music: 5 Bands, Composition & Theory. Note: Special Programs- Peer Ministry, Internships, Model U. N.; AP: English, Math, Calculus, History, Chemistry & Physics.

Athletics: Not required. Intramural Basketball. Interscholastic: Football, Basketball, Baseball, Wrestling, Golf, Track, Cross-Country, Tennis, Lacrosse, Soccer, Swimming, and Volleyball.. **Clubs**: Black Student Union, Yearbook, Model U.N., Student Council, Foreign Language. **Publications**: Newspaper, Yearbook, Literary Magazine. **Community Involvement:** 40 hour requirement in junior year as part of religion requirement.

Plant: Library 11,000 vol., Language Lab, 4 Science Labs, Art Studio, Auditorium, Gym, 3 Playing Fields, Weight Room.

Admission: Contact Director of Admissions for information and current procedures. Registration fee $220.

Tuition: (1993-94) $3,900 Books: Rental, $200 **Transportation**: one way $500, both $900. *Dress Code*: Uniform . **Financial Aid**: Available

Summer Programs: Academic: Remedial English, Science, Math, Religion. Non-Academic: Football, Basketball Baseball, Soccer Camps.

BLESSED SACRAMENT SCHOOL..........(202) 966-6682

5841 Chevy Chase Parkway, N. W., Washington, D. C. 20015
Catholic **Head** Mr. Arthur Raimo

Grades : K-8 **Enrollment**: Co-ed

Special Programs: **Extended Day** : 7:30 a.m.-6 p.m.

Tuition: (1993-94) K-8, In Parish $1,978; Non-Parish, $3,186.

BLUE RIDGE SCHOOL..........(804) 985-2811

Dyke, VA. 22935
Episcopal 1909. **Head:** Edward M. McFarlane, Education Director

Grades: 9-12. **Enrollment**: 157 Boys, All Boarding. **Average Class Size**: 9. **Faculty**: 32 full-, 4 part-time.

Special Courses: French 10-12, Spanish 10-12. Math includes 3 levels of Algebra, and pre-Calculus. Computer Programming, Introductory thru Advanced, Basic Word Processing. Biology, Chemistry, Physics, Earth Science, Anatomy, Physical Science; History: World, Modern European, U.S. History & Government, Virginia History; electives in English History; Religious Studies: World Religions (not req.) Art

Athletics: Req.; Interscholastic: Football, Cross Country, Soccer, Wrestling, Basketball, Lacrosse, Tennis, Golf, Baseball, Track & Field. **Clubs**: Glee, Dramatics, Computer, Outdoor Activity (camping, hiking, climbing, caving). **Publications**: Yearbook, Newspaper, Literary Magazine. **Community Involvement**: Recycling, Environmental-Adopt a Highway Program, County Christmas Program.

Plant: 1,000 Acre Campus. Library 11,000 vol., (augmented by easy accessed on-line data-base from U.VA Library) 3 Science Labs, Art Studio, 2 Gyms, Auditorium, 7 Playing Fields, Pool, 12 Tennis Courts (4 Indoor), Computer Lab, Student Center, Chapel, 5 acre lake for fishing, canoeing.

Admission: Rolling Admission; SSAT, ERB, Iowa, CAT SRA acceptable, WISC-R preferred. Interview and Recommendations req.; $35 Application fee.

Tuition: (1993-94) $ 16,875 Books: $150. *Dress Code*: Coat and tie. **Scholarship Aid**: 5 full, 15 partial.

Future Plans: To finish construction of the new library.

Summer Program: Remedial Academic program offered for co-ed students grades 7-12; Also individualized course of study. Non-Academic program of leisure activities in swimming, tennis, dance, weight-lifting, gymnastics, intramurals, riding, hiking, off-campus trips.

BOOK OF LIFE ACADEMY..........(410) 263-5377

913 Cedar Park Road, Annapolis, MD. 21401
Annapolis Assembly of God Church. **Head**: April Carpenter, Principal.

Grades: N3-grade 12 **Enrollment**: 210 Co-ed.

Special Courses: Spanish. ABEKA curriculum. **Extended Day**: 7:45 A.M.- 4:30 P.M.

Plant: Library, Gym

Admission: Registration fee $145; Transcript, Interview with parents.

Tuition: (1993-94) $1,550 **Extended Day**: Extra *Dress Code*: Uniform req.

BRENTWOOD ACADEMY..........(703) 780-5750

3725 Nalls Road., Alexandria, VA. 22309
Founded 1965. **Head**: Pamela Allen.

Grades: N2-grade 3. **Enrollment**: 90. **Faculty**: 12 full-time. **Average Class Size**: 15

Special Courses: General Science, Computers, Music, Art. **Extended Day**: 6:30 a.m.-6:30 p.m.

Athletics: Swimming, Softball, Ice Skating.

Plant: Library, Playing Fields, 5 wooded acres; use of nearby pool.

Admission: Interview parent and child. Registration fee $50.

Tuition: (1993-94) Half-Day $400/mo.; Full Day $500/mo. Includes Lunch, snacks, & **Extended Day**. Books: Extra.

Summer Program: Day Camp. Arts, Computers, Swimming, Field trips, Cookouts, all kinds of games. 6:30 a.m.- 6:30 p.m. Ages 2-14.

BROADFORDING CHRISTIAN ACADEMY..........(301) 797-8886

13535 Broadfording Church Road, Hagerstown, MD. 21740.
Bible Brethren, 1973. **Head**: Mr. R. William Wyand

Grades: N (2 yrs.) - grade 12. **Enrollment**: 132 Co-ed **Average Class Size**: 15.

Special Courses: French & German, as needed; Spanish, Elem. & 9-12. Math includes Calculus, Computer-Basic Programming, Word Processing, Literacy, Gen'l Business Math. General Science, Biology, Chemistry, Physics. History - World and U.S., American Gov't, World Geography. Religious Studies Req. (Bible class daily). Remedial Reading and Math. Art, Music-Vocal, Instrumental, and Handbell Choir. **Extended Day**: 7:30 a.m.-5 p.m.

Athletics: P.E. req. Intramural: Basketball, Volleyball, Flag Football, etc. Interscholastic: Basketball, Volleyball. Note: Gym class offers Fencing, Orienteering, Football, etc. **Clubs**: Yearbook, Newspaper, Home Economics. **Publications**: Yearbook, Newspaper.

Plant: Library, Science Labs, Gym, Auditorium, Playing Fields.

Admission: Interview, Test; Registration fee $60. Desire to attend the school and to receive a Christian education is important.

Tuition: (1993-94) $1,500, reduction for siblings.. Lunch: Purchase **Transportation**: one way $200 - $500; both ways $400-$850. *Dress Code*: Modest, conservative. **Scholarship Aid**: Some available.

Summer Program: Elementary tutoring in Reading, Math; other courses upon request.
Summer Daycare 7:30 a.m.- 5 p.m.

BROOKSFIELD SCHOOL....................(703) 356-5437

1830 Kirby Road, McLean, VA 22101
Founded 1987 **Head** : Mary Ann Duffus

Ungraded: Ages 2 1/2 to 2nd grade **Enrollment**: 70 Co-ed **Faculty**: 11 full-,6 part-time.
Average Class Size: Pre-school, 20; grades 1 & 2, 10.

Special Courses : Montessori curriculum for pre-school and Kindegarten includes creative m movement, art, music and foreign language; Grades 1 &2, Program includes and integrated reading program, classic and contemporary literature. Accelerated math program, computer instruction. Science; Study of world cultures; Spanish, Art, Music. **Extended Day** : 7:30 a.m.-5:30 p.m.

Athletics : P.E. with special instruction in Horseback Riding and Ice Skating

Admission : For ages 2 1/2-K, Tour, Interview, Informal Evaluation; grades 1 & 2: Tour, Interview, Transcripts, Recommendations.

Tuition: (1993-94) Registration fee $25; Ages 2 1/2-K, $3,200-$7, 100 (depends on hours); Grades 1 & 2, $5, 950-$7,550 (depends on hours); 10% discount for siblings. Note: Tuition may be paid on monthly installments. For occassional **Extended Day Care,** fee is $5/hr.,separate charge of $3 for Lunch.

Future Plans : To build own site to allow for expansion.

Summer Program: Summer camp with swimming instruction daily, nature study, art, music, dance, & crafts.

BROSCHART SCHOOL.......... (301) 251-4624

14901 Broschart Road, Rockville, MD 20850
Developmental School Foundation 1981 **Head**: Dr. Sheila Kaler

Grades: K-12 **Enrollment**: 150 Co-ed **Faculty**: 25 full-time. **Average Class Size**: 8-10

Special Courses: Foreign Language tutoring available; Biology, Chemistry, Gen'l Science, Earth Science. History: U.S., World, Contemporary Issues. Psychology, Sociology, Street Law, Government. Art, Drama, Computer, Typing. Career Education. AP.: Math, English, Social Studies, Science. Note: Also LD/ED

Athletics: P.E. Individual & Dual Sports; Volleyball, Basketball, Weight Training, Softball.
Publications: School Newsletter and Magazine.

Plant: Library, Science Lab, Art Studio, Gym, Auditorium Playing Fields.

Admission: All adolescents admitted to the Psychiatric Institute of Montgomery County are enrolled in the Broschart School; Day Student-any student who does not require hospitalization but needs a more restrictive environment than offered by public schools. Students enrolled in the residential treatment program at the Psychiatric Institute of Montgomery County (Fairbridge). Tests- Education evaluation; Transcripts; Interview with parents & student.

Tuition: (1993-94) $100 per day. **Transportation**: Day Students- no charge, provided by county school bus. *Dress Code*: Appropriate school attire; may include jeans.
Financial Aid: Available.

Summer Program: Full academic/ enrichment; outings related to course of study.

BROWNE ACADEMY...........(703) 960-3000

5917 & 5923 Telegraph Road, Alexandria, VA. 22310
Founded 1941. **Head**: Dr. Lois Ferrer.

Grades: Pre-School- grade 8. **Enrollment**: 275 Co-ed. Pupil/Teacher Ratio: 9:1
Faculty: 30 full-, 5 part-time.

Special Courses: Individualized Reading and Math, French, Computer, Art, Music (includes Violin, Piano Lessons); Physical Education, Study Skills. Emphasis on dynamic academic program in relaxed, country setting. Special programs for the gifted.
Extended Day: 7 a.m.- 6 p.m.

Athletics: Req. Intramural & Interleague: Soccer, Track & Field, Softball, Basketball, Ballet, Jazz, & Gymnastics. **Clubs**: Arts,Chess, Cooking, Spanish, Scouting, Chorus, Student Government. **Publications:** Newspaper, Literary Magazine, Yearbook.

Plant: Library 10,000 vol., Math-Science Lab, Computer Lab, Art Lab, Music Building, Swimming Pool, Playing Fields, 11 Acres, Stream, Basketball Court, Outdoor Amphitheater, Par Cours Trail.

Admission: Transcript, Interview, Testing - Seek diversified student body. Application fee $35.

Tuition: (1993-94) Pre-School, $2,450-$6,600; K- 8, $7,463: Lunch for K-4 included, 5-8 bring. **Transportation**: $802-$1,400. **Scholarship Aid** : Available

Future Plans: New Library, Multi-purpose Auditorium/Gym. Expansion of student body to 300.

Summer Program: Day Camp - 9 week program ages 2-15. Includes Red Cross swimming instruction, arts & crafts, music, gymnastics, drama, "outdoor education", field sports, pony rides. Summer Studies offering Enrichment and Remedial courses. **Transportation & Extended Day** Available.

BULLIS SCHOOL..........(301) 299-8500

10601 Falls Road, Potomac, MD. 20854.
Founded 1930. **Head**: Dr. Richard K. Jung

Grades: 4-12 & PG. **Enrollment**: 460 Co-ed. **Faculty**: 45 full-time **Average Class Size**: 14.

Special Courses: Latin 7-8, French 8-12 (I-IV), Spanish I-IV, German I-III. Math thru Calculus. Biology, Chemistry, Physics, I.P.S., Earth Science. History: Latin-American, Ancient, Modern European, U.S., English, Far Eastern, Western Civ., American Economic Development, U.S.Constitution, etc. Art & Music required 4-8. Driver's Ed, Mechanical Drawing, Drama, Computer Science-req. 4-8. elective 9-12. Studio Art, Art History, Music. AP.: Biology, Chemistry, English, U.S. History, Modern European History, Computer Science, French, Spanish, Calculus

Athletics: Intramural & Interscholastic. Cross Country, Basketball, Wrestling, Track, Tennis, Baseball, Lacrosse, Football, Soccer, Golf. **Clubs**: Drama, Model U-N, Chorus, Computer, A.F.S. Key, Outing, Honor Society, Student Council. **Publications**: Newspaper, Yearbook,

Literary Magazine. **Community Involvement**: Varsity B Club assistance to area disadvantaged youth. Key Club projects in conjunction with Kiwanis.

Plant: Library 15,000 vol., 4 Science Labs, Playing Fields, Indoor & Outdoor Tennis Courts. Football Stadium, all weather 8 lane track; 3 faculty residences. Athletic Center includes 2 Gyms, Wrestling Center, Physical Fitness Center.

Admission: SSAT or ERB, Interview, Transcript, personal Recommendations. $35 Application fee.

Tuition: (1993-94) Grades 4 & 5, $8,200; 6-8, $9,600; 9-12, $10,025; includes Lunch. Books: $300. **Transportation** : one way - $650; both ways - $1,200. *Dress Code*: Uniform req. **Financial Aid**: 6 full, 50 partial.

Summer Program: 6 week review, preview, enrichment, make-up, Grades 7-P.G.; 2 week computer science course. Camps: 1-6 weeks, soccer, wrestling, tennis, basketball, baseball. Discovery Day Camp for children.

Future Plans: Building a Fine Arts Center on campus in partnership with the Potomac Community Foundation

BURGUNDY FARM COUNTRY DAY SCHOOL..........(703) 960-3431

3700 Burgundy Road, Alexandria, VA. 22303.
Founded 1946. **Head**: Gerald Marchildon
Note: Co-op Parents/Staff Members participate in policy-making & work.

Grades: Pre K-8. **Enrollment**: 250 Co-ed. **Faculty**: 27 full-, 5 part-time, **Average Class Size**: 16-26; PreK-5, 2 teachers full time, per class.

Special Courses: French & Spanish, Transition-8; Computer, Gen'l Science, Biology. Art & Music,Drama Interdisciplinary, hands on approach. Note: Transition class K/1; Grades 1-5, cross-age grouping in two year spans. Middle School grades 6-8. **Extended Day** : until 6 p.m.; Holiday care available.

Athletics: Req.; Intramural Softball, Swimming, Soccer, Basketball. **Publications**: School Magazine, Weekly Newsletter.

Plant: Library 10,000 vol., Middle School Science Lab, Gym/ Auditorium, Art Studios, Heated Pool, Fields. Barnyard farm animals, pond, & woods. Note: 300 acre campus in West Virginia with three buildings used by grades 2-8 fall & spring.

Admission: Individual Testing with school referred psychologist; References, Student Visit, Parent Interviews and Visits classes; School seeks diverse student body.

Tuition: (1993-94) $7,630-$8,430. **Transportation**: One way $835; both ways $1,250 **Extended Day**: Extra. **Financial Aid**: Available.

Future Plans: New Elementary Classroom Building

Summer Program: Natural Science Camp at mountain campus in W. Va. (Residential). **Day Camp** (Alexandria campus)- emphasis on performing and visual arts, natural science, sports - Red Cross swimming, computers. Ages 3-14. **Extended Day**

BUTLER SCHOOL...(301) 977-6600

15951 Germantown Road, Darnestown, MD 20874
Founded 1971 **Head**: Rilla Spellman

Grades: N-6. **Enrollment**: 175 Co-ed. **Faculty**: 16 full- 5 part-time.
Average Class Size: 27 primary, 22 elementary.

Special Programs: Spanish K-6. Remedial Reading and Math available. Art, Music, Piano lessons. Equestrian program. **Extended Day**: 8:00 a.m.- 5:15 p.m.

Athletics: All grades, K-6. Intramural. **Publications**: Newspaper

Plant: Library 6,000 vol., Art Studio, Playing Fields, Swimming Pool, Stables, Tennis Courts, 22 acre campus.

Admission: Parent Interview and Classroom Observation.

Tuition: (1993-94) $3,200 half-day; $4,800 full-day. **Transportation** : $700 one way, $1,400 both . *Dress Code*: Uniform req. for elementary grades. **Scholarship Aid**: Available.

Summer Program: Full day camp, 11 weeks- June through August for ages 6-13; Outdoor adventures, equestrian, performing arts, swimming, tennis. Half- day camp, ages 2-4: arts & crafts, swimming, outdoor activities.

CALVARY BAPTIST CHURCH ACADEMY..........(410) 768- 5324

407 Marley Station Road, Glen Burnie, MD. 21061.
Independent 1973. **Head**: John Bandy

Grades: K(3)-12. **Enrollment**: 300 Co-ed. **Faculty**: 11 full-, 5 part-time.
Average Class Size: 25

Special Courses: Spanish 9-12. Algebra I & II. General Science, Biology, Chemistry, Physics. History-U.S., U.S. Gov't, World Geography. Religious Studies req. Art, Music, Typing, Computer Science. **Extended Day** : 6 a.m.-6 p.m.

Athletics: req. to grade 10. Soccer, Basketball, Baseball, Softball, Volleyball. **Publications**: Yearbook. **Community Involvement**: Visit the nursing home once a month.

Plant: Library, Science Labs, Auditorium.

Admission: Interview, Individual Testing; $100 Registration fee.

Tuition: (1993-94) N-K $2,040; 1-6 $2,020; 6-8 $2,220 9-12 $2,500 **Transportation:** $300 one way, $550 round trip. *Dress Code*: Rules stated in student handbook.

Future plans: Build a gym, develop & expand library.

CALVARY LUTHERAN SCHOOL..........(301) 589-4001

9545 Georgia Avenue, Silver Spring, MD. 20910.
Lutheran 1951. **Head**: Melvin P. Schnackenberg.

Grades: K-6. **Enrollment**: 125 Co-ed. **Faculty**: 6 full-, 4 part-time.
Average Class Size: 25 or less.

Special Courses: Remedial Reading & Math, Study Skills, Art, Music. Religious Studies, Group Piano, Science Camp. School subjects taught in Christian environment. Program aimed at developing the natural talents of each child so that he may use these gifts and talents in the services of God and his fellow man. **Extended day**: 7 a.m.-6 p.m.

Athletics: Volleyball, Flag Football, Softball, Track & Field Day. **Community Involvement**: Sing at nursing home. Choir, 10:00 a.m. church service, one Sunday a month.

Plant: Library 3882 vol., Playing Field, Multi-Purpose Room.

Admission: Grades 1-6 - interview with Principal.

Tuition: (1993- 94) K-6 $3,000 (reduced rate for siblings) **Extended Day**: Extra.
Lunch: Extra. *Dress Code*: Neat & clean. **Financial Aid**: Available.

CALVARY ROAD CHRISTIAN SCHOOL...(703) 971-8004

6811 Beulah Street, Alexandria, VA. 22310.
Baptist 1973. **Director**: L. Harold Jones.

Grades: N 2 1/2-8 **Enrollment**: 200 Co-ed. **Faculty**: 15 full-, 2 part-time.
Average Class Size: 20.

Special Courses: Computer. Religious Studies req. **Extended Day** -6:45 a.m.-6 p.m.

Athletics: Not req. Basketball, Baseball, Soccer, Softball, Volleyball. **Publications**: Yearbook.

Plant: Library, Science Labs, Auditorium.

Admission: I.Q. Test, Grade Placement Test, Interview with Principal. Registration fee $100.

Tuition: (1993-94) Ages 2 1/2-4, $3,800 includes **Lunch** & **Extended Day**; Grades K-8, $2,250 **Extended Day**: Extra. Books: Extra. *Dress Code*: Neatly trimmed hair, girls dress length to top of knee.

Summer Program: Day Camp ages 2 1/2-12. $95/wk.

CALVERTON SCHOOL..........(410) 535-0216 or (301) 855-1922

300 Calverton School Road, Huntingtown, MD. 20639.
Founded 1967 **Head**: Dr. Elizabeth C. Bratton

Grades: PreK-12. **Enrollment**: 245 Co-ed. **Faculty**: 29 full-, 2 part-time.
Average Class Size: 15.

Special Courses: French PreK-12, Spanish 9-12; Math includes Calculus, Computer. General Science, Biology, Chemistry, Physics, Biochemistry, Chesapeake Bay Studies. European Civilization I & II, American Studies, American Gov't, Economics. Art, Music, Chorus. Health, Driver's Ed. AP.: English, French, History, Calculus, Computer, Chemistry, Biology.
Extended Day until 6 P.M.

Athletics: Intramural: Tennis, Golf, Volleyball. Interscholastic: Soccer, Lacrosse, Field Hockey, Basketball, Track & Field, Volleyball. **Clubs**: Photography, Drama, Mock Trial. **Publications**: Yearbook, Literary Magazine, Newspaper. **Community Involvement**: Community Service, all levels involved. 30 hrs. of community service graduation requirement.

Plant: 2 Libraries - 15,000 vol.; 2 Science Labs, Gym, Auditorium, Playing Fields, Art Studio. 23 acres with 5 acre marsh on river, 10 miles away.

Admission: Rolling admissions. PreK- grade 2: individual assessment. Grades 3-12, Student Visits class, Testing. $35 Application fee. Student's academic achievement, character, and potential taken into consideration.

Tuition: (1993-94) PreK- Full day: $6,200. Grades K-12, $7,200. Bring lunch.
Transportation & Extended Day Extra. *Dress Code*: Uniform req. **Financial Aid:** Some

Future Plans: Outdoor Environmental Camp, Amphitheater, Fine Arts Building.

Summer Program: Day and Specialty camps for ages 5-18.

CANTERBURY SCHOOL..........(301) 292-5535

P.O. Box 509, 600 Farmington Road West, Accokeek, MD. 20607
Episcopal 1961. **Head**: Heinz Bondy

Grades: 7-12. **Enrollment**: 93 Co-ed. **Faculty**: 4 full-, 5 part-time.
Average Class Size: 10.

Special Courses: French 7-12, Spanish 9-12; Math: Algebra 7-9, Geometry 8-11, Trig 9-12, Calculus 11-12,, and Computer 9-12. General Science, Biology, Chemistry, Physics. History: Civics, American, Geography, Anthropology, Western Civilization; Environmental Studies. Studio Art, Music, Related Arts, Drama. AP.: Biology

Athletics: Not required. Intramural & Interscholastic: Basketball, Soccer, Softball; Volleyball Intramural only. **Clubs**: Bicycling **Publications**: Yearbook. **Community Involvement**: River clean-up, Work with the Homeless, Tutoring at local elementary school.

Plant: Library 8,000 vol., Science Labs, Art Studio, Pavilion/Multi-purpose room, 10 acres of Playing Fields.

Admission: $25 Application Fee; Interview, Class Visitation, Record Review, In-school Testing when indicated.

Tuition: (1993-94) $5,800 Books approx. $200. **Transportation** : $95-$140/ mo., depending on zone. *Dress Code*: Must not be offensive. **Financial Aid**: Some available.

CAPITOL CHRISTIAN ACADEMY ....(301) 336-2200

610 Largo Road, Upper Marlboro, MD. 20772
Baptist 1961 **Head**: Wayne P. Baker

Grades: K4-12. **Enrollment**: 350 Co-ed **Faculty**: 16 full-, 7 part-time.
Average Class Size: 22

Special Courses: Spanish K4-12, Remedial Reading and Math. Algebra I & II, Geometry, Computer. General Science, Biology, Chemistry, Physics. Religious studies req. Art, Music, Band, Choir, Typing. Alpha Omega program offers supervised individual progress for accelerated learning, grades 2-8. **Extended Day**: 6:30 a.m.-6 p.m.

Athletics: Req. 7-12. Interscholastic: Soccer, Basketball, Softball, Baseball. **Publications:** Newspaper, Yearbook.

Plant: Library 4,000 vol., Science Lab, Auditorium, Gym, Playing Fields.

Admission: Test, $150 Registration fee, Interview with parents.

Tuition: (1993-94) $2,755 (Reduction for siblings). **Transportation**: $968. *Dress Code*: Uniform req. K4-grade 8; grades 9-12, No jeans, Girls must wear dresses; boys traditional haircut. **Scholarship Aid**: Some available.

Summer Program: Summer school grades 1-12; Math, English, Reading for elem./jr. high. Some academic subjects for high school. "Super Summer" Program for ages 5 through grade 6:

swimming, organized games, outdoor recreation, field trips etc.

CAPITOL HILL DAY SCHOOL........... (202) 547-2244

210 South Carolina Avenue, S.E., Washington, D.C. 20003.
Founded 1968. **Head**: Catherine Peterson.

Grades: PreK-8. **Enrollment**: 225 Co-ed. **Faculty**: 32 full-, 4 part-time.
Average Class Size: 20.

Special Courses: French Pre K-8. Algebra, Computers; General Science; There is a central subject at each grade level around which much of the social studies and science is centered including: Life cycles, patterns; Native Americans and Environment; African Cultures and Rain Forests; Anthropology, Ancient Civilizations; American History. Extensive field trips integrated with curriculum. **Extended Day**: 3-6 p.m.

Athletics: Rigorous physical education program that includes games and creative movement activities for young children. Competitive sports for upper grades including Basketball, Soccer, Softball. **Clubs** : Drama, Chorus. **Publications**: Yearbook. **Community Involvement**: Students work in and provide food for local soup kitchens. parent run community involvement program.

Plant: Library 7,500 vol.; Audio-Visual equipment, Art Studio. Use playing fields in 7,000 acre park across the street.

Admission: Parent Interview, Tour, Application fee $35 (Apply between October and February). Test, Transcript, and Class visit

Tuition: (1993-94) $7,350-$8,300 Lunch: Bring Books 6-8, $285. **Transportation**: $535 one-way, $845 both ways. *Dress Code*: Neat & clean appearance. **Financial Aid**: Some Partial Available.

Summer Program: Day Camp: 2 week sessions June-July, ages 4-14, Swimming at nearby pools, field trips to historic sites and playgrounds; special programs for older children coordinated with such places as Genesee Valley Outdoor Center/Belle Haven Sailing Marina.

CHARLES E. SMITH JEWISH DAY SCHOOL..........(301) 881-1400

1901 East Jefferson Street, Rockville, MD. 20852
Founded 1965. **Head**: Dr. Elliot Prager

Grades: K-12. **Enrollment**: 1,020 Co-ed. **Faculty**: 61 Full-, 111 part-time.
Average Class Size: no larger than 23.

Special Courses: French 7-12, Spanish 7-12; Hebrew Language and Literature req. K-12. Math thru Calculus; Computer. Science: General Science, Biology, Chemistry, Physics. History-

Geography, U.S., Modern European, Jewish; Senior Seminars: Vietnam and the 60's; Human Growth & Development. Religious Studies req. Remedial Reading & Math. Art & Music, K-9. Choir 4-6, Drama. Business Management, Computer Keyboarding AP: Biology, Physics, French, Spanish. Note: Israel Work/Study Program Senior year.

Athletics: Req.; Intramural & Interscholastic. Soccer, Softball, Basketball, Tennis, Baseball, Volleyball, Cross-Country. **Clubs**: Social Action, Student Council, Cooking. **Publications**: Newspaper, Literary Magazine (in Hebrew & English), Yearbook. **Community Involvement**: Service program required in upper school; community involvement in resettlement of Soviet immigrants.

Plant: 2 Libraries- 27,500 vol., 3 Science Labs, Art Studio, 2 Gyms, Auditorium, Playing Fields, Chapel. Note:; newly equipped playground.

Admission: Interview, Screening Tests, Transcript, Teacher Recommendation. Openings expand at K, 1, and 7th grade.

Tuition: (1993-94) K-6, $6,420; 7-11, $7,630; grade 12, $3,815 for 1st semester; $4,200. 2nd semester work/study program in Israel. Books: Extra Lunch: Bring. **Transportation**: one way, $650; both ways $985. *Dress Code*: Neat and Clean , no cut-offs, halter tops; no short shorts in grade 7-12. **Scholarship Aid**: Full and partial available.

Summer Program: Academic and Enrichment, concurrent co-op program with Jewish Community Center Day Camp.

CHATHAM HALL...........(804) 432-2941

Chatham, VA 24531
Episcopal, 1894 **Head**: Mr. Jerry A. Van Voorhis, Rector

Grades: 9-12 **Enrollment**: 113 Girls (102 Boarding) **Faculty**: 27 full-, 1 part-time.
Average Class Size: 8

Special Courses: Latin, French, Spanish: levels I-AP; Science: Introductory Science, Biology, Chemistry, Physics - tri-mester electives: Ethnology, Comparative Anatomy, Genetics. History: World Geography and Cultures, U.S. History, Modern European; Senior tri-mester electives: Economics, Government, World Affairs. Math: Algebra I, intermediate, and II; Geometry, Pre-Calculus, Math V (Statistics, Mathematical Modeling, Intro. to Calculus) AP Calculus, SAT Math Review trimester elective: Math in Nature. Computer 1 (Literacy Basic Programming), Keyboarding and Word Processing. AP: English, US History, French, Spanish, Calculus, Biology, Chemistry. Religion: 1 year req; Fine or Performing Arts (1 yr. req.-Art, Music (Choir, Voice, Organ, Instrumental), Dance. Special Opportunities: Sophomore Service Project, St. Independent Project, Woodberry Forest in Britain, English Speaking Union.

Athletics: Req. Intramural (all sports) & Interscholastic- Field Hockey, Basketball, Tennis. Also offered-Riding, Swimming, Lacrosse, Softball. **Clubs**: French, Spanish, Latin, Ecology, Photography, Riding, Athletic Council, Student Council, Student Senate, Art, Drama, Music,

Outdoor. **Publications:** Literary Magazine, Newspaper, Yearbook. **Community Involvement**: Every student is a member of the Service League-either School Life, Church Life, or Community Life.

Plant: Library 16,000 Vol.; 3 Science Labs, Computer Lab, Art Studio, Gym, Stables, 3 Playing Fields, Swimming Pool, 8 Tennis Courts, Greenhouse, 3 Dorms, Community Center, Infirmary, Chapel, New Fine Arts Center, new Gym, new Library with on-line system.

Admission: $30 Application fee; Essay, Questionnaire, Recommendations from English & Math teachers, Transcripts, Campus Visit, Interview, SSAT. First Choice Plan-acceptance date late January, others notified early March.

Tuition: (1993-94) Day $7,000; Boarding $17,500 Books: $750 deposit *Dress Code*: Neat appearance req. for classes, Chapel & Dinner. **Scholarship Aid**: 3 full, 33 partial.

CHELSEA SCHOOL..................(301) 585-1430

711 Pershing Drive, Silver Spring, MD. 20910.
Founded 1976. **Head**: Margaret E. Gray, Ph.D.

Grades: 1-12. **Enrollment**: 87 Co-ed. **Faculty**: 27 full-, 6 part-time.
Average Class Size: 5-8

Special Courses: Algebra, Geometry, Trig., Computer Programming, Keyboarding. Science Gen'l Science, Biology, Chemistry, Physics, Environmental Science, Nature Skills. History: U.S., World, Government, Geography. Psychological and Social Issues. Remedial Reading. Art, includes Independent Seminar, Pottery. Advanced Language Seminar, Journalism, Child Development. College & Careers, Library Skills, Office Practice. Note: Services for LD students including: tutorials, speech & language pathologist, occupational therapist, social skills groups. **Extended Day**: Monday-Friday: 12:10 p.m.-5 :00 p.m.

Athletics: Not req.; Interscholastic competition; member of Small Schools League - Soccer, Basketball, Softball, Tennis, **Clubs**: Music, Trail, Cinema, Student Government, Pan African Society, Cheerleading. **Publications**: Yearbook, Newspaper. **Community Involvement**: Senior Internship Program, Community Service and Newspaper.

Plant: Library 8,000 vol., Science Lab, Art Studio, Pottery Studio, Darkroom, Gym, Auditorium.

Admission: Interview and one day Visit. Review of Transcript and Testing. Note: Students must be of average or above average intelligence with a learning disability.

Tuition: (1993-94) $ 16,888. Lunch: Bag, vending; hot pizza, Tuesdays.
Dress Code: Clean, neat and presentable clothing. **Scholarship Aid**: Some partial available

Future Plans: Expanded use of existing building & grounds.

Summer Program: 5-week Program Half- day or full- day for make-up credit, and enrichment. (SAT Prep and Internships) Non-Academic Program: Outdoor adventure course, nature skills, field trips, athletics, community service.

CHESAPEAKE ABILITY SCHOOL..........(703) 256-1900

5533 Industrial Drive, Springfield, VA 22151
Founded 1979. **Head**: Lois A. Gloor

Grades: K-12; parent/adult education. **Enrollment**: 70 Co-ed. **Faculty**: 11 full-, 3 part-time. **Average Class Size**: 15

Special Courses: Individualized instruction;" how to learn", study and communication courses for students at elementary through high school ages, as well as adults. Licensed by Applied Scholastics International to use the study methods developed by L. Ron Hubbard. Emphasis on 100% comprehension and practical application in all subjects. Students move at own rate, and gradiently increase to their full potential as study methods learned and used. Remedial actions determined by testing and interview with student and parent; routinely work done to repair weak areas in student's earlier education.

Innovative Reading Program raises student literacy level to new heights through individual instruction. Starting with phonics, the program then shifts to include dictionary and learning instruction and having the child read great quantity of good literature by himself. Emphasis is on having child read lots of good books that gradiently increase in difficulty so child meets many of the important and valuable individuals of his society, culture and heritage through reading.

High school students expected to do apprenticeship in area of career interest. Students routinely exposed to a moral code. The Way to Happiness, which is based wholly on common sense and is the basis for school counseling services. Graduating student receives diploma certifying competency. College bound program available. Foreign language offered: French, Spanish, & German. Some electives are: Typing, Home Skills, Art, Computer Keyboard, Word Processing, Basic Programming. Personal Economics, Photography. Note: Adult education component includes how to read effectively, study & communication courses, and parent workshops.

Athletics: P.E. daily. **Publications**: Quarterly Newsletter. **Community Involvement**: Participation in environmental clean-ups; Visit senior citizen homes; Volunteer Service at homeless/community centers; other Way to Happiness Projects.

Plant: 4 1/2 acre campus, Soccer Field, Outdoor Basketball Courts (half court), Library, Film room, Dark Room.

Admission: Interview with student and parents. $50 Application Fee Student's own interest and goals for education important. Year round enrollment.

Tuition: (1993-94) $500/mo. Materials Fee: $270/$330. Lunch: Bring. *Dress Code*: Casual but neat. **Financial Aid**: Available on limited basis.

Future Plans: Parent workshops development to institute of Parent Education; Teacher/Tutor Institute.

Summer Program: 8 weeks (4 week min.); Morning: academics, how to study, communication courses; Afternoon camp: bowling, ice skating, swimming, field trips, fun outings, pony rides.
Extended Day : Available

CHESAPEAKE ACADEMY.........(301) 647-9612

1185 Baltimore Annapolis Boulevard., Arnold, MD. 21012
Founded 1980. **Head**: Jane C. Pehlke

Grades: N3-grade 5. **Enrollment**: 185 Co-ed. **Faculty**: 22 full-time, 4 part-time.
Average Class Size: 14.

Special Courses: French N-5; Computer, General Science; American & Ancient History, World Geography; Art, Music. Individualized programs. **Extended Day**: 7:15 a.m.- 6 p.m.

Athletics: P.E. Req.; Volleyball, Basketball, Soccer, Field Hockey. **Clubs**: French, Drama, Crafts, Gymnastics. **Community Involvement:** Children help support community projects such as Severna Park Assistance Network (SPAN) Chamber of Commerce Projects, etc.

Plant: Library 6,000 vol., Auditorium, Playing Fields, Computer Lab.

Admission: Application fee $55; Tour, Interview, Testing: Preschool-Early Learning Screening and Diagnostic test; Elementary Grades, 2 day visit includes Otis Lennon and Brigance testing.

Tuition: (1993-94) $1,600-$6,200 **Extended Day** Extra *Dress Code*: Uniform req.
Scholarship Aid: 1 full, 10 partial.

Summer Camp: "Super Summer" 9 a.m.-3 p.m., Care provided 7:30 a.m.-6 p.m.. Arts and crafts, sports, swimming, nature study, games, drama, music, cooking, field trips, overnights.

CHESAPEAKE MONTESSORI SCHOOL..........(410) 757-4740

30 Old Mill Bottom Road North, Annapolis, MD. 21401
Founded 1977. **Head**: Anne Locke.

Ungraded: Ages 2-1/2 to 11. **Enrollment**: 95 Co-ed. **Faculty**: 4 full-, 3 part-time.
Average Class Size: 20.

Special Courses: French - all ages, Art, Music, Athletics K-5, Montessori Method;
Extended Day Care: 7 a.m.-6 p.m.

Publications: Yearbook **Community Involvement**: Jump Rope for Heart

Plant: Central Library & Libraries in classrooms, Playing Fields, Swimming Pool, Multi-purpose Room.

Admission: Interview with parents and child; Observation; Test age 6 and over; $25 Application fee, $250 Registration fee. Note: Child must be at least 2-l/2 and toilet trained to be admitted.

Tuition: (1993-94) Half- day N, $3,210; full day K $4,520; Elementary $4,790. **Extended Day**: additional charge. **Financial Aid**: Available

Summer Program: Three 2-week sessions late-June through July for ages 3-8; includes swimming, singing, nature walks, field trips, arts & crafts. Morning or full day programs.

CHILDREN'S LEARNING CENTER............(301) 871-6600

4511 Bestor Drive, Rockville, MD 20853
Jewish 1978 **Head**: Ms. Rena Popkin

Grades: N, 2-4yrs, Elementary, K-5 **Enrollment**: N: 260 Co-ed; K-5, 57 Co-ed
Faculty: N, 54 part-time; K-5, 10 full, 5 part-time. Resource teachers in P.E., Science, Art, & Music.

Special Programs: Judaic/Hebrew Curriculum inclusion. After School: Computer tots, Group Piano Lessons, Dance Lessons. **Extended Day**: 7 a.m.-6 p.m.

Admission: Registration fee, $75-$100. Interview with parents.

Tuition: (1993-94) K, $550/mo.; grades 1 &2, $450/mo.; grade 3-5 $400/mo. Reduction for Nursery, depends on number of days (2,3, or 5) and full or half day. **Financial Aid**: Available.

CHRISTCHURCH SCHOOL...........(804) 758-2306

Christchurch, VA 23031
Episcopal 1921 **Head**: Reverend R.S. Phipps, Jr.

Grades: 9-PG **Enrollment**: 220 Coed (190 Boys, 30 Girls) 160 Boarding, 60 Day.
Faculty: 24 full-, 14 part-time. **Average Class Size**: 10-12.

Special Courses: Latin, French, Spanish: 9-12. Math includes Trig, Calculus, Basic & Advanced Computer. Science: Introduction to Physical Science, Biology, Chemistry, Physics, Marine Science I,II. History: World, U.S., U.S. Gov't, 20th Century World, World Geography, Comparative Idealogies, Future Studies. Economics. Religious Studies, req.; Art, Music, Drama. Remedial Reading and Math . Learning Skills Program for students diagnosed as having a learning skills disability Note: Complete program for Learning Disabled. AP: Chemistry; Honors English.

Athletics: Req.; Intramural: Softball, Volleyball. Interscholastic: Soccer, Football, Wrestling, Basketball, Cross Country, Track, Baseball, Lacrosse, Tennis, Golf, Indoor Soccer, Weight Lifting, Indoor Track, Sailing. **Clubs**: Social Activities, Sailing, Scuba, Marine Science. **Publications**: Newsletter, Yearbook, Literary Magazine. **Community Involvement**: Work with Local civic club & organizations, nursing homes; Participate in Adopt a Highway Program.

Plant: Library, 7,000 vol.; 2 Science Labs, 2 Gyms, Art Studio, 4 Playing Fields, 2 Swimming Pools, 5 Tennis Courts. Waterfront location used for Marine Science projects and Sailing.

Admission: Interviews are conducted all year. Recommendations: teachers, counselor and family friend. Note: Candidates for the Learning Skills Program may use outside tests administered within the last two years.

Tuition : (1993-94) Boarding $16,450; Day, $ 8, 150, Includes Lunch Books: $300-$400. *Dress Code:* Boys: Shirts with collars, trousers with belt, shoes & socks (No jeans, running shoes, etc. for classroom dress). **Scholarship Aid:** 17 full, 22 partial.

Future Plans: Refurbishment of Dormitory, Construction on waterfront of new field house and Marine Science classroom with lab facility.

Summer Program: Academic classes in Math, History, Languages, etc.
Summer Camp: Junior Marine Science Institute which studies Chesapeake Bay Ecology. Also an all sports Camp which includes sailing, scuba, soccer, & tennis.

CHRIST CHURCH DAY SCHOOL..........(301) 934-1477

East Charles Street, (P.O. Box 1467) La Plata, MD 20646
Head: Barbara Merrick

Grades: PreK-5 **Enrollment**: 80 Co-ed

Special Programs: **Extended Day**: 7:30 a.m.-6 p.m.

Tuition: (1993-94) Pre K, Half-day, $750; K, $1,400; Grades 1-5, $2,150.

CHRIST EPISCOPAL SCHOOL.........(301) 424-6550

109 S. Washington Street, Rockville, MD. 20850
Episcopal 1966. **Head**: Dana F. Beane

Grades: N-8. **Enrollment**: 159 Co-ed. **Faculty**: 12 full-, 7 part-time.
Average Class Size: 18.

Special Courses: Spanish K-8; Algebra, Computer K-8. General Science. Social Studies 5-8 Great Books K-6; Shakespeare. Library Skills K-8. (Learning Resource teacher on staff).

Art, Music (Recorders, Chimes), Chapel req. (daily), Drama. Builders Club. **Extended Day**: until 6 p.m..

Athletics: Required and includes Soccer. **Publications**: Yearbook, Monthly Newsletter. **Community Involvement**: Outreach programs

Plant: Library, Science Lab, Art Studio, Playing Fields, Chapel (located in church).

Admission: Interview, Transcripts, Testing, Class Visit. Fee for Screening. Recommendations from previous schools.

Tuition: (1993-94) N,3 mornings, $1,620; N 5 mornings, $2,700; K-8, $4,975. Books: $150. *Dress Code*: Uniform req. **Financial Aid**: Some Available.

CHRISTIAN ASSEMBLY ACADEMY.....(703) 698-7458

8200 Bell Lane, Vienna, VA 22182
Founded 1984. **Head**: Martin R. Reeve, Principal; Richard W. Alley, Administrator

Grades: K-8 **Enrollment**: 96 Co-ed **Faculty**: 7 full-, 8 part-time.
Average Class Size: 14

Special Courses: Algebra, Music, Art

Athletics: P.E., Basketball and Soccer, 5-8

Admission: Application (open to non-church members)

Tuition: (1993-94) Call for information in summer.

CHRISTIAN CENTER SCHOOL..........(703) 971-0558/0559

5411 Franconia Road, P.O. Box 10274, Alexandria, VA. 22310
Interdenominational 1976. **Head**: Mercedes S. Morrison, Principal

Grades: K4-grade 6. **Enrollment**: 157 Co-ed. **Faculty**: 27 full-, 1 part-time.
Average Class Size: 20.

Special Courses: Art, Bible, Computer, Co-Curricula Studies, Health Safety and Manners; History and Geography, Language Arts, Math, Music, Science, Science Lab, Spanish; Morning & Afternoon Extended Learning Center, Speech Therapy.
Extended Day : 7 a.m.-6 p.m.

Athletics: P.E. req. all grades: Intramural: Basketball, Baseball, Volleyball, Softball, Soccer, Dance (Tap, Jazz, Ballet), Gymnastics. **Clubs**: Art **Publications**: Yearbook.

Plant: Gym, Playground, Classrooms

Admission: Parent/child Interview with Principal, Test, Transcript.

Tuition: (1993-94) K4 & K5, $3,250 ($325/mo.); Grade 1-6 $2,400 ($240/mo.); Reduction for siblings. Books, Material and Lab fees, Lunch. Extra. **Transportation**: depends on distance, reduced rates for siblings. *Dress Code*: Uniform req.

Future Plans: Possible pre-school.

Summer Program: Day camp, late June-mid August.

CHRISTIAN FAMILY MONTESSORI SCHOOL..........(301) 927-7122

3628 Rhode Island Avenue, Mt. Rainier, MD. 20712
Christian, 1982. **Head**: Vernice Townsend

Ungraded: Ages 2 1/2-12. **Enrollment**: 100 Co-ed. **Faculty**: 4 full-, 4 part-time.
Average Class Size: 25.

Special Courses: Montessori method. Elementary Math and Science studies. History and Social Science included in cultural areas. Religious Studies req.; Art and Music. Note: Catechesis of the Good Shepherd, a religious education program based on Montessori, developed by Sophia Cavaletti, that stress the spiritual life and child's relationship with God, offered after school, one day a week.

Athletics: P.E. req. in elementary grades only.

Plant: Library 2,400 Vol.; Atrium

Admission: Observation by parents recommended; Interview for parent and child. Rolling admission. (Parents are expected to co-op and regularly participate in non-classroom activities).

Tuition: (1993-94) N & K, Half-day, $1,540, 1-6, $2,120 **Financial Aid**: Some available.

CLINTON CHRISTIAN SCHOOL..........(301) 599-9600

6707 Woodyard Road., Upper Marlboro, MD. 20772.
also: Bannister Circle, Waldorf, MD 20601
Baptist 1966. **Head**: William G. Spence

Grades: N-12. **Enrollment**: 600 Co-ed. **Faculty**: 33 full-, 6 part-time.
Average Class Size: 20.

Special Courses: French 1-6. Computer Instruction 1-12. Religious studies req. Bible; Piano, Chorus, Drama. **Extended Day**: 7 a.m.-6 p.m.

Athletics: Req. 1-12. Interscholastic. Flag Football, Volleyball, Basketball, Softball, Cheerleading. **Clubs**: Journalism, Yearbook. **Publications**: Yearbook. **Community Involvement**: MS Read-a-Thon, Thanksgiving Basket project.

Plant: Auditorium, Playing Fields, Gym.

Admission: Registration (conference before child is registered). Testing. Registration fee $100.

Tuition: (1993-94) Half- day, $1,680; Full Day, $2,727 includes hardback Books. **Extended Day & Lunch**: Extra. **Transportation**: $940 plus zone charges. *Dress Code*: Specific regulations.

Summer Program: Summer school - Elementary level work in Phonics, Reading & Math. Summer Camp - Day program offering Swimming, Riding, Fishing, Field trips, Organized games, Bible stories.

CLOVERLAWN ACADEMY..........(703) 538-4022

3455 North Glebe Road (at Ditmar Rd.), Arlington, VA 22207
Founded 1953. **Head**: Mary Harper Clark.

Grades: N-7. **Enrollment**: 65 Co-ed. **Faculty**: 6 full-, 3 part-time.
Average Class Size: 11.

Special Courses: French, Holt Unlimited Math; Computer; Enrichment Reading, Creative & Expository writing; Accelerated Science Program; Social Science & Geography; History. Art, Music. Humanities. **Extended Day**: 7 a.m.-5:30 p.m.

Athletics: P.E. req. **Clubs**: Newspaper & Science. **Publications**: Newspaper.
Community Involvement: Services to the community including sandwich making for the homeless. Environment.

Plant: Science Lab, Computers, Playing Fields, & Auditorium.

Admission: Interviews; Referrals; some Testing; Transcript. Classroom visits.

Tuition: (1993-94) $2,500-$4,500 *Dress Code:* Uniform req. in grades.
Scholarship Aid: 2 full, 2 partial.

Summer Program: Combined recreational and academic program .

CONCORD HILL SCHOOL..........(301) 654-2626

6050 Wisconsin Avenue, Chevy Chase, MD. 20815.
Founded 1965. **Head**: Mrs. French McConnaughey

Grades: N-3. **Enrollment**: 90 Co-ed. **Faculty**: 11 full, 3 part-time.
Average Class Size: 18.

Special Courses: Art, Music, Computer, General Science, Social Studies, Field Trips. Note: Small classes allow much individual attention: a ratio of 1/9 teacher/ pupil maintained throughout the program.

Plant: Library 3,000 vol.; Computer Lab, Playground. Spacious classrooms and indoor play/assembly facilities.

Admission: $50 Application fee; Transcripts and Teacher Recommendations; Parent Interview, then child visits . Interviews begin in Oct. 1. for following year, notification mid-March..

Tuition: (1993-94) N $4,900; K $6,300; Grades 1-3 $6,600, includes Books. Lunch: Brown bag, milk provided. *Dress Code*: Comfortable, appropriate school clothes.

Summer Program: Day Camp for 4-5 yr. olds, 3 two-week sessions.

CONCORDIA LUTHERAN SCHOOL..........(301) 927-0266

3799 East-West Highway, Hyattsville, MD. 20782.
Lutheran 1944. Head: Mr. Norman A. Hoerauf.

Grades: Age 3-grade 8. **Enrollment**: 268 Co-ed. **Faculty**: 12 full-, 1 part-time.
Average Class Size: 26.

Special Courses: Spanish, 7 -8. Algebra, Computer. Gen'l Science. World & U.S. History; World & U.S. Geography. Religious studies req. Note: Language Arts & Math, grouped according to performance. **Extended Day** : 7 a.m. - 6 p.m.

Athletics: P.E. Req. grades 1-8. Interscholastic Basketball. **Clubs**: Computer, Odyssey of the Mind. **Publications**: Yearbook. **Community Involvement**: Students participate in various charity drives, Hyattsville Clean-up, Canned goods for needy, etc.

Plant: Library 10,000 vol., Science Labs, Computer Lab (27 networked computers), Gym, Playing Field.

Admission: Apply any time. Interview, Transcript, Teacher & Principal Recommendations.

Tuition: (1993-94) Half-Day N & K, $2,330; grades 1-8, $2,680 **Transportation**: one way, $320; both ways $640. *Dress Code*: Neat and in good taste. **Scholarship Aid:** 8 partial.

Future Plans: New addition to provide space for early childhood program.

Summer Program: Summer program for age 3 & 4, daily 7 a.m.-6 p.m.; Summer camp for K-grade 6 daily, 7 a.m.-6 p.m.

CONGRESSIONAL SCHOOLS OF VIRGINIA...........(703) 533-9711

3229 Sleepy Hollow Road, Falls Church, VA 22042
Founded 1939. **Head**: Eugene C. Rose

Grades: N (infant)-grade 8. **Enrollment**: 384 Co-ed. **Faculty**: 39 full-time.
Average Class Size: Pre -school (Age 2-5), Teacher/pupil ratio 1/7, 1/9; grades 1-8, 15-22.

Special Courses: French l-8, Spanish 6-8. Computer Pre-K- grade 8, Algebra 8. General Science 6, Life Science 7, Physical Science 8; Art, Music. **Extended Day**: available 7 a.m. -6 p.m., for Pre-school-grade 8.

Athletics: P.E. Program. Note: after-school program for grades 5-8. Soccer, Basketball, Softball, Track and Field, Swimming. **Clubs**: Service, Student Gov't, Drama, Art, Chess. **Publications**: Yearbook, Literary Magazine. **Community Involvement**: Through Service Club: Recycling project, Volunteer at W.S.P.C.A. (Humane Society), Nursing Homes, and Ronald McDonald House; Collect canned goods for local shelters.

Plant: 2 Libraries, 2 Science Labs, Art Studio, Assembly Room, 3 Playing Fields, 2 Swimming Pools.

Admission: Interview, Transcript & Recommendation from previous school. Testing. Application fee $50.

Tuition: (1993-94) $5,400-$7,020. **Extended Day** : Extra. Lunch: $395-$498. **Transportation**: $1,539-$2,,169. *Dress Code*: Uniform req. grades 1-8.

Summer Program: Recreation for ages 2 1/2-14 ; Swimming, riding, archery, art, music, outdoor sports.

CONNELLY SCHOOL OF THE HOLY CHILD..........(301) 365-0955

9029 Bradley Boulevard., Potomac, MD. 20854.
Catholic 1961. **Head**: Sister Margaret Doyle, SHCJ.

Grades: 6-12. **Enrollment**: 200 Girls. **Faculty**: 18 full-, 7 part-time.
Average Class Size: 15 Note: 20% of students, non Catholic.

Special Courses: Latin 10-11, French & Spanish- 7-12. Math includes Calculus, Computer. Gen'l Science, Biology, Chemistry, Physics. History: Western Civilization, U.S. History, Gov't. & Social Issues, Geography, International Relations.. Religious studies req.; Art Appreciation, and 4 yrs. Studio Art. Music, Photography; Note Multidisciplinary Humanities Course and two Consortium Courses open to 11 & 12. AP.: Spanish, French, U.S. History, Biology, Calculus, English, Chemistry.

Athletics: Intramural & Interscholastic: Basketball, Tennis, Cross-Country, Swimming, Volleyball, Soccer, Lacrosse, Hockey, Softball. **Clubs**: Art, Debate, GAA, Pep, Library, Nat'l

Honor Society, Black Awareness, Environmental, SADD, Service, Drama, Model OAS. **Publications**: Newspaper, Yearbook. **Community Involvement**: Service Program.

Plant: Library 10,000 vol., 3 Science Labs, 2 Art Studios, Gym, 2 Playing Fields, 2 Tennis Courts. Campus is in a pastoral setting.

Admission: Archdiocese Entrance Test or SSAT; School Visit, Interview. Recommendations; $35 Application Fee.

Tuition: (1993-94) 6-8, $7,250; 9-12, $8,250 **Books**: Extra. *Dress Code*: Uniform req. **Transportation**: reached by #36 Ride on and T-2 Metro bus. **Scholarship Aid**: 4 full, 46 partial.

CORNERSTONE CHRISTIAN ACADEMY..........(301) 262-7683

16010 Annapolis Road, Bowie, MD 20715
Head Mrs. Grace Sheleheda

Grades: PreK-12 **Enrollment**: Co-ed

Special Programs: ABEKA; small classes, individual attention **Extended Day**: 7:30 a.m.-6 p.m.

Tuition: (1993-94) $2,100

The COUNTRY DAY SCHOOL OF JEFFERSON COUNTY..........(304) 725-1438

P.O. Box 659, Charles Town, West VA 25414
Founded 1982 **Head**: Thomas H. Gast

Grades: K-9 **Enrollment**: 112 Co-ed **Faculty**: 17 full-, 8 part-time
Average Class Size: 18

Special Courses: Academic oriented: French K-9; Latin 6-9; Computer K-9; Art, Music, Math through Geometry; Science through Biology. Drama. Field trips: one per grade, per month and grade 3 visits Williamsburg, Jamestown, Yorktown. Latin Certamen 6-9; National Mythology Exam and National Geography Bee.

Athletics: P.E. K-9; Intra-mural programs for girls & boys in soccer and basketball. Skiing, Swimming, Horseback Riding, and Roller Skating.

Plant: Library, Language Lab, Computer Lab, Art/Music Facility, Playing Fields, Basketball Court

Admission: Interview parent & child; Placement Testing; Transcript. Application fee $25.

Tuition : (1993-94) $3,200-4,340 Books: extra **Financial Aid** : Some available

Future Plans: Addition of a sports/auditorium

Summer Program : Two week summer/sports camp; 3 sessions available. Tutoring by faculty members also available.

DeMATHA CATHOLIC HIGH SCHOOL..........(301) 864-3666

4313 Madison Street, Hyattsville, MD. 20781
Catholic 1946. **Head**: Mr. John L. Moylan.

Grades: 9-12. **Enrollment**: 820 Boys. **Faculty**: 52 full-, 2 part-time.
Average Class Size: 25.

Special Courses: Latin I-II, French I-IV, Spanish I-IV, Math through Calculus BC, Basic I-II, Fortran I-II, Pascal, Cobol; Biology, Chemistry, Physics, Economics, Business Law, Accounting Typing, Journalism, Mech. Drawing, Art History, Religious Studies req. Extensive Music program: Music Theory, 7 performing bands; Concert Band I-II, Wind Ensemble, Percussion Ensemble. Fundamental Art & Color Ceramics, Advanced Drawing, Architectural Drawing. AP.: English, History, Biology, Chemistry, Physics, Calculus: Regular and Honors courses also offered in these areas. Students are ability grouped and performance determines mobility. Strong counseling program to help students evaluate own potential both educationally and vocationally. Levels of Courses: Some students attend University classes; some take courses at DeMatha to earn college credits by examination; can participate in specialized study.

Athletics: (Not req.) Intramural & Interscholastic. Football, Basketball, Baseball, Cross-Country, Track, Ice Hockey, Softball, Soccer, Swimming, Wrestling, Lacrosse, Tennis, Golf. **Clubs**: Nat'l Honor Society, Science, Black Student Union, etc. **Publications**: Yearbook, Newspaper, Literary Magazine. **Community Involvement**: Social Action Groups and campus ministry program.

Plant: Library 12,000 vol., 5 Science Labs, Art Studio, Gym. Use of public parks for playing fields. Large new addition to academic building.

Admission: For grades 9 & 10 - Students in Catholic Elementary schools apply through Elementary schools; those in public school take High School Entrance Exam. School Records, standard Test scores, and character References. Grades 11 & 12 - Students must submit Transcript, References, High School Entrance Exam. Upon acceptance, $125 Registration fee.

Tuition: (1993-94) $3,780, plus fees.. *Dress Code*: Uniform Blazer and Gray Dress Trousers. Books: $175. Lunch: Cafeteria. **Financial Aid**: Available.

Summer Program: 5-week program for high school level repeat and preparatory courses; Typing.

DIFFERENT DRUM, INC..........(703) 971-0778

7150 Telegraph Road, Alexandria, VA. 223410
Founded 1973. **Director**: Mrs. Robin Harviel

Ungraded: Ages 14-18. **Enrollment**: 25 Co-ed. **Faculty**: 7 full-, 5 part-time.
Average Class Size: 8.

Special Courses: LD & ED Program. Remedial Reading & Math Program is individualized -student is taught at his level. Computer, General Science, Biology. All required Va. Social Studies, History, Math, English courses on secondary level. Elective courses include Typing, Vocational Class, Photography. Individualized curriculum for students who have been unsuccessful in public schools. Note: additional services include individual, group, and parent counseling.

Athletics: Informal sports program - all grades. **Publications**: monthly newsletter.

Plant: Basic Science Lab, Volleyball Court.

Admission: Social history, previous Testing (psychological & academic). Transcript req. prior to Interview with parents and students.

Tuition: State & County contract fees. **Transportation**: Available

DIVINE PEACE LUTHERAN CHURCH SCHOOL...........(301) 350-4522

1500 Brown Station Road, Upper Marlboro, MD 20772
Lutheran, 1983 **Head**: John Mittlestaedt

Grades: 1-8 **Enrollment**: 23 Co-ed **Faculty** : 2 full, 1 part-time **Average Class Size**: 4

Tuition: (1993-94) $1,900 **Financial Aid**: Some available

DuPONT PARK SCHOOL..........(202) 583-8500

3942 Alabama Avenue, S.E., Washington, D.C. 20020
Seventh Day Adventist, 1914. **Head**: Mrs. Lafese Quinones

Grades: Pre K-10. **Enrollment**: 215 Co-ed. **Faculty**: 15 full-, 3 part-time.
Average Class Size: 20.

Special Courses: Biology, Gen'l Science; America: Its People and Values, History. Bible K-10 (req.); Classroom worship service. Choir, Band, Typing, Home Ec. **Extended Day** : 7 a.m - 6 p.m.

__Athletics__: Req. Clubs: Many older students participate in Pathfinders (church-sponsored - like Scouts). __Publications__: Weekly newsletter.

Admission: Transcript, Interview, Test. Healthy children with no disciplinary problems.

__Tuition__: (1993-94) Averages $200/mo.(Discount for Siblings)
__Extended Day__: Extra. *Dress Code*: Uniform req. Books: Included in Registration Fee.

EARLY YEARS MONTESSORI...........(703) 237-0264

3241 Brush Drive, Falls Church, VA 22042
Founded 1990 __Head__: Mrs. Ahmad

__Ungraded__: Age 2-8 (grade 3) __Enrollment__: 50 Co-ed

__Special Programs__: __Extended Day__: 7 a.m.-6 p.m.

__Tuition__: (1993-94) $400/mo.

__Summer Camp__: Ages 2-8; Call for information

EDLIN SCHOOL...........(703) 758-1855

10922 Vale Road, Oakton, VA 22124
Founded 1989 __Head__: Elaine Mellman & Linda Schriebstein

__Grades__: K-8 __Enrollment__: 60 Co-ed __Average Class Size__: 12

__Special Courses__: Latin & French K-8. Extensive Math program with many computer courses. Science. History. English Language Arts program with emphasis on Shakespeare. Art, Music, Drama, Dance. Note: An alternative school for gifted students. __Extended Day__: 3:30- 6 p.m. __Athletics__: P.E. req. all grades. Racquet ball.

__Admission__: IQ. & Achievement Tests, Testing fall and spring. Child spends 3 days visiting in class.

__Tuition__: (1993-94) $6,100

__Future Plans__: A summer program.

EDMUND BURKE SCHOOL..........(202) 362-8882

2955 Upton St., N.W., Washington, D.C. 20008
Founded 1968. __Head__: (Mr.) Jean Mooskin and Richard Roth.

Grades: 7-12. **Enrollment**: 250 Co-ed. **Faculty**: 29 full-, 6 part-time.
Average Class Size: 15.

Special Courses: Rigorous college preparatory studies with full attention to basic skills, innovative course offerings, and intellectual challenge. Writing Center & Math Center for students of all grades; Math program integrates Algebra, Geometry, and Higher Mathematics; 7th Grade Linguistics Course; large array of Upper School electives, ranging from Peace Studies to Japanese History to Pascal Programming; AP courses in all disciplines; extensive use of city and the surrounding outdoor area.

Athletics: Intramural & Interscholastic. 20 Varsity, Jr. Varsity, and Middle School Teams for males and females in 8 sports (Potomac Valley Athletic Conference winner in Girls Cross Country, Soccer, & Basketball and Track & Field in 1989/90. PE and Health req. to 11th grade; Outdoor program. Full range of extracurricular activities including a thriving Theater program. **Clubs:** Debate Team, Model U.N. **Publications** : Yearbook, Literary Magazine, Newspaper. **Community Involvement**: Community Service Program for all grades.

Plant: Library 8000 vol., 4 Science Labs, Computer Lab, Art and Pottery Rooms, Gym, Playing Fields, Dark Room. School's center is an architecturally attractive atrium that is used for assemblies, meetings, recitals, etc.

Admission: SSAT or equivalent, plus Essay; Interview with parents; Student Visits for a day. Application fee $40. Transcript and Teacher Recommendations.

Tuition: (1993-942) $9,975. *Dress Code*: Neatness & cleanliness. **Scholarship Aid**: Available.

Summer Program: Academic: Developmental and College Preparatory Math; Verbal Skills, Study Skills. SAT Review, Computer courses among others. Camp: Summer Sports Camp in Pennsylvania.

ELFLAND SCHOOL..........(703) 971-4337

4511 Glenwood Drive, Alexandria, VA. 22310
Head: Elizabeth Hathorn

Grades: N2-l. **Enrollment**: 75 Co-ed. **Faculty**: 9 full-time, 5 part-time.
Average Class Size: 10.

Special Courses: **Extended Day** : 7 a.m.-6 p.m.

Plant: 2-l/2 acres of playing area.

Tuition: (1993-94) $375/mo. includes Lunch & **Extended Day**. Discount for 2nd child..

Summer Program: Arts & Crafts, Field Trips, Sports. June - Labor Day. 7 a.m.-6 p.m.

ELIZABETH SETON HIGH SCHOOL.......... (301) 864-4532

5715 Emerson Street, Bladensburg, MD. 20710
Catholic 1959. **Head**: Mrs. Geraldene Buckley

Grades: 9-12. **Enrollment**: 500 Girls. **Faculty:** 66 full-time. **Average Class Size**: 20-23

Special Courses: Besides the general college prep offerings: Careers in Art, Ceramics, Sculpture, Drawing and Painting; Business Education Word processing and Basic programming; Honors Program Latin, French and Spanish; Chorus, Concert Band, Symphonic Band; Nutrition, Clothing-Interior Design, Consumer Survival, The Family and the Child. Religious Studies. Honors Psychology, Introduction to Philosophy/ Theology, Sociology. AP: Biology, U.S.History, English, Government, Spanish, French, Calculus..

Athletics: Interscholastic. Basketball, Softball, Soccer, Volleyball, Track, Swimming, Cheerleading. **Clubs**: French, Spanish, Latin, Ecology, Mock Trial, Drama, Art, National Honor Society, SADD, Photography, Dance, Lacrosse. **Publications**: Newspaper, Yearbook. **Community Involvement**: Tutor in public schools, visit aged and help in Day Care centers; charity drives and involvement with S.O.M.E. and organizations helping the homeless in D.C..

Plant: Library 17,000 vol., Computer Center, Language Lab, Science Labs, Art Studio, Gym-Auditorium, Playing Fields, Tennis Courts, Home Economics Labs.

Admission: Arch-Diocese Entrance exam (call 202-853-4597 for dates)
Transcript. Registration fee $100.

Tuition: (1993-94) $3,650. Books: $150 *Dress Code*: Uniform: Req. **Scholarship Aid**: Available through Archdiocese and work/study.

EMERSON PREPARATORY SCHOOL..........(202) 785-2877:

1324 18th Street, N.W., Washington, D.C. 20036
Founded 1852. **Head**: Dr. John J. Humphrey.

Grades: 9-12 & PG. **Enrollment**: 150 Co-ed (over 3 terms including summer) **Faculty**: 2 full-, 12 part-time. **Average Class Size**: 12; Students are assigned to classes on basis of preparation and ability.

Special Courses: Note Intensive and accelerated program, ages 13-20; French, Spanish, German, Japanese & Russian: all 9-12. Math includes Calculus, Computer Programming. General Science, Ecology, Biology, Chemistry, Physics. History: U.S., World Geography, American Government; Law, Economics. The Individual & Society. Remedial Reading & Math. Typing, AP.: Math & Foreign Languages. There are two terms each year. (There are no extra-curricular activities). Small classes .

Plant: Library 5000 vol., Science Lab, Recreation Area.

Admission: Personal Interview, placement Exam - ETS, Math & English, Formal Application ($35 fee), Transcripts.

Tuition: (1993-94) $3,700 per term. Books: $200/term. *Dress Code*: Good taste. **Scholarship Aid**: 3 partial.

Summer Program: Intensive 6 week academic program, $1,600.

ENGELSIDE CHRISTIAN SCHOOL..........(703) 780-4332

8428 Highland Lane, Alexandria, VA. 22309
Baptist 1972. **Head**: Pastor, Robert Purdue

Grades: K4-12. **Enrollment**: 150 Co-ed. **Faculty**: 15 full-, 3 part-time. **Average Class Size**: 13.

Special Courses: Spanish, 9-12. Math includes Calculus, Computer. Gen'l Science, Biology, Chemistry, Physics. History-Geography, World, Government, U.S., World Studies, New Republic. Religious Studies, req.; Speech, Music, Choir & Ensemble. **Extended Day**: 7 a.m.- 5:30 p.m.

Athletics: P.E. Req. to Grade 10. Boys: Soccer, Basketball, Baseball; Girls: Volleyball, Basketball, Softball, Cheerleading. **Publications**: Yearbook.

Plant: Library 5,000 vol., Science Lab, Auditorium, Playing Fields.

Admission: Application, Interview, Testing. Registration fee.

Tuition: (1993-94) K, $1,850; 1-12, $2460 **Transportation**: $58-$72/mo. both ways *Dress Code*: Conservative.

EPISCOPAL HIGH SCHOOL..........(703) 379-6530

1200 N. Quaker Lane, Alexandria, VA. 22302
Episcopal 1839. **Head**: Lee S. Ainslie, Jr.

Grades: 9-12. **Enrollment**: 395 Co-ed (Boarding Only). **Faculty**: 64 full-, 4 part-time. **Average Class Size**: 12-15.

Special Courses: Latin, French, Spanish, Russian, Greek, all 9-12. Science: Biology, Chemistry Physics; Computer Science, Math through Calculus. History: English, U.S., Western Civilization, Modern, Russian. Anthropology, Economics. Art, Music. Religious Studies req. Driver's Ed., Art, Dance, Drama, Photography, Study Skills. AP.: History, English, Biology, Physics, Chemistry, Calculus, Computer Science, Latin, Spanish, French. Note: Washington Intern Program for Seniors. Study Abroad.

Athletics: Req. Interscholastic - Football, Track, Golf, Basketball, Lacrosse, Tennis, Squash, Baseball, Soccer, Volleyball, Wrestling, Cross Country. **Clubs**: E Club, Vestry, Debate, Science, Chess, Model U.N., Model Judiciary, Philanthropy. **Publications**: Yearbook, Newspaper, Literary Magazine.

Plant: Library 24,000 vol.; Computer Lab, Science Lab, Art Studio, Auditorium, Gym, Tennis Courts, Playing Fields, Swimming Pool, Chapel, Indoor Track, Outdoor All-weather Track.

Admission: SSAT, Interview; additional Tests if needed.

Tuition: (1993-94)) $17,900 Comprehensive Fee. **Books**: $100-$200. *Dress Code*: Boys: Shirt & tie to classes, Coat & tie for meals; Girls: Blazer and collared shirt for meals.
Financial Aid: Available

Future Plans: Renovation of campus theater.

Summer Program: Academic-three week program.

ETS CHAIYIM SCHOOL..........(301) 424-0721

215 W. Montgomery Avenue, Rockville, MD 20850
Head: Lee Cooperman

Grades: K4-8 **Enrollment**: Co-ed

Special Programs: ABEKA; small classes, individual attention, students advance at own speed.

Admission: Registration, $75

Tuition: (1993-94) K, Half-day, $1,692; 1-4, $2,472; 5-8 $2,688; reduction for siblings.
Transportation: Vans for Germantown, Gaithersburg area.

EVANGEL CHRISTIAN SCHOOL..........(703) 670-7127

14836 Ashdale Avenue, Dale City, VA 22193
Head: Dr. Dick Schimkus

Grades: K-12 **Enrollment**: 234 Co-ed **Faculty** 12 full-, 6 part-time
Average Class Size : 15

Special Programs: Traditional College Preparatory Program in High School.
Extended Day: 6 a.m.-6 p.m.

Athletics: Interscholastic. Soccer, Volleyball, Baseball, Basketball, Softball, Track & Field.

Tuition: (1993-94) Half-day K $1,077; High School $2,196.

EVERGREEN MONTESSORI SCHOOL..........(301) 942-5979

10101 Connecticut Avenue, Kensington, MD. 20895
Founded 1964. **Head**: Lynn Pellaton.

Ungraded: Ages 2-1/2 to 12 (N-grade 6). **Enrollment**: 110 Co-ed. **Faculty**: 9 full-, 2 part-time
Average Class Size: primary 22, elementary, 18.

Special Courses: Integrated curriculum taught using the Montessori method, including (on elementary level): Language Arts, Spanish, Geography, Computer, History, Science, Music, Art, Math, Parent education. **Extended Day**: 7:30 a.m.- 6 p.m.

Athletics: P.E. req. for all grades-Includes Volleyball, Soccer, Kickball, Gymnastics.
Community Involvement: Elementary children spend time with younger children as part of the Student Service Corps.

Plant: Library; Playground: adjacent to public park with fields, basketball court, and play equipment for ages 6-12.

Admission: $50 Application fee. Interview; preference given to siblings and children with Montessori experience.

Tuition: (1993-94) N-K, $4,250-$6,450 depending on number of days, hours, etc.;
Grades 1-6, $6,750. Lunch: Bring. **Transportation**: Available. **Scholarship Aid**: Available.

Future Plans: Long range plan to purchase school building.

Summer Program: 9-10 week summer component: 2 1/4- 12 years, Montessori based program with field trips, swimming, fishing, and fun.

FAIRFAX BAPTIST TEMPLE ACADEMY..........(703) 323-8100

9524 Braddock Road, Fairfax, VA. 22032
Baptist 1976. **Head**: Gil Hansen, Administrator.

Grades: K4 - Grade 12. **Enrollment**: 250 Co-ed. **Faculty**: 5 full-, 10 part-time.

Special Courses: Strong Phonics Program: Grades K4-1, based on Pensacola Curriculum; Grades 2-12, Accelerated Christian Education, ABEKA and Bob Jones curriculum. Higher Math & Science, Piano & instrumental instruction available. Note: Emphasis on individual learning based on diagnostic testing. Child's ability determines level. Purpose of the Academy is to give academic training throughout with a solid Bible foundation.

Athletics: P.E. req. in Jr. & Sr. High. Intramural: Softball, Volleyball, Basketball, Soccer.
Clubs: Choir K-12. **Publications**: Yearbook. **Community Involvement**: All through association with the Fairfax Baptist Temple and ODACS.

Plant: Use church facilities which include 4 acres, Auditorium, Resource Center.

Admission: Interview, parent & child. Transcript & Recommendations. Registration fee, $75.

Tuition: (1993-94) K4 & 5, $1,860; 1-12, $2,490: Discount for Siblings. Books: Extra. *Dress Code*: Uniform req.

FAIRFAX-BREWSTER SCHOOL..........(703) 820-2680

5860 Glen Forest Drive, Baileys Crossroads, VA. 22041
Director: Mr. & Mrs. William Brill, Jr.

Grades: Age 4-grade 6. **Enrollment**: 215 Co-ed. **Faculty**: 15 full-, 3 part-time; 4 teacher aides. **Class Size**: 20 Maximum.

Special Features: Spanish, Music, Computer instruction for grades Jr. K -6.
Extended Day: 6:30 a.m.-6 p.m.

Athletics: P.E., Basketball, Soccer, Cheerleading, **Clubs**: Spanish, Girl Scouts and Brownies, Cub Scouts, Tiger Cubs, Jr. and Sr. Chorus, Cheerleading.

Plant: Pre-primary building and elementary school building; separated Playgrounds; modern classrooms with computers, Cafeteria.

Admission: Interview, parent & child; Transcript; Evaluation

Tuition: (1993-94) $385/mo.; all supplies included. Lunch: $45/mo. (Breakfast $10.75/mo.) **Transportation**: $65/one way, $120/both ways. 10% reduction for siblings. *Dress Code*: Uniform grades 1-6. **Extended Day**: Extra.

Summer Camp: ages 4-12. "SAFARI" program ages 6-11. Swimming, extended field trips, sports, arts & crafts, June-August.

FAIRFAX CHRISTIAN SCHOOL...(703) 759-5100

1624 Hunter Mill Road, Vienna, VA. 22182
Founded 1961. **Head**: Robert L. Thoburn II

Grades: K4-12. **Enrollment**: 300 Co-ed. **Faculty**: 15 full-, 5 part-time.

Special Courses: French 1-12, Russian 8-12. Math includes Calculus, Computer (8-12). General Science, Biology, Chemistry, Physics, Economics, History - U.S., World. Music-Choral & Instrumental, Band. Religious Studies req. Driver's Ed. Note: Advanced curriculum offered.
Extended Day: to 6 p.m.

Athletics Req., Intramural. Baseball, Basketball, Soccer.

Plant: 28 acre campus off Dulles Toll Rd.; Playing Fields, Basketball Courts.

Admission: $150 Registration fee; Interview req.; Possible Testing; Transcript.

Tuition: (1993-94) K-1,$3,600; 2-7, $3,750; 8-12, $5,500; (can be paid in 10 installments)
Books and Milk: Included **Transportation:** $1,400 first child, $700 each additional child
Extended Day: Extra

Future Plans: Additional Buildings, Expand Student Body.

FAITH CHRISTIAN SCHOOL..........(703) 430-0499

21393 Potomac View Road, Sterling, VA. 20164
Independent Bible. Founded 1980. **Head**: David K. Duffy.

Grades: PreK-8. **Enrollment**: 305 Co-ed. **Faculty**: 20 full-, 2 part-time.
Average Class Size: 21

Special Courses: Religious studies req. Traditional academic program; LD (Learning Differences) Program . Band, Jr. High Student Council. **Extended Day**: 7 a.m.-5:30 p.m.

Athletics: P.E. req.; Basketball & Soccer. **Publications**: Yearbook, Student Newsletter.

Plant: Library, 16 Classrooms, Gym, Auditorium, LD Centers, Playing Fields.

Admission: Interview

Tuition: (1993-94) PreK, $700-$3,500; grades 1-5, $2,300; 6-8 $2,400; discount for siblings.
Books Extra **Financial Aid** : Available

Future Plans: Additional classrooms.

FALLS CHURCH CHILDREN'S HOUSE OF MONTESSORI...........(703) 573-7599

3335 Annandale Road, Falls Church, VA. 22042
Founded 1971. **Head**: Carol Bowers.

Ungraded: Ages 2-1/2 - 7. **Enrollment**: 92 Co-ed. **Faculty**: 6 full-, 13 part-time.
Average Class Size: 23.

Special Features: Montessori method, ungraded classes. French, Enrichment program one day a week. Children learn about nutrition, travel, science, etc. - special snack and art project always related. **Extended Day** : 7:30 a.m.-5:30 p.m.

Admission: $100 Registration fee. Not accepted after age 4 unless previously enrolled in Montessori school.

Tuition: (1993-94) Half-day, $310/mo.; Full day only - $540/mo. (includes hot Lunch and two snacks).

Summer Program: Program with special crafts, gardening and "splash pools".

FIELD SCHOOL ....(202) 232-0733

2126 Wyoming Avenue, N.W., Washington, D.C. 20008
Founded 1972. **Director**: Mrs. Elizabeth C. Ely

Grades: 7-12. **Enrollment**: 170 Co-ed. **Faculty**: 19 full-, 8 part-time.
Average Class Size: 12.

Special Courses: Latin, French, Spanish - all 7-12. Art & Music. Drama, Photography, Woodshop, Pottery. General Science, Biology, Chemistry, Physics. History: Modern European, American, Chinese History & its impact on Western Civilization in 20th Century. Note: Curriculum is integrated (Literature/ History/ History of Art/ Music History) by historical period for each grade. Language & Math are ability grouped. Composition taught as separate class for each grade. Study skills incorporated into humanities curriculum. Foreign language exchange programs to France & Spain. Theater presentations, Chorus. Typing. AP.: Physics American History, Calculus, Computer Science, & American Literature, Advanced Writing.

Athletics: Req.; Intramural & Interscholastic. Member PVAC. Soccer, Tennis, Baseball, Volleyball, Basketball, Aerobics, Track & Field, X-Country. **Publications**: Yearbook, Newspaper, Literary Magazine. **Community Involvement**: 2 week intern program for students in community service. Youth in Philanthropy program.

Plant: Library 2500 vol., Science Labs, Shop, Art Studio, Photo Studio & Darkroom, Ceramics Studio, Small Theater. Volleyball Court, Gym. Access to playing fields. Friends Meeting House is used for all school assemblies. Adjunct campus, Leesburg, VA., 93 acres.

Admission: $35 Application fee; Student spends day at school followed by Interview with Director which includes parents. SSAT strongly recommended; Essays req.

Tuition: (1993-94) $10,375 includes Books. Lunch: Bring. *Dress Code*: decent attire.
Scholarship Aid: Some available.

Summer Program: Academic- Math Summer School and Typing Class. Recreational- two week sports camp in August. In Leesburg, VA., three week summer Arts Program.

FIRST BAPTIST SCHOOL OF LAUREL...........(301) 490-1076

811 Fifth Street, Laurel, MD 20707
Head: Brenda Schilling

Grades: N-6 **Enrollment**: 135 Co-ed. **Average Class Size**: 16
Special Courses: P.E., Music, Day Care for ages 2-4; **Extended Day**: 7 a.m.-6 p.m.

Tuition: (1993-94) N $70-$90/mo; K $1,800; 1-6, $2,000. **Extended Day:** N2 $95/wk; N3 & N4 $90/wk. Lunch: Bring.

Summer Program: only for children enrolled yr. round.

FLINT HILL SCHOOL..........(703) 242-0705

10409 Academic Drive, Oakton, VA. 22124
Founded 1956. **Head**: Thomas C. Whitworth.

Grades: K-12. **Enrollment**: 500 Co-ed **Faculty**: 50 full-, 5 part-time.
Average Class Size: 11.

Special Courses: Latin 7-12, French & Spanish 8-12, German 10-12. Math includes AP Calculus. Computer-Graduation requirement. Biology, Chemistry, Physics, Field Ecology. History: U.S., Modern European, Comparative World Cultures, Soviet Studies, War & Peace in the 20th Century, Ancient Civilization. Music- Choral, Guitar; Drama. Note: Learning center available for mild learning style differences and enrichment. AP.: English, Calculus, Biology, Chemistry, Physics, U.S. History, Latin, Spanish, French. **Extended Day**: 3:30 p.m.-6 p.m.

Athletics: Req. Grade 6-11. Intramural 6-8, Interscholastic 7-12. Golf, Basketball, Baseball, Swimming, Soccer, Tennis, Football, Track, Lacrosse, Cross-Country. Clubs: Latin, Spanish, Journalism, Ski, Bird Banding, Astronomy. **Publications**: Yearbook, Newspaper.
Community Involvement: 60 hours of community service req. for graduation.

Plant: Library 30,000 vol.; Science Lab, Art Studio, Playing Fields, Multi-purpose for Music, Drama.

Admission: K-5: Entrance Test, Teacher Recommendations, Visit, Transcript; Grades 6-10: SSAT, Interview, Teacher Recommendations, Transcript. Application by March 5.

Tuition: (1993-94) K-3, $8,910; 4-12, $10,235. **Transportation**: $800-$1,560. Books: Extra. *Dress Code*: Uniform req. **Scholarship Aid**: 80 partial.

Future Plans: New Activities Center for Fall 1993.

Summer Program: Enrichment & Summer Studies for all grades, end of June-1st week of Aug, Trips to Mexico & Costa Rica. Day Camp: grades 4-12, 9 a.m.- 3 p.m. **Extended Day Care**: 7:30 a.m.-6 p.m.; Summer Sports Academy: Baseball, Softball, Soccer, Lacrosse, Golf, Tennis, Field Hockey, Basketball, Football.

FORCEY CHRISTIAN SCHOOL...(301) 622-2281

2130 E. Randolph Road, Silver Spring, MD. 20904
Founded 1977 **Head**: Mr. T. Kenneth Roussey, Jr.

Grades: N3-grade 6 **Enrollment**: 450 Co-ed. **Faculty**: 22 full-, 8 part-time.
Average Class Size: 18

Special Courses: Religious Studies req.; Language Arts, Math, Social Studies, Science, Bible, Art, Music. After School Programs in Piano, Band.

Athletics: P.E. required in all grades. Publications: Yearbook.

Plant: Library, 8,000 vol.; Gym.

Admission: Registration fee, K $160, grades 1-6 $200. Achievement Tests. Open enrollment, March 6 until classes fill.

Tuition: (1993-94) K, $1,400; 1-6 $2,200 (includes Books) Note: 20% discount for siblings.

Summer Program: Day camp for grades 1-6. Call 301-622-3498

FORK UNION MILITARY ACADEMY............(804) 842-3212

P.O. Box 278, Fork Union, VA 23055
Baptist 1898 **Head**: Col. Charles T. Clanton

Grades: 6-12, PG **Enrollment**: 625 Boys, 26 Day, 599 Boarding (all grades).
Faculty: 45 full-time **Average Class Size**: 14

Special Courses: Spanish, French, German, all 9-PG; Gen'l Science, Biology, Chemistry, Physics, Astronomy; History: World, U.S.; Economics, World Geography, Asian Studies, U.S. Gov't, Sociology. Religious Studies req. of all 11th graders or new 12th graders. Band, Chorale, Computer Science, Health & P.E.; Driver's Ed. AP: U.S.History, Calculus, English, Biology.

Athletics req. Intramural, Interscholastic. Football, Basketball, Baseball, Lacrosse, Wrestling, Track, Cross-Country, Swimming and Diving, Tennis, Golf, Soccer, Riflery. **Clubs**: (According to student interest) Boy Scouts, Explorers, Bicycling, Canoeing, Computer, Civil Air Patrol, Flight Training, Art, Bayonet, Military History, Debate, Fishing, Weight Lifting, Model Building, Fellowship of Christian Athletes,National Rifle Assoc., Jr. Rifle, Chess, Science, Quadrille (arranges school dances). **Publications**: Newspaper, Yearbook. **Community Involvement**: Cadets participate in Community activities for various churches & charities.

Plant: Library, 19,000 vols.; 5 Science Labs, 3 Gyms, Auditorium, 6 Playing Fields, 2 Swimming Pools, 4 Tennis Courts.

Admission: Interview recommended; $50 Application fee; Two letters of Recommendation req.; Quotas established for each grade level. Applicants accepted on basis of character and ability.

Tuition: (1993-94) Day $3,200 includes Lunch; Boarding $10,500 Books and fees: $195. *Dress Code*: Uniform req.(approx. $1,500) **Financial Aid**.: Available

Summer Programs: Summer School, non-military; grades 7-12 for enrichment, remediation, and review. Summer Camp: One week Basketball Camp for Boys.

FOXCROFT SCHOOL..........(703) 687-5555

Middleburg, VA. 22117
Episcopal 1914. **Head**: Mary Louise Leipheimer.

Grades: 9-PG. **Enrollment**: 136 Girls (108 Boarding, 28 Day). **Faculty**: 27 full-time. **Average Class Size**: 10-12

Special Courses: French, Spanish, Latin: all 9-P.G. Math includes advanced Algebra & Trig, Calculus, Computer; General Science-Biology, Chemistry, Physics, Anatomy, and Physiology, Ecology; History- U.S., World Civilizations, European, Africa, World Cultures, Nazi Germany. Art includes Drawing, Painting, Art History, Printmaking; Music includes History, Theory, Chorus, Ballet, Dance, Drama. Independent Study in grades 11-12. E.S.L. Program, Interim term with Senior Projects. AP.: in all disciplines.

Athletics: Req. to grade 12.; Intramural & Interscholastic: P.E.; Hockey, Soccer, Basketball, Tennis, Lacrosse, Softball, Riding, Volleyball. **Clubs**: Art, Drama, Outing, Athletic, Activities, Riding, Camera, Vaulting, Social Service, Octet, Blue Planet Society, Afternoon Delights.. **Publications**: Yearbook, Literary Magazine, Newspaper. **Community Service**: Students must complete a certain amount of community service each year.

Plant: Library 50,000 vol., Science Labs, Math Lab, Computer Lab, 4 Playing Fields, 5 Dormitories, Dance Studio, Pool, Art Studio, Gym, Stables (Trails & Rings), 8 Tennis Courts, Indoor Riding Ring, Fields, Observatory, 500 Acres, Auditorium.

Admission: SSAT req., Transcript & personal information req. Applications due mid-Feb.-early March but Rolling Admission. Fee $35, $45(foreign). Interview at school req. of U. S. students, recommended for overseas students. (Parent asking financial aid must complete SSS form).

Tuition: (1993-94) $12,600 Day; $19,400 Boarding. Books: $300-$350 **Transportation**: Available, Cost varies. *Dress Code*: Neat and orderly appearance, no jeans, no printed T-shirts. **Financial Aid**: Available.

Summer Program: Co-ed, 5 Day Residential Camp for ages 9-13; Adventure Program, for ages 11-13; Day Camp for ages 5-13: Riding, swimming, canoeing, arts & crafts, sports, music, hiking, & camping.

FREDERICK ACADEMY OF THE VISITATION..........(301) 662-3322

200 East Second Street, Frederick, MD. 21701
Catholic 1846. **Head**: Sister Mary Paula.

Grades: K4-8. **Enrollment**: 125 Girls - Boarding (grades 5-8) & Day

Special Courses: French, Computer, Dance. Special language department for foreign students.
Extended Day: 7 a.m.-7 p.m.

Tuition: (1993-94) Day $1,700; Boarding $9,000-$10,000.

FREDERICK CHRISTIAN ACADEMY..........(301) 473-8990

6642 Carpenter Road, Frederick, MD. 21702
Founded 1974. **Head**: Rev. Roger Salomon.

Grades: K3-12. **Enrollment**: 300 Co-ed. **Faculty**: 20 full-, 3 part-time.
Average Class Size: 15-22

Special Courses: Foreign Languages; English; History, Government, Geography; Science, Math, Computer; Accounting, Business Law, Business Procedures; Drama ,Speech, Drafting, Photography; Fine Arts. **Extended Day**: 6:45 a.m.-6 p.m.

Athletics: Req.; Intramural sports. Soccer, Basketball, Volleyball, Cheerleading. **Clubs**: Yearbook, Photography. **Publications**: Yearbook.

Plant: Library, Science Lab, Gym, Auditorium, Playing Fields.

Admission: Entrance Test ; $75 Registration fee

Tuition: (1993-94) $2,244 **Transportation by zone**: $540-$840. Lunch: available.
Dress Code: Uniform req. **Financial Aid** : Available

Summer Program: For pre-school, age 3-4yrs ; Super Summer camp for K5-grade 6.

FREDERICK SEVENTH DAY ADVENTIST SCHOOL..........(301) 663-0363

80-A Adventist Drive, Frederick, MD. 21701
Adventist, 1951. **Head**: Dan Goddard

Grades: K-8. **Enrollment**: 81 Co-ed. **Faculty**: 4 full-6 part-time.
Average Class Size: 18-22

Special Courses: Remedial Reading & Math. Economics. Religious Studies, req. Art, Music, Bell Choir; Computer. **Extended Day**: 7:30 a.m.-5:30 p.m.

Athletics: P.E. req. **Clubs**: Yearbook staff. **Publications**: Yearbook **Community Involvement**: Students visit Nursing Home

Plant: Library 3,500 Vol., Science Lab, Gym, Auditorium, Playing Fields.

Admission: Iowa Test of Basic Skills, grades 3-8. $125 Registration fee.

Tuition: (1993-94) $130/mo for Frederick S.D.A. Church member; $220/mo for non- member. *Dress Code*: No tank tops; No tight jeans, No shorts in grades 4-8. **Scholarship Aid**: Some partial available.

Future Development: Add new library and additional classrooms.

Summer Programs: Special tutoring by a certified teacher on fee basis. Instrumental music lessons; Band. Bell Choir.

FREEDOM CHRISTIAN ACADEMY..........(301) 736-2500

2916 East Avenue, Forestville, MD 20747
Head: Willetta Langon

Grades: PreK-12 **Enrollment**: Co-ed

Special Courses: **Extended Day** to 6 p.m.

Tuition: Call for information

FRENCH INTERNATIONAL SCHOOL..........(301) 530-8260

9600 Forest Road, Bethesda, MD. 20814
Founded 1967. **Head**: Pierre Hudelot

Grades: N-13. **Enrollment:** 980 Co-ed. **Faculty**: 70 full-time. **Average Class Size**: 20-25.

Special Courses: Latin 8-12, French K-13, Spanish 9-13, German 9-13, Remedial Reading, Art, Music, Biology, Chemistry, Physics, General Science, Economics. American History, French History & Geography. Computer Learning; Video Tape. Note: All classes are taught in French. The academic program follows the French School system except for additional English.

Athletics: Req. Intramural: Soccer. Interscholastic: Volleyball, Basketball.
Publications: Yearbook.

Plant: Library 10,000 vol., Language Lab, Art Studio, Gym, Playing Fields, Media Center.

Admission: Interview, Tests. Registration fee $110. Note: Students must be fluent in French except in N. Student body represents 52 nationalities.

Tuition: (1993-94) K $6,000; Primary $5,620; Junior High $6,530. High School $7,450
Transportation: $350 round trip.

Summer Program: Two Sessions- Ages 4-14;

FRIENDS COMMUNITY SCHOOL..........(301) 699-6086

4601 Calvert Road, College Park, MD. 20740
Quaker 1986 **Head**: Jane Manning

Grades: K-6 **Enrollment**: 100 Co-ed **Faculty**: 6 full-, 5 part-time.
Average Class Size: 15

Special Courses: Spanish; Math: Their Way; Science. Social Science is integrated with field trips. Writer's Workshop, Whole Language Approach, Great Books; Art, Music; Multi-age classes; conflict resolution program. **Extended Day** : 8 a.m. -5:45 p.m.

Athletics: Gymnastics, Swimming, Co-operative Games, Skills. **Publications**: Weekly Newsletter **Community Involvement**: visit to Nursing Home; donations to soup kitchens; Ecology projects.

Plant: Library, Playing Fields.

Admission: Application Fee $40; Interview, Visit.

Tuition: (1993-94) $4,700 includes Books. Lunch: Bring
Scholarship Aid: Some Available.

FROST SCHOOL AND COUNSELING CENTER..........(301) 933-451

4915 Aspen Hill Road, Rockville, MD. 20853
Founded 1975. **Head**: Sean McLaughlin

Ages: 11-19 **Enrollment**: 35 Co-ed. **Faculty**: 5 full-, 2 part-time. **Average Class Size**: 6.

Special Courses: Spanish. Business Math, Consumer Math, Algebra, Geometry. Remedial Reading & Math. U.S. History I-II, Ancient & World History; Psychology, Sociology, Economics, Anthropology; Art. Advanced work provided when needed. Typing. Note: Teachers trained to work with students with emotional problems. Great flexibility at individualizing a program. Aim is to bring students up to grade level and to motivate students to become involved in academics. Program is operated on year-round basis. Counseling is integrated into daily schedule; students may work part-time and receive credit for same. School is approved by both Maryland, Virginia, & D.C. Boards of Education.

Athletics: Req. Variety of intramural sports.

Plant: Library 4000 vol., Science Lab, Art Studio, Playing Fields, Gym.

Admission: Interview-exchange information, 3 evaluation sessions . Students may be referred by physician, social service agency or school system.

Tuition: May be paid in part or in full by local school system. Counseling fee may be covered by family's health insurance. Scholarships may be arranged.

GAITHERSBURG INTERNATIONAL SCHOOL ....(301) 840-9335

429 West Diamond Avenue. Gaithersburg, MD. 20877
Founded 1977. **Head**: Mrs. Sandhoo

Ungraded: Ages 2-1/2 -6. **Enrollment**: 52 Co-ed.(Capacity 75) **Faculty**: 4 full-time, 7 assistants. **Average Class Size**: 22.

Special Courses: Montessori method. French, Computer, Creative Movement, Music.
Extended Day: 7 a.m.-6 p.m.

Plant: Library in each room, Playing Field.

Admission: Interview parent & child; Application & Registration $50

Tuition: (1993-94) Half-day, $325/mo; Full, $490/mo. Bring Lunch. **Extended Day**: included

Summer Program: Camp - ages 2-1/2 -8. Swimming, arts & crafts, nature study, music, drama. Hours: 7 a.m.-6 p.m.

GARRISON FOREST SCHOOL..........(301) 363-1500

300 Garrison Forest Road, Owings Mills, MD 21117
Founded 1910. **Head**: Elsa M. Bowman

Grades: Pre K-12. **Enrollment**: Note: N & K is Co-ed. Grades 1-12, Girls only. Total enrollment, 489, Day-404, Boarding 85 (Boarding begins grade 8) **Faculty**: 65 full-, 15 part-time. **Average Class Size**: 14.

Special Courses: Latin 7-12, French & Spanish, 1-12. Algebra -Calculus; Computer-practical, programming; Finite Math. Biology, Chemistry, Physics, Physical Science, Field studies in Ecology, Current Issues in Science, Animal Behavior, Geology. History- World, U.S., Contemporary World Issues, Ethnicity in 20th Century America, Major Religions, Modern

China, Russian/Soviet History; America since 1945. Anthropology, Psychology, Child Development. Art, Music, Theater Arts, Dance. AP. English, French, Spanish, Latin, U.S. History, Calculus, Biology, Studio Art, Art History. **Extended Day** : 3:30 p.m.-6:30 p.m.

Athletics: Req.; Interscholastic. Riding, Polo, Field Hockey, Basketball, Lacrosse, Tennis, Cross Country, Badminton, Soccer, Softball. **Clubs**: Activities, Athletics, Chapel Committee, Cultural Awareness, Singing Groups, Foreign Language Clubs, Drama, Outing, Riding, Ski, Tour Guides, Model U.N., Community Service. **Publications** : Yearbook, Newspaper, Literary Magazine. **Community Involvement**: Comprehensive Community Service Program run by students with a faculty advisor.

Plant: Library 16,000 vol., 3 Science Labs, Art Studio, Auditorium, 2 Gyms, Weight Training Center, Dance Studio, 3 Dorms, Tennis Courts, Chapel, Stables, Playing Fields.

Admission: Apply by Feb. 1; Testing-SSAT, Upper School; ERB, Otis Lennon Middle School; Stanford Achievements Lower School. Interview on campus, req., Transcript, Teacher Recommendations. Application fee: Upper & Middle School, $35.

Tuition: (1993-94) $1,260-$9,970 Day; $19,260 Boarding. Lunch: $2.50/day-Lower; $3.00/day, Middle & Upper. Books $200 **Transportation**: $325-$600 for day students.
Dress Code: Uniform req. **Scholarship Aid**: 80 partial.

Future Plans: Fine Arts Center, Student Center. Master plan to improve all sections of the campus.

Summer Program: Camp for Pre and Lower School Children; Pony Club.

GEORGE SCHOOL..........(215) 579-6547 Fax (215) 579-6604

Admissions Office, Box 4000, Newtown, PA 18940
Quaker, 1893 **Head**: David L. Bourns

Grades: 9-12 **Enrollment**: 532 Co-ed (295 Boarding) **Faculty**: 70 full-, 8 part-time.
Average Class Size: 15

Special Courses: College Preparatory, AP & International Baccalaureate Programs; ESL, IB, Fine Arts, Performing Arts Courses; Outdoor Adventures.

Athletics: 101 Team Sports for Boys and Girls, including: Basketball, Football, Baseball, Softball, Lacrosse, Field Hockey, Soccer, Swimming, Diving, Riding, Tennis, Track & Field, Cross-Country, Cheerleading, Dance, Wrestling; **Clubs** : 40 Clubs and **Community Service** Workcamps.

Plant: 265 Acre Campus: Library, 25,000 vol.; 5 Classroom Buildings, Meeting House; 2 Girls Dorms, 4 Boys Dorms; Word Processing Center; 9 Playing Fields, 14 Outdoor Tennis Courts, Indoor Tennis Courts, 2 Gyms, Cross-Country Course, Cinder Track, Swimming Pool, Stables, Barn; Alternate Energy Center houses Solar Greenhouse & Dance Studio.

Admission: SSAT, Application, Essay, 3 School Recommendations, Interview, Transcript

Tuition: (1993-94) Day $11,650; Boarding $17,900 **Financial Aid**: Available

GEORGETOWN DAY SCHOOL..........(202) 333-7727, H.S. (202) 966-2666

4530 MacArthur Blvd., N.W., Washington, D.C. 20007
4200 Davenport Street, N.W., Washington, D.C. 20016 (H.S.)
Founded 1945 (parent owned). **Head**: Gladys M. Stern.

Grades: Pre K-12. **Enrollment**: 992 Co-ed. **Faculty**: 114 full-, 16 part-time.
Average Class Size: Lower/Middle - 20; High School - 15.

Special Courses: French & Spanish 4-12; Latin 6-7, 9-12. Math includes Calculus. Computer Programming. Gen'l Science, Biology, Chemistry, Physics, Human Behavior. History- U.S. Gov't & Politics, Western Civilization to Middle Ages, Global History, U.S., European, Anthropology, Cultural Anthropology. Art, Music Drama, Band, Photography. AP.: Art, Computer Science, French Literature, Spanish Literature, Calculus, Biology, Chemistry, Physics, U.S. History. **Extended Day** : 3 p.m.-6 p.m.

Athletics: Req. through 4 semesters of H.S.; Intramural & Interscholastic. Soccer, Basketball, Track & Field, Volleyball, Lacrosse, Cross Country, Softball, Tennis. **Clubs**: Debate, Newspaper, Literary Magazine, Chess, Math, Model U.N, Model Congress, " It's Academic", SADD, Amnesty International, Women's Issues, Black Issues, Yearbook. **Publications**: Yearbook, Newspaper, Literary Magazine. **Community Involvement**: Each High School student is Req. to complete 60 hrs. of community service.

Plant: 2 Libraries - Lower/Middle; 12,000 vol., H.S. 12,000 vol. Science Labs, Art Studio, Gym, Auditorium, Theater, Playing Field. Photography Lab, Computer Labs.

Admission: Parents Interview and Tour; Student Visit. $50 Application fee. SSAT req. grades 7-12. Committee begins meeting March 1.

Tuition: (1993-94) $10,162-$11,438; Extra fees $300 for first 3 yrs. Bring Lunch.
Financial Aid: 144 partial.

Summer Program: "Hop into Summer", all day program for grades PreK-5; Explore and Discover for grades 5-8; Counselor apprentice program; **Extended Day** and early morning programs.

GEORGETOWN PREPARATORY SCHOOL..........(301) 493-5000 FAX (301)493-5905

10900 Rockville Pike, North Bethesda, MD. 20852
Catholic 1789. **Head**: Rev. Thomas E. Roach, SJ

Grades: 9-12. **Enrollment**: 400 Boys, 100 Boarding. **Faculty**: 50 full-time. **Average Class Size**: 17.

Special Courses: Latin, French, Spanish, German: all 9-12; Greek. Math through Calculus Computer. Biology, Chemistry, Physics. History-American, Western Civilization. Economics. Religious Studies req.; Art, Music. ESL program. AP: English, Calculus, Biology, Physics, Computer Science, Chemistry, Modern European History, Art History, Studio Art, Music, Economics.

Athletics : Not req. Intramural & Interscholastic: Football, Track, Basketball, Cross Country, Swimming, Tennis, Golf, Lacrosse, Soccer, Wrestling, Baseball. **Clubs**: Forensics, German, French, Russian, International Relations, Math Team, Chess Team, Drama, Fencing, Computer, Photography, Student Council. **Publications**: Yearbook, Newspaper. **Community Involvement**: Required Service Projects for all students.

Plant: Library 15,000 vol., Language Lab, 3 Science Labs, Theater, Art Studio, Gym, Playing Fields, Swimming Pool, Indoor Tennis Courts, Chapel, Golf Course, Synthetic Track.

Admission: Application Deadline Feb. 1.; SSAT, Interview, Transcripts, Recommendations from 2 teachers, auto-biographical essay. Reply date March 1.

Tuition: (1993-94) Day, $10,300; Boarding, $19,000 includes Lunch. Books: $350. *Dress Code* : Jacket and tie req. **Scholarship Aid**: 70 full or partial.

Summer Program: Summer Day Camp - co-ed, ages 6 to 13.
Summer School: For foreign students, co-ed, ages 14-18, Day & Boarding; intense English language and academic enrichment program.

GEORGETOWN VISITATION PREPARATORY SCHOOL.........(202) 337-3350

1524 35th Street, N.W., Washington, D.C. 20007
Catholic 1799. **Head**: Daniel M. Kerns, Jr.

Grades: 9-12. **Enrollment**: 403 Girls. **Faculty**: 32 full-, 19 part-time. **Average Class Size**: 20.

Special Courses: AP courses in the following subjects: English, Modern European History, U.S. History, Comparative Politics, Calculus, Biology, Chemistry. Electives in Creative Writing, Anthropology, Law, Psychology, among others. Bridge Program with Georgetown University enables selected students to take courses for college credit. Language Consortium with area high schools in Chinese, Japanese, and Russian.

Athletics: P.E. Req.; Interscholastic athletic teams: Volleyball, Basketball, Soccer, Field Hockey, Cross Country, Track, Swimming, Diving, Softball, Lacrosse, Tennis. **Clubs**: Co-curricular activities include over 35 Clubs: Model U.N., Prism Multicultural, Photography, Forensics Team, Madrigal Choir, Environmental Awareness, Chorus, Drama, Dance, Great

Books, Service, Black Women's Society, Language; Speakers Forum.. **Publications**: Yearbook, Newspaper, Art & Literary Magazine.

Plant: 24 acre campus includes four-story main academic building; Library 10,000 vol., 4 Science Labs, Art Studio, Auditorium, Gym, 4 Tennis Courts, 3 Playing Fields; Lodge & cabin.

Admission: Applications should be filed by Dec.15; Process includes a personal statement, student Interview, Recommendations from Math & English teachers; Transcript; Archdiocesan Entrance Exam..

Tuition: (1993-94) $7,450. Lunch: Catered, may be purchased. Books: $300 approx. *Dress Code*: Uniform req. **Financial Aid**: Available, based on need and merit..

Summer Program: Courses offered in pre-Algebra, English, and Word-processing, U.S. History, SAT Prep Course, First Aid and CPR. Note: Week prior to Labor Day: Camps in Field Hockey, Soccer, Tennis, and Volleyball.

GERMAN SCHOOL..........(301) 365-4400

8617 Chateau Drive, Potomac, MD 20854-4599
Founded 1961. **Head**: Peter Kasper

Grades: K-13. **Enrollment**: 560 Co-ed. **Faculty**: 41 full-, 8 part-time.
Average Class Size: Lower School, 20; Upper School, 20-24.

Special Courses: Art 5-13, Music 5-13, Latin 9-11, French 7-13, German l-13, English l-13. General Science 5 & 6, Biology, Chemistry, Physics. History-World, American History, Social Science. AP.: 11-13 English, French, German, Math, Biology, Chemistry. Computer Science. Religious studies. Typing, Drama, Choir, Orchestra. Note: Grades 5-13 are University preparatory; curriculum taught in German similar to that of a University preparatory school within Germany.

Athletics: Req. Swimming, Basketball, Soccer, Volleyball. **Publications**: Yearbook.

Plant: Library 25,000 vol., Science Lab, Art Studio, Auditorium, 2 Gyms, Playing Fields, Swimming Pool, Photography Lab, Music Lab.

Admission: Test, Interview, Transcript. Must be German speaking.

Tuition: (1993-94) K, $2,400; 1-13, $3,000-$3,500 **Transportation**: $60-$90/mo. both ways. Books: Extra.

GESHER JEWISH DAY SCHOOL..........(703) 998-6733

2908 Valley Drive, Alexandria VA 22302
Jewish, 1982 **Head**: Rabbi Reuven Taff

Grades: K-6. **Enrollment**: 105 Co-ed **Faculty**: 16 **Average Class Size**: 15.

Special Courses: General Studies & Judaic program, Hebrew Language; Resource Program. Religious Studies req.; Art, Music, Band, Computer. **Extended Day**: Monday through Thursday, until 6 p.m.

Athletics: P.E. req.; Intramural. **Publications**: Community Newsletter. **Community Involvement**: Perform at Senior Citizens Home, various synagogues in Northern Va; participate in certain activities sponsored by Alexandria Recreation Dept.

Plant: Library 4,500 vol,; Classes held in school wing of a synagogue.

Admission: Interview with parents & child; Testing, Transcripts when applicable; Consultation req. when child's fifth birthday falls after Oct. 1st; Final determination by Admission Committee.

Tuition: (1993-94) $5,460 **Transportation**: Available-cost varies with distance. **Scholarship Aid**: Available.

GIBSON ISLAND COUNTRY SCHOOL..........(410) 255-5370

5191 Mountain Road, Pasadena, MD 21122
Founded 1947. **Head**: John Hewett.

Grades: Pre K-5. **Enrollment**: 96 Co-ed. **Faculty**: 12 full-, 4 part-time. **Average Class Size**: 15.

Special Courses: French, Pre K-5. Art, Music, Environmental Studies, 4-5.

Athletics: Req. Intramural **Clubs**: Science, French, Student Gov't. **Publications**: Weekly Newspaper, Literary Magazine.

Plant: Library 6,000 vol.; Computer Lab, Science Lab, Gym, Art Studio, Playing Fields.

Admission: Parent Visit; Testing; Interviews.

Tuition: (1993-94) $5,750, includes Books. *Dress Code*: Uniform req. **Transportation**: $600 both ways **Scholarship Aid**: 16 partial.

GLENELG COUNTRY SCHOOL..........(410) 531-2229

Folly Quarter Road, (P.O. Box 190) Glenelg, MD 21737
Founded 1954 **Head** Ryland O. Chapman, III

Grades: PreK-12 **Enrollment**: 400 **Faculty**: 55 full-time **Average Class Size** :18

Special Courses : French, Latin, Spanish; Computer Science, Art, Music, Chorus, Drama; Remedial Reading; Philosophy & Religion. Ecology.

Athletics: Req.; Intramural & Interscholastic; Soccer, Field Hockey, Cross- country, Basketball, Lacrosse, Tennis. **Publications**: Yearbook, Newspaper, Literary Magazine.

Plant: 2 Libraries, 3 Science Labs, Gym, 3 Art Studios, Fields, Pool, Performing Arts Room, 2 Computer Rooms.

Admission: Interview, Tests req.; class visits optional.

Tuition: (1993-94) PreK, $3,500; K $6,350; 1-12, $6,950-$8.350 Books: Extra. **Transportation**: $1,300 both ways. *Dress Code*: Good taste. **Financial Aid**: Available

Summer Program: Summer School - Grades 1-9, Remedial or Enrichment. Summer Day Camp - Ages 6-13. Pre-K Camp, ages 4-5.

GONZAGA COLLEGE HIGH SCHOOL..........(202) 842-1650

19 Eye Street, N.W., Washington, D.C. 20001
Roman Catholic/ Jesuit 1821. **Head**: Dr. Joseph Ciancaglini/ Rev. Bernard Dooley (President)

Grades: 9-12. **Enrollment**: 750 Boys. **Faculty**: 62 full-, 8 part-time. **Average Class Size**: 25.

Special Courses: Latin, French, Spanish, German - all 9-12; Greek 3 yrs. Math thru Calculus, Computer Science, Math Analysis and Statistics. Biology, Chemistry, Physics, Psychology. History- World Cultures, European and American. Politics, Economics, and Social Justice. Religious Studies req.; Art, Music, Learning Development; Driver's Ed., Band, Drama, TV. Communications. Extensive Retreat Program. AP.: Languages, Science, Math, History, English, Computer Science.

Athletics: Not Req. Intramural & Interscholastic. Football, Soccer, Basketball, Baseball, Softball, Cross-Country, Track & Field, Tennis, Golf, Swimming, Diving. **Clubs**: Languages, Forensics, Drama, TV Communications, Booster, Chess, Bridge, Math, Science. etc. **Publications**: Newspaper, Yearbook, Literary Magazine. **Community Involvement**: Mandatory Social Justice Program for all Seniors. Enrichment program for neighborhood children. Appalachian project. Summer project-working in orphanage in Mexico.

Plant: Library 15,000 vol., Language Lab, Science Lab, Art Studio, Gym, Auditorium, Playing Fields, Tennis Courts, Track.

Admission: Grade 9: Application, Achievement Test, Transcript, Recommendations of teacher. Apply by Dec. 15. For other grades, contact Director of Admissions.

Tuition: (1993-94) $6,550. Lunch: Extra. Books: Extra. *Dress Code*: Dress pants, shirts, shoes. **Scholarship Aid**: 230 full & partial, need based.

Summer Program: Academic but remedial for those who may need to review or complete a course; Academic enrichment program. Also Purple Eagle Basketball Camp, Football Camp.

GOOD COUNSEL HIGH SCHOOL..........(301) 942-1155

11601 Georgia Avenue, Wheaton, MD. 20902
Catholic 1958. **Head**: Mr. Michael E. Murphy

Grades: 9-12. **Enrollment**: 950 Co-ed **Faculty**: 50 full-time. **Average Class Size**: 26

Special Courses: Latin, French, Spanish; Art, Instrumental Music, Math; Religion Req. Typing, Driver's Ed., Mechanical Drawing. Honors level available, AP.: English Literature, French, Spanish, Calculus Biology, Physics, U.S., European History, Politics.

Athletics: P.E. req. through Grade 10. Intramural & Interscholastic. Football, Basketball, Soccer, Cross Country, Track & Field, Indoor Track, Swimming, Wrestling, Tennis, Baseball, Softball, Golf, Lacrosse. **Clubs**: Booster, Drama,Chess, Spanish, French, Math, Political Science, Volunteers, Speech & Debate, Sportsmen, National Honor Society, Student Council. **Publications**: Yearbook, Newspaper, Literary Magazine. **Community Service**: Project req. for Seniors; underclasses encouraged to volunteer in day camp or recreation programs for the underprivileged.

Plant: Library, Language Lab, 3 Science Labs, 2 Art Studios, Music Center, College Resource Room, Computer Center, Cafeteria, Gym, Auditorium, Playing Fields, Weight Room, Lighted Field, Chapel.

Admission: Contact Director of Admissions.

Tuition: (1993-94) $5,300 Lunch: Cafeteria. Books: Extra. **Financial Aid**: Available

Summer Program: Full academic credit and extra credit courses. **Camp**: Boys and Girls Basketball camps. Day Camp for underprivileged children; Driver's Ed.

GRACE ACADEMY..........(301) 733-2033

530 N. Locust Street, Hagerstown, MD. 21740
Founded 1976. **Head**: George F. Michael

Grades: K-12. **Enrollment**: 290 Co-ed. **Faculty**: 13 full-, 1 part-time.
Average Class Size: 22

Special Courses: Gen'l Science, Biology, Chemistry, Physics. History: U.S. & World. Gov't, Economics; Religious Studies, req.-Study of the Bible in grades 9-12. Remedial Reading & Math-limited. Computer Science, Accounting, Typing Emphasis on Grammar, Language, Literature.

Athletics: Not Req. Soccer (Jr. High), Softball (Girls), Volleyball (limited basis). **Clubs**: Christian Service Club (student leadership) **Publications**: Yearbook **Community Involvement**: Christian Service Club projects.

Plant: Library 10,550 Vol.; Science Labs, Gym/Auditorium

Admission: Interview, Achievement Test for placement, Recommendations; Note: emphasis is on Christian character development and on developing a Christian world-view for students.

Tuition: (1993-94)) $1,700; reduced rate for siblings. Bring Lunch. *Dress Code*: Modest & clean.

GRACE BRETHREN CHRISTIAN SCHOOL...(301) 894-2444, 630-3300, 868-1600

5000 St. Barnabas Road, Temple Hills, MD 20748 (N-K)
6501 Surrets Road, Clinton, MD. 20735 (N-12)
5214 Temple Hills Road, Temple Hills, MD.(K-5)
Highway 5, P.O. Box 283-1, Waldorf, MD. 20601 (N-5)

Grace Brethren Church 1965. **Head**: Pastor Howard Mays.

Grades: N-12. **Enrollment**: 950 Co-ed. **Average Class Size**: 25

Special Courses: Spanish 6-12, French 8-12; General Science, Biology, Chemistry, Physics; Computer Literacy and Math. Art, Music, Religion req., Bible; Chapel once a week. Drama, Band, Typing, Yearbook Note: L.D. Therapy Program; Talented & Gifted Program; College Classes-11 and 12; Dinner Theater. **Extended Day**: 6:30 a.m.-6 p.m.

Athletics: Req. to grade 9. Soccer, Basketball, Baseball, Softball Volleyball.

Plant: Library, Playing Fields, Chapel, Gym, Science Labs.

Admission: Parent/child interview. Registration fee $60. Required Testing.

Tuition: (1993-94) Half day $186/mo.; K-8 $302/mo.; 9-12 $330/mo. **Extended Day** : $463/ mo; Lunch: Bring. Books: $50-$110. *Dress Code*: Neat.

GRACE CHRISTIAN SCHOOL..........(301) 262-0158

7210 Race Track Road, Bowie, MD 20715
Baptist 1975. **Head**: Mrs. Kathy Brown

Grades: K 5 - grade 8. **Enrollment**: 230 Co-ed. **Faculty**: 19 full- time.
Average Class Size: 25

Special Courses: Algebra, 8. Computer Science & Lab all grades. Art, Music-Vocal & Instrumental. Religious Studies req.; P.E.

Athletics: Not req. Interscholastic: Boys Soccer (grades 6-8) in fall; Girls Volleyball in fall; Boys/Girls Basketball (grades 6-8) in winter; Softball, Baseball, Track.. **Publications**: Yearbook. **Community Involvement**: MS. Readathon competition, Community Service Programs.

Plant: Library 9,000 vol., Computer Lab, Auditorium, Playground, Large Indoor Multi-purpose Room.

Admission: Screening Tests all students. Application & Testing Fee $50. Enrollment Conference.

Tuition: (1993-94) K half-day $1,840; K(all day)- grade 8, $2,440 (Discount for siblings) Lunch: Bring . **Transportation**: Privately contracted. *Dress Code*: Uniform req.

GRACE EPISCOPAL SCHOOL..........(703) 549-5067

3601 Russell Road., Alexandria, VA. 22305
Episcopalian 1959. **Head**: Mrs. Shirley N. Tyler.

Grades: N-5. **Enrollment**: 101 Co-ed. **Faculty**: 13 full-, 3 part-time.
Average Class Size: 14-17 Pre-school, 8:1 ratio

Special Courses: Grades-Strong individualized academic program. French, grades. 4-5; Art, Music. Religious Studies req.; Computer literacy. Note: Small instructional groups, low pupil/staff ratio, and Developmental Pre-school Program; **Extended Day**: 7:30 a.m.- 5:30 p.m.

Athletics: P.E/ Creative Movement req. **Publications**: Newsletter
Community Involvement: Outreach Projects

Plant: Library 2,500 vol. Auditorium (shared) Multi-purpose rooms. Playgrounds, including semi-wooded area for nature study.

Admission: Application fee $50; Parent/Child Interview; Transcript, Testing as necessary.

Tuition: (1993-94) $1,275-$4,800. Supplies/Activities fee: $125-$160; Grades Bring Lunch, Milk Fee. **Extended Day**: Extra *Dress Code*: Comfortable, washable clothing; no sandals. **Financial Aid**: Full and partial on Tuition only.

GRACE EPISCOPAL DAY SCHOOL..........(301) 949-5860

9411 Connecticut Avenue, Kensington, MD. 20895 (1-6)
9115 Georgia Avenue, Silver Spring, MD. 20910 (N- K)
Episcopalian 1960. **Head**: Mrs. Carol Hjortsberg.

Grades: N-6. **Enrollment**: 225 Co-ed. **Faculty**: 16 full, 15 part-time.
Average Class Size: 10-15.

Special Courses: Spanish K-6, Latin 5 & 6, Gen'l Science, Computer, Math Enrichment class grade 4-6. Geography. Religious Studies req., one semester in grades 5 & 6. Library, Music, Art, Group Piano. **Extended Day** : 7:45 a.m..- 6 p.m.

Athletics: P.E. req. **Publications**: Yearbook, Literary Magazine of Children's Work.
Community Involvement: Community out-reach programs.

Plant: 11 Acre Campus with Playing Fields and woodlands; All-purpose room, Library, Science room, Art room, Computer Lab.

Admission: Parents Interview and Tour School; Testing K-6 and child visits class for a day. Teacher Recommendations and Transcripts. Earliest admissions decisions made by March 1.

Tuition: (1993-94) $5,700 Lunch: Bring Books and milk included. *Dress Code* : Uniform req.
Financial Aid: Some available.

Summer Program: Day camp for age 3 -5, (in Silver Spring) two three-week sessions each with thematic program. For ages 6 -10, (in Kensington)program includes environmental and natural sciences, arts & crafts, rehearsal & performance of a play.

GRACE LUTHERAN SCHOOL..........(703) 534-5517

3233 Annendale Road, Falls Church, VA. 22042
Head: Steve Lauber

Grades: K-8. **Enrollment**: 30 Co-ed.

Tuition: (1993-94) $1,500 **Transportation**: Some available

GRANITE BAPTIST CHURCH SCHOOL..........(410) 761-1118

7823 Oakwood Road, Glen Burnie, MD. 21061
Head: Rick Scarfi

Grades: K4-12 **Enrollment**: 232 Co-ed

Special Programs: **Extended Day**: to 5:30 p.m.

Tuition: (1993-94) K, Half-day, $1,360; full day, $2,095; 1-6, $2,050; 7-12, $2.200
Reduction for siblings

GREEN ACRES SCHOOL..........(301) 881-4100

11701 Danville Drive, Rockville, MD. 20852
Founded 1934. **Head**: Dr. Arnold S. Cohen

Grades: N-8. **Enrollment**: 290 Co-ed. **Faculty**: 22 full-, 14 part-time. **Cooperative**: Parent/teacher owned, team teaching, small instructional groups. **Average Class Size**: 28 in the grades.

Special Courses: Spanish. Algebra, Computers; General Science, Biology; Contemporary & American History, Global Issues; Art, Music, Drama, Family Life Education, Library, Outdoor Education, Physical Education, Research & Study Skills. Note: Older students work with younger students.

Athletics: Req.; Soccer, Basketball, Softball, Volleyball, Gymnastics, Track & Field, Creative Movement, Outdoor Education. **Clubs** : After school enrichment classes. **Publications:** Yearbook. **Community Involvement:** 20 hours of community service for grades 7 & 8 other grades participate in community drives for food & clothing, etc.

Plant: Library 11,000 vol., Science Lab, Art Studio, Swimming Pool, Playing Fields, Wooded area, Basketball Courts, Gym/Theater Building.

Admission: Parent Interview/Tour; Child Interview. Child must be age 4 by June 1 for PreK Applications due by Feb. 1st.

Tuition: (1993-94)Full Day PreK-8, $7,330; Lunch: Bring. Books: grades 7-8, Extra. **Transportation**: $1,260 Round Trip, $785 one way; reduced rate for siblings. **Financial Aid**: Some Available.

Summer Program: Summer Day Camp ages 4-12. One 6 week session.

GREEN HEDGES SCHOOL..........(703) 938-8323

415 Windover Avenue, Vienna, VA. 22180
Founded 1942. **Head**: George Schumacher

Grades: N3 -grade 8. **Enrollment**: 175 Co-ed **Faculty**: 28 full-, 4 part-time. **Average Class Size**: 15

Special Courses: Latin, French K-8, Spanish 5-8. Computer 1-8. Individualized Reading, Drama, Art, Music. Note: School offers accelerated Math, Science and English courses at least one year ahead of grade level. Pre-school Montessori Program; Enriched Elementary 1-5, Innovative Middle School. **Extended Day**: until 6 p.m.

Athletics: Req.; Daily P.E., after school sports club available. Publications: Yearbook, Monthly Newsletter.

Plant: Library 6,000+ vol.; Auditorium, Playing Fields, Science Lab, Computer Lab.

Admission: Children must be able students who would benefit from enriched curriculum. Admission based on Transcripts, Recommendations, Testing, and Interview.

Tuition: (1993-94) 1/2 Day $5,600; Full Day -up to $8,600. *Dress Code*: Uniform req. for special occasions. **Financial Aid**: Available.

Summer Program: Enrichment program, ages 3-10. **Extended Day and Transportation**: Available.

THE GRIER SCHOOL..........(814) 684-3000 FAX (814) 684-2177

Tyrone, PA. 16686 (165 miles from Washington, D.C.)
Chartered 1853. **Head**: Angelica Wutz

Grades: 7-PG. **Enrollment**: 136 Girls Boarding **Faculty**: 21 full-, 4 part-time.
Average Class Size: 8

Special Courses: French and Spanish 9-12. Math includes Algebra I-III, Geometry, Calculus, Computer Science and Appreciation. Science : General Science, Biology, Chemistry, Physics Human Anatomy, Science & Literature, Earth Science. History: U.S., World Cultures, Modern Global Issues. Remedial Reading and Math. Art: Ceramics, Painting, Design, Jewelry, Weaving. Note: Learning Skills and ESL. AP. Calculus.

Athletics: Required all grades; Intramural: Volleyball, Soccer. Interscholastic: Soccer, Horseback Riding, Basketball, Softball. Swimming. **Clubs**: Ecology, Spanish, French. **Publications**: Yearbook, Newspaper, Literary Magazine. **Community Involvement**: Young Life Christian Group, Adopt a Grandparent Program.

Plant: Library 10,000 vol., 2 Science Labs, Language Lab, 3 Art Studios, Gym, Auditorium, Playing Field, 5 Tennis Courts, 2 Swimming Pools, 2 Stables, Dance Studio.

Admission: Application, Two References, Parent Essay, School Transcript, Interview, PSAT optional.

Tuition: (1993-94) $17,250 Boarding. **Dress Code**: Informal, clean and neat.
Financial Aid: Available

Summer Program: Allegheny Riding Camp, Girls 8-16. intensive ESL program for 15 students who will be enrolled in September.

GUNSTON SCHOOL............(410) 758-0620

P.O. Box 200 Centerville, MD. 21617
Founded 1911. **Head**: Peter A. Sturtevant, Jr.

Grades: 9-12. **Enrollment**: 90 Girls (80 Boarding). **Faculty**: 15 full-, 2 part-time. **Average Class Size**: 9.

Special Courses: Note: College Preparatory & Chesapeake Bay Studies. Latin I & II, French I-V, Remedial Reading, Art, Music; Adv. Biochemistry, General Science, Biology, Computer, Chemistry, Physics. History: American, Modern European, Eurasian Studies, Political Science, World Geography. Photography, Ecology, Advanced Composition, House Management, Drama, Piano, Guitar, Art, Music History, Typing, Music Appreciation; Honors courses offered. Independent study week, Individualized instruction, Private tutoring. Full range of English and Mathematics courses.

Athletics: Req.; Intramural & Interscholastic. Field Hockey, Biking, Volleyball, Sailing, Basketball, Riding, Dance, Tennis, Softball. **Clubs**: Drama, French, Candy Stripers, Photography, Pep Club, Library. **Publications**: Literary Magazine, Yearbook. **Community Involvement**: Teachers' aides, Candy Stripe program, Church & civic aides.

Plant: Library 5000 vol., Science Labs, Language Lab, Auditorium, Art Studio, Stables, Playing Fields, Tennis Courts, Field House. Note: Located on the Corsica River for swimming, canoeing and sailing.

Admission: Interview, (fall or winter) $50 fee with application -credited toward tuition. No senio applicants.

Tuition: (1993-94) 5 Day Boarding $16,300, 7 day Boarding $18,300. Lunch: Included. Books: Included. *Dress Code*: Uniform req. **Scholarship Aid**: 12 partial.

HADLEY ACRES SCHOOL..........(301) 926-0337

20101 Woodfield Road, Gaithersburg, MD. 20882
Seventh Day Adventist 1957. **Head**: David L. Gardner

Grades: K-8. **Enrollment**: 75 Co-ed. **Faculty**: 5 full-, 1 part-time. **Average Class Size**: 15.

Special Courses: Spanish K-8. Religious studies req.; Art, Music. **Extended Day**: 7 a.m. -6:15 p.m., Mon.-Thurs; 7 a.m.- 4 :30 p.m. Friday.

Athletics: P.E. Req.; Gymnastics, Swimming **Publications**: Yearbook Newsletter. **Community Involvement**: Participate in functions of soup kitchen, nursing homes, and individua needs.

Admission: Registration fee $100, before June 7, $50. All new students are accepted on a 30 da probationary period. For entrance to K, must be 5 by Sept. 15; for grade 1, 6 by Sept. 15. Reading readiness testing.

Tuition: (1993-94) Church member, $1,625; Adventist, non-constituent, $2, 320; Non-Adventist, $2,785; includes Lunch. Books: $150. *Dress Code*: Neat & modest.

HARBOR SCHOOL..........(301) 841-6410

6601 Bradley Boulevard, Bethesda, MD. 20817
Founded 1972. **Head**: Judith Knotts

Grades: N3-grade 2. **Enrollment**: 155 Co-ed. **Faculty**: 21 full-, 2 part-time.
Average Class Size: 14. Reading and Computer Specialist on staff.

Special Courses: French, all classes; Computer; Art, Music, Remedial Reading and Math. Optional full day Nursery (9:30 a.m.-3:30 p.m.) **Extended Day** : 8:15 a.m. - 3:30 p.m.; 5 yrs. and up may stay until 6 p.m.

Plant: Library, Computer room, Playing Fields

Admission: $40 Application fee. Parent visits and observes.

Tuition : (1993-94) Half Day N, $3,745; K, $7,280; Grades 1-2. $7,580 **Extended Day**: Extra. **Financial Aid** : Available

HARBOUR SCHOOL..........(410) 974-4248

1277 Green Holly Drive, Annapolis, MD 21401
Founded 1982 **Head**: Dr. Linda Jacobs

Grades: N-12 **Enrollment**: 53 Co-ed **Faculty**: 23 full-, 3 part-time
Average Class Size: 4

Special Courses: Algebra, Computer. General Science, Biology, Chemistry, Physics. American History (2 yrs.), Government, World History, Economics. Remedial Reading and Math. Art, Drama Note: School is ungraded N-8 and is designed for Learning Disabled; program is completely individualized to meet each student's needs.

Athletics: Not required. **Clubs**: Drama, Computer, Crafts, Student Council. **Publications**: Yearbook, Newspaper. **Community Involvement**: Seniors are required to complete a Senior Community Service project.

Plant: Library, 5,000 vol.

Admission: Application Fee, Submit all previous Test Records; Interview and School Visit for half-day. Note: Student should have some type of learning problem.

Tuition: (1993-94) Lower/Middle School, $16,500; High School, $17,500. Books & Lunch: included. *Dress Code:* No holes, No Sex, Drugs, Alcohol on T-shirts or other apparel. **Scholarship Aid**: 8 partial.

Future Plans: Expansion: new building construction to include playground and playing fields.

Summer Program: Tutoring & Recreation.

HARGRAVE MILITARY ACADEMY..........(800) 432-2480

Military Drive, Chatham, VA 24531
Southern Baptist 1909 **Head**: Colonel Thomas Cunningham

Grades: 7-12, PG **Enrollment** : 320 (Girls, 17 Day); Boys, 303 (250 Boarding)
Faculty: 33 full-, 3 part-time, **Average Class Size**: 12

Special Courses: Spanish, French, German, & Latin; Math thru Calculus; Science: Physical Earth ,Enviornmental, Biology, Chemistry, Physics; Computer I & II, Pascal; American & World History, Government; Mechanical Drawing, Art; Bible, Health, Public Speaking, Business Law, Journalism; English as a Second Language; How to Study, SAT Prep.; Band, Horsemanship.

Athletics: P.E.; Football, Soccer, Cross-Country, Riflery, Basketball, Wrestling, Baseball, Track, Golf, Tennis, Lacrosse.

Plant: 240 Acre Campus;Library, Computer Lab, 2 Science Labs, Chapel, Auditorium, 2 Gyms, Outdoor Pool, 4 Athletic Fields, Weight & Nautilus Room, Rifle Range, Skeet Range, Stables, Outdoor Track, 5 Dormitories.

Admission : $50 Application fee, Transcripts, Campus visit or interview

Tuition: (1993-94) $12,275 includes Books, Laundry, Uniforms, Haircuts, Lab pass, Accident insurance. **Financial Aid**: Available

Future Plans: To build a Science Building and Aquatic Center

Summer Program: 5 week, non-military summer school

HEBREW ACADEMY OF GREATER WASHINGTON..........(301) 587-4100

2010 Linden Lane, Silver Spring, MD. 20910
Orthodox Jewish 1943. **Head**: Principal, Pinchos Hecht

Grades: N3-12. **Enrollment**: 530 Co-ed. **Faculty**: 25 full-, 50 part-time.
Average Class Size: 20.

Special Courses: Remedial Reading, Remedial Math, Art, Music, Religious studies req., Hebrew N-12, Half- day; Academic studies, Half- day. **Extended Day**: until 5:30 p.m.

Athletics: Req.; Intramural & Interscholastic: Tennis, Touch Football, Basketball, Volleyball, Softball.

Plant: Library 12,000 vol., Science Lab, Auditorium, Gym, Playing Fields, Tennis Courts.

Admission: Interview, req.; Transfer student-require knowledge of Hebrew.

Tuition: (1993-94) Half-Day N, $2,400; K-12, $4,828-$8,207 Lunch: Extra.
Transportation $700 both ways. *Dress Code*: No extreme styles.

HEBREW DAY INSTITUTE...........(301) 984-2111

11710 Hunters Lane, Rockville, MD 20852
Jewish, 1973 **Head**: To be announced

Grades: N2-grade 6 **Enrollment**: 280 Co-ed **Faculty**: 9 full, 35 part-time.
Average Class Size: N, 13; Grades K-6, 18

Special Courses: Hebrew K-6; Enrichment programs in Science and Math; Computer K-6. Religious Studies req. Remedial Reading & Math. Art, Music, Library Science. Note: Skills Augmentation Program for gifted & talented. **Extended Day** : 7:30 a.m.-6 p.m. except Friday in winter, then day ends earlier.

Athletics: P.E. req. **Clubs**: Chorus, Chess, Science. **Community Involvement**: Chorus performs regularly throughout the community at nursing homes, etc. Students participate in special projects related to Jewish & Israeli causes.

Plant: Library, 6,000 vol. Gym, Auditorium, Playing Fields. Recent renovation to Nursery School.

Admission: Application fee $55 for N, $85 for K-6; Interview req. for placement in K-6. (Registration fee applied to tuition).

Tuition: (1993-94) N-6, $5,500 . Lunch: Bring Books: $115 **Transportation**: $965 Mornings only. *Dress Code:* Modest attire. **Scholarship Aid**: Need based.

HEBREW DAY SCHOOL OF MONTGOMERY COUNTY..........(301) 649-5400

1401 Arcola Avenue, Silver Spring, MD 20902
Jewish **Head**: Rabbi Yitzchak Charner

Grades: K-6. **Enrollment**: 145 Co-ed. **Faculty**: 9 full-, 11 part-time.
Average Class Size: 15.

Special Courses: Hebrew. Religious Studies req. -full curriculum of Judaic Studies. Remedial Math & Reading. Art, Music, Choir, Drama. Individualized instruction in all areas-child progresses at own rate. **Extended Day**: to 6 p.m.

Athletics: P.E. req. all grades. Soccer. **Publications**: Weekly and quarterly Newsletter.

Plant: Library 3,000 vol., All-purpose room, Playing Fields, Auditorium.

Admission: Interview with parents & student; Testing where indicated.

Tuition: (1993-94) K - $4,800; Grades 1-6 $5,250. Note: Registration Fee for K-6, $150.
Scholarship Aid: Available.

THE HEIGHTS SCHOOL..........(301) 365-4300 FAX (301) 365-4303

10400 Seven Locks Road, Potomac, MD. 20854
Catholic, 1969 **Head**: Joseph W. McPherson, J.D.

Grades: 3-12. **Enrollment**: 220 Boys **Faculty**: 18 full, 2 part-time. **Average Class Size**: 20.

Special Courses: Latin 9-12, Spanish 6-10, Greek 11 & 12. Biology, Chemistry, Physics, Nature Study. U.S. & European History. Physiology, Art History, Economics, Logic, Shakespeare Seminar. Religious studies for Catholic students. Band 3-8. Entire program has traditional liberal arts orientation - program pace requires academically-motivated students - all courses at secondary level are accelerated.

Athletics: Req.; Intramural & Interscholastic: Tennis, Soccer, Basketball, Baseball,
Clubs: Drama, Computer, Chess **Publications**: School Yearbook, Newspaper.

Plant: 3 Classroom Buildings, Playing field, 3 Tennis courts, Gym.

Admission: Application, Transcript, Recommendations, Interview. $25 fee.

Tuition: (1993-94) grades: 3-5 $5,500; 6-8, $6,400; 9-12 $7,000, includes Books, milk.
Dress Code: Jacket & Tie. **Financial Aid**: Available.

Future Plans: Additional buildings.

Summer Program: Natural History Camp - boys grades 2-5 - includes classes, collecting expeditions, nature drawing, etc. Exploration Camp-boys, grades 6-8, enrichment classes.

HELLENIC AMERICAN ACADEMY.........(301) 365-2308

7108 Oak Forest Lane, Bethesda, MD 20817
Greek Orthodox **Head**: Dr. Devereaux Weld

Grades: N2-5 **Enrollment**: 70 Co-ed **Faculty**: 6 full-, 4 part-time. **Average Class Size**: 10

Special Features: Greek all grades, taught as a second language, one hour daily. Computer, General Science. Religious Studies req. Piano instruction available. Note: Students develop at own pace. **Extended Day**: 7 a.m.-6 p.m.

Athletics: P.E. all grades. **Publications**: Newsletter. **Community Involvement**: Visit & sing in Nursing Homes.

Plant: Library, Auditorium, Playground.

Admission: Interview parent/child; Child Visits classroom. Registration fee $200.

Tuition: Half-day N, $1,900; K-5,$4,600 includes Books *Dress Code*: Uniform req.
Financial Aid: Some Available.

HENSON VALLEY MONTESSORI SCHOOL..........(301) 449-4442

7007 Allentown Road, Temple Hills, MD. 20748
Founded 1965. **Head**: Mr. Gordon Maas

Ungraded: Ages 2-1/2 -12. **Enrollment**: 210 Co-ed. **Faculty**: 11 full-2 part-time, 5 aides.
Average Class Size: 25.

Special Features: Montessori primary and elementary ungraded programs. Computers in Elementary classes. Spanish all ages. Art, Music, P.E. Comprehensive integrated program in Math, Science. Note: LD Specialist on staff. **Extended Day**: 7:30 a.m.-6 p.m.

Plant: 4 acres of land for play and study. Library. Building especially designed to accommodate Montessori Classes.

Admission: Interview, $25 Application fee. Not accepted after age 4-1/2 unless previously enrolled in Montessori school.

Tuition: (1993-94) Half-day, $2,836; Full day, $3,597-$3,809 Equipment fee, Books: $125. Bring Lunch. *Dress Code*: Clean & Neat. **Financial Aid**: Available after one year.

HERITAGE ACADEMY CHRISTIAN SCHOOL..........(301) 582-2600

12215 Walnut Point West, Hagerstown, MD 21740
Founded 1969. **Head:** Kathleen Mallory.

Grades: K4-12. **Enrollment**: 210 Co-ed. **Faculty**: 17 full-, 4 part-time.
Average Class Size: 24; Resource Room in elem., 20.

Special Courses: Spanish 9-10, Science through Physics, Computer science, Math includes Advanced Math & Business Math. Typing, Music, Art, Journalism.

Athletics: P.E. req.; Intramural & Interscholastic. Boys - Soccer, Basketball, Baseball. Girls - Volleyball, Softball, Basketball, Cheerleading.

Plant: Library, Science Lab, Gym - All purpose room, Playing Fields, Auditorium.

Admission: Interview & Testing, Registration fee $60.

Tuition: (1993-94) Age 4-Grade 6, $1,700; Grades 7-12, $1,800. Books: Extra.
Transportation: Depends on distance & number of students in family. Lunch: Cafeteria.
Dress Code: Uniform req. **Scholarship Aid**: Details on Request.

HERITAGE ACADEMY & CHILD CARE CENTERS, INC...........(703) 922-6600

6318 May Boulevard, Alexandria, VA. 22310

Note : Child Care Facilities also located at:
7136 Telegraph Road, Alexandria, VA. 22310
6215 Roberts Parkway, Burke ,VA.

Founded 1948 **Head**: Dr. & Mrs. C. Wheeler.

Grades: Age 4-Grade 6. **Enrollment**: 140 Co-ed. **Faculty**: 15 full-time.
Average Class Size: 12

Special Courses: French, Spanish, Music, Computer Studies. Remedial Reading (Phonovisual method used for reading) Individual Learning Program for special needs.
Extended Day : 6:30 a.m.- 6:30 p.m.

Publications: School paper monthly.

Plant: Library 1,300 vol., Playing Fields, Swimming Pool, Tennis Courts, Computer Lab, Gym.

Tuition: (1993-94) $3,900; With **Extended Day**: $5,100 includes Books & Lunch.
Transportation : $90-$130/mo.

Summer Program: Day Camp- swimming, tennis, archery, arts & crafts, competitive sports, hikes, 6:30 a.m.-6:30 p.m.

HIGHLAND SCHOOL..........(703) 347-1221

597 Broadview Avenue, Warrenton, VA 22186
Founded 1928. **Head**: David P. Plank

Grades: PreK-8. **Enrollment**: 162 Co-ed. **Faculty**: 20 full-, 4 part-time.
Average Class Size: 15.

Special Courses: Latin , French, Spanish. Algebra, Geometry, Computer. Grammar, Science, Social Studies. **Extended Day**: 2:15 p.m.-5:30 p.m..

Athletics: Required; Intramural & Interscholastic: Skiing, Riding, Softball, Tennis, Soccer, Field Hockey, Lacrosse, Basketball, Track and Field. **Clubs**: Yearbook **Publications**: Yearbook, Literary Magazine.

Plant: Library , C.D. Room/ 8,000 vol.; Science Lab, Art Studio, Gym, Playing Fields.

Admission: Interview, Placement Test. $50 Testing fee. Transcript,

Tuition: (1993-94) K-2 $5,320; Grades 3-8, $5,820 includes Books. **Transportation**: Available. **Financial Aid**: Available.

Future Plans: Possible addition of 9-12 campus; adding counselor part-time.

Summer Program: Art; Day camps, soccer & lacrosse; science & math.

HIGHLAND VIEW ACADEMY..........(301) 739-8480

10100 Academy Drive, Hagerstown, MD 21740
Seventh Day Adventist 1949. **Head**: Mogan Hellgren

Grades: 9-12. **Enrollment**: 160 Co-ed, (70 Boarding). **Faculty**: 12 full-time.
Average Class Size: 20.

Special Courses: Physical Science, Chemistry, Biology, Human Physiology, Physics; Math, Mini-Business Courses. History: U.S., World, Civil War, Government. Computers. Religious Studies req. Typing, Mechanical Drawing, Shop, Home Economics, Architectural Drafting, Photography, Woodworking, Band, Automechanics, Small engines. Note: Grades 9 & 11 have classes from 1:00 p.m.-5:30 p.m. -work in the morning either in school maintenance jobs, in the school office, or assisting the teachers. Grades 10 & 12 have classes 7 a.m.-11:30 a.m., and work in the cafeteria or other jobs. Opportunities available to work in Pretzel Factory or Bakery. Complete combination of work experience with educational experience
Extended Day: 6:45 a.m.-7:30 p.m.

Athletics: Boys: Varsity & Jr. Varsity Basketball, Varsity Soccer; Girls Varsity Volleyball and Basketball. Clubs: Boys & Girls Club, Student Association. **Publications** Newspaper, Yearbook.

Plant: Gym, Computer Lab, Dormitories, Cafeteria, Music Building, Playing Fields.

Admission: Application, Interview, Transcript.

Tuition: (1993-94) $4,100; Room & Board $3,250 Lunch: Extra for day students. Books: Extra. *Dress Code*: Girls, Dresses; Boys - No jeans; sports shirts slacks.

HILL SCHOOL..........(703) 687-5897

P.O. Box 65, Middleburg, VA 22117
Founded 1926. **Head:** Thomas Northrup.

Grades: K-8. **Enrollment**: 180 Co-ed. **Faculty**: 22 full- time. **Average Class Size**: 12.

Special Courses: Spanish 8, Latin 7-8. Algebra 8, Computer 1-8. General Science 1-8. Art & Music, K-8.

Athletics: Req.; Intramural, K-8; Interscholastic 4-8. Soccer, Field Hockey (Girls), Basketball, Volleyball, Gymnastics, Lacrosse, Track & Field. **Clubs**: Outing, Skiing. **Publications**: Yearbook, Literary Magazine.

Plant: Library 8,000 vol.; Science Labs, Art Studio, Gym, Playing Fields, Auditorium, Music Building, 20 Computers.

Admission: Interview, Achievement Testing, $20 fee.

Tuition: (1993-94) K $4,300; Grades 1-8, $7,200-$7,500 *Dress Code*: No blue jeans, T shirts, sweatshirts. **Financial Aid**: Available.

The HILL SCHOOL ....(215) 326-1000

717 East High Street, Pottstown, PA 19464
Founded 1851 **Head**: Mr. David R. Dougherty

Grades: 8-12, PG **Enrollment**: 456 Boys (Boarding 385) **Faculty**: 71 full-, 4 part-time **Average Class Size**: 11

Special Courses: Latin, Greek , French, Spanish, German, Russian; Math, Computer, Pascal History: European, U. S. (req); Economics; Science: Biology, Chemistry, Physics; Theology/Philosophy (one yr, req.), Judeo-Christian roots; Discussion of Dimensions, Encounters Beyond and Within, Religion through Literature, The Nature of Religious Experience, Philosophy Seminar, Psychology; Transitional English, Study Skills. Theatre I, II; Music Theory, Photography, Studio Art, Wood shop, AP: English, Humanities, Math, Pascal, French, Spanish, History: European and U.S., Economics, Biology, Chemistry, Physics. Note The Hill School is an an associate member of The School Year Abroad Program: Open to Juniors who have completed two years of French (program in Rennes, France) or Spanish (Barcelona, Spain).

Athletics: Req.; Interscholastic and Intramural; Soccer, Football, Cross Country, Water Polo, Basketball, Ice Hockey, Wrestling, Swimming, Squash, Ski-racing; Winter Track, Lacrosse, Baseball, Golf, Tennis, Track. **Clubs**: Model U.N., Spanish, Glee, Chamber Orchestra, Jazz Ensemble, Hilltones, String Quartet, Drama, Radio Station. **Publications** : Newspaper, Yearbook **Community Service** : Students participate in various ways.

Plant Library, Extensive Athletic Facilities, Large Physical Plant

Admission : Apply by Feb. 15; Transcript, Recommendations from English & Math teachers, SSAT. and Interview on campus.

Tuition: $19,000 **Financial Aid**: Available

Future Plans : 150th Anniversary Celebration and Capital Campaign

Summer Program: Academic Enrichment

HOLTON ARMS SCHOOL..........(301) 365-5300

7303 River Road, Bethesda, MD 20817
Founded 1901. **Head**: Diana Coulton Beebe

Grades: 3-12. Enrollment: 620 Girls, expands at Grades 7 & 9. **Faculty**: 69 full-, 10 part-time. **Average Class Size**: 15.

Special Courses: Latin, French & Spanish, all 7-12. Math through Calculus & Computer, Statistics; Discrete Math. General Science, Biology, Chemistry, Physics, Botany, Environmental, Earth Science. History & Social Science- Western Civilization, History of U. S. and Europe, Asian History, Anthropology, Western Philosophy, Contemporary History, Geography, Government & Economics. Art, Art History, Art & Music. AP.: English, U.S. History, Biology, Calculus, Computer Science, French Literature, Spanish, Latin. **Extended Day**: 3:30 - 6 p.m.

Athletics: Req.; Intramural & Interscholastic. Field Hockey, Soccer, Tennis, Softball, Track, Volleyball, Cross Country, Basketball, Swimming, Lacrosse. **Clubs**: Amnesty International, Boosters, Community Service, Cultural Awareness, Debate, Environmental Awareness, Model U.N., Peer Counseling, It's Academic, Drama, Chorus, Swing Choir, Orchestra. **Publications**: Literary, Newspaper, Yearbook. **Community Involvement**: Long tradition of service by graduation requirement requiring 30 hours of voluntary service during one 12 month period of four years of high school.

Plant: Library: Upper School 22,000 vol., Lower School, 6,000 vol.; Language Lab, 2 Computer Centers, Science Labs, 2 Art Studios, 2 Gyms, Playing Fields, Tennis Courts, Dance Studio, Swimming Pool, Theater, Amphi-Theater.

Admission: SSAT Req. 7-12. Individual aptitude and achievement testing 3-6; Tour and Interview. Application fee $50; Feb. 1 deadline.

Tuition: (1993-94) Gr.3/4, $10,380; Gr. 5/6, $10, 480; Gr. 7-12, $11,015 includes Lunch Books: $300. *Dress Code*: Uniform req. **Transportation**: one way $425, both ways $750. **Scholarship Aid**: Available.

Summer Program: Creative Summer - Programs for boys and girls ages 7-14; Art, Music, Dance, Drama, Tennis, Swimming, Computer, Science. Creative Sixes: day program for age 6. Creative Morning: half-day program for ages 4-6.

HOLY COMFORTER SCHOOL..........(202) 547-7556

1503 East Capitol Street, S. E., Washington, D. C. 20003
Catholic **Head**: Mr. Charles Robinson

Grades: K4-8 **Enrollment**: Co-ed

Special Courses : **Extended Day** : 7 a.m.-6 p.m.

Tuition: (1993-94) $180/mo.

HOLY CROSS ELEMENTARY SCHOOL..........(301)949-1699

4900 Strathmore Avenue, Garrett Park, MD 20896
Catholic **Head**: Sister Miriam R. Brosnan CSC

Grades: K-8 **Enrollment**: 227 Co-ed

Special Programs: Emphasis on Reading, Writing, Math, Science & Social Studies; Enrichment courses in Art, French, Drama, Music, Spanish, Computer Science, Library Skills. Religion req.
Extended Day: 7:15 a.m.- 6 p.m.

Athletics: P.E. req.

Plant: Library, 10 acre park-like campus

Admission: Interview, child Visits school for day, Transcript.

Tuition: (1993-94) In parish, $2,300; Out of parish, $2,900

HOLY FAMILY SCHOOL..........(301) 894-2323

2200 Callaway Street, Hillcrest Heights, MD 20748
Catholic **Head** : Sister Elizabeth Ferguson, SSJ

Grades: K4-8 **Enrollment**: Co-ed

Special Courses: **Extended Day** : 7 a.m.-6 p.m.

Tuition: (1993-94) Catholic, $1,870; Non-Catholic, $2,670; Reduction for siblings.
Extended Day: Extra

HOLY NAME SCHOOL..........(202) 397-1614

1217 West Virginia Avenue, N. E., Washington, D. C. 20002
Catholic **Head** : Sister Owen Patricia Bonner, SSJ

Grades: K4-8 **Enrollment**: Co-ed

Special Courses: **Extended Day** : until 6 p.m.

Tuition: (1993-94) K4, $1,950; K-8, $1,750; Reduction for siblings.

HOLY REDEEMER SCHOOL...........(301) 942-3701

9715 Summit Avenue, Kensington, MD 20895
Catholic 1951 **Head** : Mrs. Rosemarie Garten

Grades: K-8 **Enrollment**: 315 Co-ed **Faculty** : 19 full-, 6 part-time.
Average Class Size: 22

Special Courses : French, Spanish,.Math, Social Studies, Science, English. Religion req.: Art, Music, Learning Center (Enrichment & Remedial). **Extended Day**: 3-6 p.m.

Athletics: P. E.; Soccer, Basketball, Football, Baseball, Softball, T-Ball. **Clubs** : Drama, Chorus, Hands on Science Program

Admission : Interview, Testing

Tuition : Parishioner, $1,800; Non-Catholic, $3,000. *Dress Code*: Uniform req.
Financial Aid: Available

Summer Program : Camp & Academic Summer Classes

HOLY REDEEMER SCHOOL..........(301) 638-5789

1135 New Jersey Avenue, N. W., Washington, D. C. 20001
Catholic, 1954 **Head**: Gerald R. Fields

Grades: Pre K-8 **Enrollment**: 258 Co-ed **Faculty**: 13 full-, 2 part-time
Average Class Size: 26

Special Courses Reading, Math, Language Arts, Science, Social Studies, Computer. Religion req: Conformity of Christian Doctrine. **Extended Day**: 3 p.m.-6 p.m.

Athletics: P.E.; Basketball, Double Dutch, Track and Soccer.

Admission: Birth Certificate. Testing, Health Records.

Plant: Computer Lab, Use of nearby Gym for athletic program.

Tuition: (1993-94) $!,700 yr. or $170/mo. Family rates available.

Future Plans: Expand physical plant to include an Art and Computer Lab.

Summer Program: Summer Camp, 7 a.m.-6 p.m.; Summer School, 7 a.m.-noon, 5-7 wks.

HOLY TRINITY EPISCOPAL DAY SCHOOL..........(301) 262-5355

13106 Annapolis Road, Bowie, MD. 20720
Episcopal 1963. **Head**: Margaret C. Reiber

Grades: K-6. **Enrollment**: 270 Co-ed. **Faculty**: 15 full-, 8 part-time.
Average Class Size: 16-20

Special Courses: French , Art, Music. Computer, Gen'l Science, Pre-Algebra, P.E.. Religious studies req. **Extended Day**: 7 a.m.-6 p.m.

Athletics: P.E. K-6, Req. Intramural.

Plant: Library 5,000 vol., All Purpose Room, Playing fields.

Admission: Free Application; As openings occur applicants are called in order and Tested; $50 fee; Interview. Preference given to siblings & parish children.

Tuition: (1993-94) $3,895. **Extended Day**: Extra. Lunch: Purchased daily, Beverage provided.
Transportation: Limited; Queen Ann School bus service, car pools. *Dress Code*: Suitable.
Scholarship Aid: Available.

HOLY TRINITY SCHOOL..........(202) 337-2339

1325 36th Street, N.W., Washington, D.C. 20007
Catholic 1860's **Head**: Ms. Ann Marie Santora

Grades: N-8 **Enrollment**: 330 Co-ed **Faculty**: 23 full, 6 part-time.
Average Class Size: 15-30

Special Features: French 2-8. Algebra, Geometry, Computer. General Science, Biology. Religious Studies req; Remedial Reading & Math Note : LD tutoring/ Speech & Language Therapy/ Developmentally appropriate ED program. Art, Music. **Extended Day**: 7:30 a.m. -6 p.m.

Athletics: P.E. req. 1-8 **Clubs**: Student Council, Environmental Club. **Publications**: Yearbook, Newspaper. **Community Involvement**: Food collections for hungry; Special events for seniors; Recycling.

Plant: Library, Science Lab, Art Studio, Auditorium, Computer Room, Tutoring and Resource Rooms.

Tuition: (1993-94) Parish member, N-K $4,400; 1-8, $2.900; Non-parish member, $3,400 Reduction for siblings. Fees, 1-8, $325. *Dress Code*: Uniform req. **Scholarship Aid**: Some Available.

Summer Program: 4 week programs in subject skills and study skills.

HOPE CHRISTIAN ACADEMY..........(301) 982-6405

5301 Edgewood Road, College Park, MD 20740
Head: V. Michele Jackson

Grades: K4-grade 6 **Enrollment**: Co-ed

Special Programs: Small classes for maximum individual attention. Program structured around family involvement. Students are challenged to their fullest potential. ABEKA academic program. **Extended Day**: 6:30 a.m.- 6:30 p.m.

Tuition: (1993-94) $2, 125

IDEAL SCHOOL OF WASHINGTON..........(202) 726-0313

1501 Gallatin Street N. W., Washington, D. C. 20011
Head: Mr. Taiwo Inman

Grades: N 2 1/2- Grade 6 **Enrollment**: Co-ed
Special Programs: LD/ED program, **Extended Day**: 7:30 a.m.-6 p.m.

Tuition: Call for information

IMMACULATE CONCEPTION SCHOOL..........(202) 234-1093

711 N Street, N. W., Washington, D. C. 20001
Catholic **Head**: Sister Donna Marie Coward, RSM

Grades: K4- grade 6 **Enrollment**: Co-ed

Special Courses: **Extended Day**: Until 6 p.m.

Tuition: (1993-94) $1,300

IMMANUEL CHRISTIAN SCHOOL..........(703) 941-1220

5215 Backlick Road, Springfield, VA. 22151
Founded 1976 **Head**: Stephen Danish

Grades: Pre K-8 **Enrollment**: 235 Co-ed

Special Programs: Well-rounded academic program. Daily Bible. Computer Science program. High parent involvement. Strong music program. Sports and other activities in the upper grades.

Tuition: (1993-94) N $700-1,000; K $1,550; 1-5 $3,100; 6-8, $3,250. **Transportation** : Some Available

IMMANUEL LUTHERAN SCHOOL.......... (703) 549-7323

109 Belleaire Road, Alexandria, VA. 22301
Missouri Synod, Lutheran 1945. **Head**: Nancy Moen

Grades: K-6. **Enrollment**: 90 Co-ed. **Faculty**: 7 full-time. **Average Class Size**: 19.

Special Courses: General Science. Music Program. Religious studies req. Strong academic & religious programs. **Extended Day**: 7 a.m.- 6 p.m.

Athletics: Req., all grades. Softball, Volleyball.

Plant: Library 5000 vol., Playing Fields.

Admission: Interview, Application fee $25. Placement test in Math & Reading.

Tuition: (1993-94 $2,200, Reduction for siblings. **Extended Day**: Extra Books: $150. *Dress Code*: Uniform req. **Scholarship Aid**: Partial scholarships available.

INDEPENDENT BAPTIST ACADEMY..........(301) 856-1616

P.O. Box 206, 9255 Piscataway Road, Clinton, MD. 20735
Independent Baptist 1972. **Head**: Mr. William Anker

Grades: K4-12. **Enrollment**: 100 Co-ed. **Faculty**: 10 full-, 1 part-time.
Average Class Size: 20.

Special Courses: Spanish, Math thru Pre-Calculus. Biology, Chemistry, Physics. Religious studies required. Typing, shorthand. **Extended Day** : 7 a.m.-6 p.m.

Athletics: Req.; Flag Football, Basketball, Softball, Volleyball.

Plant: Gym; use of nearby Library & Playing Fields.

Tuition: (1993-94) $2,340; Reduction for Siblings. **Books**: $120. **Registration Fee**: $125

INDIAN CREEK SCHOOL.........(410) 987-0342

Evergreen Road, Crownsville, MD. 21032
Founded 1973. **Head**: Anne Chambers.

Grades: PreK-8. **Enrollment**: 415 Co-ed. **Faculty**: 37 full-, 1 part-time.
Average Class Size: PreK & K, 1:10; grades 1-5, 1:20; grades 6-8, 1:15.

Special Courses: Spanish N-8th. Algebra, Computer. General Science, Biology. History includes Maryland, American, European. Civics, World Geography. Remedial Reading and Math(within classroom). Art, Music, Library. note: Learning Specialist on staff, parallel program for grade 6-8; Enrichment Program. **Extended Day**: 7:30 a.m.- 6 p.m.

Athletics: Required all grades. Intramural: Soccer, Field Hockey, Lacrosse, Basketball, Wrestling. **Clubs**: Grades 1-5 meets Friday afternoon; Swimming, Mind Olympics, Drama, Cooking, Crafts, Computer. **Publications**: Yearbook, Newspaper. **Community Involvement**: Extensive holiday sharing program.

Plant: Library, Science Lab, Gym, Art Studio, Auditorium, Playing Field, Computer Lab.

Admission: Application fee $30; In-House Testing(fee $30): Brigance Metropolitan Readiness, Iowa Achievements; Transcript, Teacher Recommendations.

Tuition: (1993-94) $3,350, half-day PreK; $4,680 full day PreK; K-grade 8, $4,975-$6,435. Lunch: $1.50 day. *Dress Code*: Uniform req. **Transportation**: $425, one way, $850 both-ways; Reduction for siblings. **Extended Day** Extra, several plans offered. **Financial Aid**: Available.

Summer Program: Summer Art Camp

ISLAMIC SAUDI ACADEMY...........(703) 780-0606

8333 Richmond Highway, Alexandria, VA 22309
11121 Popes Head Road, Fairfax, VA 22309
Muslim **Head**: Dr. Saad H. Al Adwani

Grades: K-12 **Enrollment**: 1,150

Special Courses: Advanced academic program all grades for Muslim students. Arabic Language, Islamic Studies Program.

Tuition: (1993-94) $1,000

JEWELS OF ANN SCHOOL..........(202) 529-5446 or 529-2278

2011 Bunker Hill Road, N.E., Washington, D.C. 20018
Founded 1970. **Head**: Dr. Ruth H. Baxter.

Grades: N-6. **Enrollment:** 70 Co-ed. **Faculty**: 10 full-, 2 part-time.
Average Class Size: 10.

Special Courses: Foreign Language K-6, Remedial Reading & Math as needed; Art, Music; British method - reading readiness program at 4 yrs. - open education, ability grouping. **Extended Day Care**. 7 a.m.-6 p.m. and in and out of the country trips.

Admission: Registration fee $60. K Interview, 1-6 Interview & Aptitude Test. Fee $75.

Tuition: (1993-94) N-3 $300/mo.; 4-6, $350/mo.; Tuition includes **Extended Day**. Books: (rental fee) K-3 $50, 4-6 $70. *Dress Code* Uniform req. Pre-K-6.

Summer Program: Day Camp ages 3-12; (End of June - end of August). Arts & crafts, swimming, physical education.

JEWISH PRIMARY DAY SCHOOL of ADAS ISRAEL..........(202) 362-4449

2850 Quebec Street, N. W., Washington, D. C. 20008
Head: Susan Koss, Director

Grades: K-3 **Enrollment**: 60 Co-ed **Faculty**: 8 full-, 6 part-time. **Average Class Size**: Maximum, 16

Special Courses: Integrated curriculum combining General and Judaic studies along with Hebrew as a modern spoken language. Developmental orientation. Hands- on- Learning. Writer's Workshop, Journals, Math Their Way, Computers. Music, Art; Frequent Field Trips. **Extended Day Care**: Provided on site by the DCJCC; Monday-Thursday, 3-6:30 p.m.; Friday , until 6 p.m.; Also available for special programs, school holidays and vacations.

Athletics: P.E. **After School**: Science, Cooking(program changes every year) **Publications**: Monthly Community Newsletter

Admission: Parents visit at Open Houses Nov.-Jan.; Application fee $50; Child visits for a play session and a Kindergarten Readiness Screening (fee).

Tuition: (1993-94) $5,730; Activities fee: $125 **Financial Aid**: Some Available, pending acceptance into school

Future Plans: Second playground in planning stage.

JOHN NEVINS ANDREWS SCHOOL..........(301) 270-1400

117 Elm Avenue, Takoma Park, MD. 20912
Seventh Day Adventist 1907. **Head**: Dr. Leroy Kuhn, Principal

Grades: N-8. **Enrollment**: 286 Co-ed. **Faculty**: 20 full-time. **Average Class Size**: 23.

Special Courses: French, grade 4. Algebra, Computer. Gen'l Science, Remedial Reading & Math. Steel Band, Weaving. Religion req. - General Bible program for all grades.
Extended Day: until 6 P.M.

Athletics: Req.; Intramural Basketball, Full P.E. Program. **Clubs**: Student Council.
Publications: Yearbook, Newspaper. **Community Involvement**: Musical programs, Nursing Home visits.

Plant: Library 10,000 vol., Gym, Playing Fields.

Admission: Interview, Transcript, Achievement/readiness tests req. of all new students. Gesell testing for admission to K.; Metropolitan testing for grade 1; WRAT testing for all new students. Additional testing may be given to identify children with learning disabilities.

Tuition: (1993-94) $1,500-$3,000. Books: $85-$100. Lunch: $2.50 / day. **Transportation**: $350-$700 one way; $500-$1,000 both ways. *Dress Code*: Must be neat & clean; No jewelry or heavy make-up. **Scholarship Aid**: Some available

JULIA BROWN MONTESSORI SCHOOL...........(301) 498-0604

9540 Madison Avenue, Laurel, MD 20723 (N-3)
1300 Milestone Drive, Silver Spring, MD 20904 (N-K)
Head: Julia Brown

Grades: N-3 **Enrollment**: 185 Co-ed

Special Programs: **Extended Day**: 7 a.m.-6 p.m.

Tuition: (1993-94) Call for information.

JUNIPER LANE SCHOOL.............(703) 533-8890

3106 Juniper Lane, Falls Church, VA. 22044
Head: Mrs. Christine Bishton

Grades: N-3 **Enrollment**: 40 Co-ed

Tuition: (1993-94) $200/mo.- $455/mo. Depends on days and number of hours in school.

KENWOOD/GRASSHOPPER GREEN SCHOOLS..........(703) 256-4712

4955 Sunset Lane, Annandale, VA. 22003
Founded 1957/1939. **Head**: Nancy Griffin.

Grades: N-6. **Enrollment**: 200 Co-ed. **Faculty**: 20 full-, 5 part-time.
Average Class Size: 16.

Special Courses: Computer, Spanish, Music; High priority placed on mastery of Reading skills and Math concepts as basis for ongoing educational development. Small classes and groups with individual attention. P.E. Before & after school supervision & activities available. **Extended Day** 7 a.m.-6 p.m.

Plant: 3 Classroom Buildings, Library, Gym, Playing Fields.

Admission: Interview, $30 Registration fee; Testing for placement.

Tuition: (1993-94) 1/2 Day $220/mo.; All Day $490-$495/mo. Lunch: Provided for Pre-School; Kenwood-Bring. Books: Extra. *Dress Code*: Neat, no jeans or tee shirts.

Summer Program: Year round program for pre-school. School age, Day Camp 12 weeks, ages 5 1/2-12. Swimming instruction, field trips, ice & roller skating, soccer, picnics, camp-out & overnights, arts & crafts. **Extended Hours** 7 a.m.-6 p.m.

KEY SCHOOL..........(410) 263-9231

534 Hillsmere Drive, Annapolis, MD. 21403
Founded 1958. **Head**: Ronald S. Goldblatt

Grades: Pre-K - grade 12. **Enrollment**: 510 Co-ed. **Faculty**: 48 full-, 19 part-time.
Average Class Size: 15.

Special Courses: Latin 8 & 9, French 1-12; Greek & Spanish 9-12. Math includes Calculus, Computer, Analytical Geometry, Logic, Economics. Biology, Chemistry, Physics, Earth Science, Estuarine Biology, Physiology. History- Ancient, European, American, American Civilization. Education/ Psychology, Introd. to Philosophy. Russian Studies. Remedial Reading & Math. Art, Music. AP.: French, Calculus, Biology, Physics, Art History. **Extended Day** : to 5:30 p.m.

Athletics: Req. thru grade 11. Intramural & Interscholastic: Soccer, Lacrosse, Field Hockey, Basketball, Softball. Clubs: Chess, Journalism, Drama, Chorus, Ensemble, Dance, Typing. Publications: Yearbook, Newspaper, Literary Magazine.

Plant: 2 Libraries, 2 Language Labs, 3 Science Labs, 2 Art Studios, 4 Playing Fields, Gym, Auditorium, Amphitheater, 2 Computer Labs.

Admission: Rolling (yr. round); $35 Application fee; Testing (ERB)

Tuition: (1993-94) $4,200-$8,200 Lunch: Bring or buy **Transportation:** Available. **Scholarship Aid**: Available

Future Plans: Expansion in progress-new building, expansion at 5th grade level.

Summer Program: Pre K-grade 5, Day Camp; Ages 10-15, Outings and Overnight trips. Tutoring.

THE KINGSBURY DAY SCHOOL...........(202) 232-5877

2138 Bancroft Place N.W., Washington, D.C. 20008
Founded 1984 Note: 1938, founded as Kingsbury Center **Head**: Judith Zangwill

Grades: K-5 **Enrollment**: 48 Co-ed **Faculty**: 7 full-time, 5 part-time. **Average Class Size**: 6-8

Special Courses: "Hands on Science", Art, Music. Remedial Reading & Math. School offers intensive intervention for students with learning disabilities. Occupational therapy and l language therapy are available on site and integrated with classroom learning. Note: The Kingsbury Center offers assessment and tutoring for all ages.

Athletics: P.E., non-competitive games.

Plant: Library 5,000 Vol.; New Arts Studio; Computers in classrooms.

Admission: Rolling admissions: applicants should apply as early as possible; $50 fee. Submit any previous tests or arrange for Testing to be done at parent expense. Child must Visit school for minimum of two days. The school seeks students who have diagnosed learning disabilities and who would benefit from early intervention. Students accepted as old as 9 in September of school year.

Tuition: (1993-94) $12,250 plus $150 Activities fee. Lunch: Bring. **Financial Aid**: Limited.

Summer Program: For students ages 5-11.

LAB SCHOOL OF WASHINGTON..........(202) 965-6600

4759 Reservoir Road, N.W., Washington, D.C. 20007
Incorporated, Non-profit 1967. **Head**: Mrs. Sally L. Smith.

Grades: Ages 5-18, ungraded in elementary. **Enrollment**: 250 Co-ed. **Faculty**: 102 **Average Class Size**: Individualized tutortials and small groups (3-10).

Special Features: Program designed for primary, elementary, junior and senior high school students of average or better intelligence with learning disabilities. Primary and elementary students spend half-day in classrooms with highly individualized prescriptive programs taught by master teachers; half-day learning academic skills through art forms (Graphics, Woodwork, Ceramics, Photography, Music, Dance, Drama, and Film making) with outstanding artists trained in learning disabilities. History, Geography, Civics, and academic readiness skills are taught through a unique method called Academic Clubs in the elementary school. The junior - senior high school programs emphasize college preparatory courses, arts, electives, and sports. Spanish offered in High School. Math includes Calculus & Computer; General Science, Biology; History-U. S. and D. C.; Remedial Reading & Math.

Athletics: Req. (2 yrs. high school). Basketball, Soccer, Softball.

Plant: Modern 3-story classroom building, an historic mansion, a carriage house, and an occupational therapy annex. Media Center with extensive tape and cassette library of books. Library, 6,000 vol.

Admission: Registration fee $50, Educational, Neurological, Psychological Tests; Interview : child visits school for half day. Child must be of average to superior intelligence with specific learning disabilities (i.e., dyslexia, attention deficit) that impede academic success.

Tuition: (1993-94) Age 5-12 $14,393; Jr. High $15,393; Sr. High $15,923. **Financial Aid**: Tuition funded through D. C. & MD if approved by the public school system.

Summer Program: 6 weeks of Arts, Recreation, Remedial Instruction and Study Skills, mid-June through July. Scholarships available.

LAKE SHORE CHRISTIAN ACADEMY..........(410) 437-3529

860 Swift Road, Pasadena, MD. 21122
Head: Bill Natzer

Grades: K4-10 **Enrollment**: 50 Co-ed.

Special Features: ACE Program.

Tuition: (1993-94) K4-K5, $1.000; 1-8, $1,500; 9-10, $1.600.

LANDON SCHOOL...........(301) 320-3200 FAX (301) 320-2787

6101 Wilson Lane, Bethesda, MD. 20817
Founded 1929. **Head**: Damon F. Bradley

Grades: 3-12. **Enrollment** 615 Boys; Enrollment increases 4 through 9.
Faculty: 60 full-, 4 part-time. **Average Class Size**: 10.

Special Courses: French , Latin, Spanish all 7-12. Math through Calculus, Computer. General Science, Biology, Chemistry, Physics. History- Geography, Ancient, Modern World, Modern Soviet, Contemporary World Issues, Term Courses. Art-History, Design, Appreciation and

Studio, Pottery, Ceramics. Photography. Music- History and Theory, Harmony, Choir, Glee Club, Jazz, Band. Drama, Film making. AP.: Languages, Calculus, Biology, Physics, Modern European and U. S. History, English, Music. Cross registration with Holton Arms School (nearby Girls School) for AP. courses.

Athletics: Req. 3-12. Intramural & Interscholastic: Football, Cross Country, Track, Basketball, Wrestling, Soccer, Baseball, Tennis, Lacrosse, Riflery. **Clubs**: Community Service, Music and Drama, School Service, and numerous special interest clubs. **Publications**: Yearbook, Newspaper, Literary Magazine. **Community Involvement**: State and nationally recognized community service projects. Recommended by the Governor of Maryland as a model program for other schools.

Plant: Library 25,000 vol., Language Lab, 5 Science Labs, 2 Art Studios, 2 Gyms, Auditorium 5 Playing Fields, 12 Tennis Courts, Performing Arts Center, All-weather track, Rifle Range, Green House, Ropes Course, 2 Computer Labs.

Admission: Interviews; Entrance Tests in January; Application fee $50, covers testing.

Tuition: (1993-94) Grades 3 -6, $10,050; Grades 7 - 12, $10,650. Lunch: $550. Books: $200
Transportation: Available *Dress Code*: Jacket, shirt & tie req. grades 7-12.
Financial Aid: 70-80 recipients.

Summer Program: Summer Sessions: Computer, study skills, enrichment, math courses. Day Camp: boys 6-11. 4-8 weeks. Tutoring available. Lacrosse. Baseball, Soccer, Basketball Tennis, & Wrestling camps.

LANGLEY SCHOOL..........(703) 356-1920

1411 Balls Hill Road, McLean, VA. 22101
Founded 1942 (parent owned co-op). **Head:** Mrs. Betty J. Brown.

Grades: N-8. **Enrollment**: 450 Co-ed. **Faculty**: 28 full-, 25 part-time.
Average Class Size: 18-22.

Special Courses: French & Spanish K-8; Gen'l Science, Earth Science, Physical Science, Life Science; History-Middle Ages & Renaissance, U. S., 20th century U.S. with emphasis on Geography, Current Events. Typing, Band, Drama, Film-making.
Extended Day: until 6 p.m.

Athletics: Intramural & Interscholastic. Basketball, Soccer, Softball, Track & Cross Country.
Publications: Yearbook, weekly Memo, Literary Magazine, Quarterly Parent Magazine.
Community Involvement: Service Projects.

Plant: New Library, 13,000 vol.; Computer Lab, AV Room. Science Labs, Greenhouse, Art Studio, Gym, Auditorium, Playing Fields, Jr. High Complex

Admission: Apply Sept.-Jan.; Parent Tour & Interview, child Visit & Testing; Transcripts & Recommendations . Application fee $30-$50;

Tuition: (1993-94) $5,4,60-$9,590 includes Books. **Transportation**: $670 one way, $1,040 both ways. *Dress Code*: Clean & neat. **Financial Aid**: Available.

Summer Program: Ages 3 - 16. 5 week program with variety of courses: Washington Art Program, Foreign Language-Spanish & French, Keyboard skills, Enrichment & Remedial Math & Reading, Study Skills. **Extended Day** Program.

LANHAM CHRISTIAN SCHOOL..........(301) 552-1156

8400 Good Luck Road, Lanham, MD. 20706
Head: Gene Pinkard

Grades: K- 12 **Enrollment**: 320 Co-ed

Special Features: Traditional program K-6; ACE curriculum 7 & 8; College Preparatory Program 9-12; Individualized Christian education for select students. Students advance at own pace with teacher/supervisor. **Extended Day**: 7 a.m.-5:30 p.m.

Tuition: (1993-94) $2,660 (Reduction for siblings).

LAUREL BAPTIST ACADEMY...........(301) 498-5060

7th & Montgomery Streets, Laurel, MD 20707
Head: Clyde Dowell

Grades: K4-12 **Enrollment**: 40 Co-ed
Special Program: ACE Program.

Tuition: (1993-94) Call for information,

LEARY SCHOOL..........(703) 573-5400

6349 Lincolnia Road, Alexandria, VA 22312
Founded 1964 **Head** President, Albert Leary, Jr. Director: Eugene Meale

Ungraded: 5-22 yrs.

Special Program: The Leary School is a private, day, co-educational, special education facility which serves students who have learning, emotional, and behavioral problems. Each child's identified learning styles, strengths, and weaknesses suggest the preferred methods of educational intervention.

An individualized educational program is formulated for each child in consultation with public school personnel, parents, and, when appropriate, the child. Psychological services, Counseling, and when needed, Career Development programs are all an intrinsic part of the Leary School program.

Admission: Most children are referred by their local public school system

Tuition Placement in the school through a public agency pays the full tuition and transportation fees.

LEESBURG CHRISTIAN SCHOOL..........(703) 777-4220

Route 1, P.O. Box 252 B, Leesburg, VA. 22075
Non-denominational 1969. **Head**: Mr. Terry Overstreet

Grades: Pre K-12. **Enrollment**: 110 Co-ed. **Faculty**: 7 full-, 2 part-time.
Average Class Size: 20.

Special Courses: German, Spanish.. Computer Literacy 1-12. General Science, World History, Remedial Reading & Math. Art, Music, Chorus. Religious studies req. Bob Jones Program.

Athletics: P.E. Req.; Interscholastic: Soccer, Baseball, Softball, Basketball.

Admission: Interview parents & child. Testing (depending on age).

Tuition: (1993-94) K-4 $2,200; 5-8 $2,300; 9-12 $2,400. Books & **Transportation**: Extra
Lunch: Bring. *Dress Code*: Good grooming stressed; no jeans or T-shirts.

Summer Program: Academic Enrichment & Fine Arts Program featuring painting, drawing & music.

LEONARD HALL JUNIOR NAVAL ACADEMY...........(301) 475-8029

P.O. Box 507, Leonardtown, MD. 20650
Catholic 1909. **Head**: Mrs. Margaret Bailey

Grades: 5-12. **Enrollment**: 80 Co-ed **Faculty**: 8 full-, 2 part-time.
Average Class Size: 15.

Special Courses: Computer. General Science. History: American, World, European. Remedial Reading. Religious Studies req. Drill Team, Marching Units.

Athletics: Req. Interscholastic Basketball. Other sports offered: Soccer, Volleyball, Softball, Kickball. **Publications**: Newspaper **Community Involvement**: Participate in local and state parades.

Plant : Library, Science Lab, Computer Lab, Drill Hall

Admission: Entrance Test by appointment, Fee $25.

Tuition: (1993-94) 5-8, $2,378; 9-12, $2,600 . Lunch: Bring. Books: $130 **Transportation**: Available *Dress Code*: Uniform req.

LEXINGTON PARK CHRISTIAN SCHOOL...........(301) 862-4355

100 South Shangri-La Drive, Lexington Park, MD 20653
Head: Mrs. Sarah T.Patterson, Administrator

Grades: 1-8 **Enrollment** : 150 Co-ed **Faculty**: 8 full-, 4 part-time. **Average Class Size** :20

Special Courses : Academic acceleration and remediation available. Band, Ensemble, Keyboard Piano, Orchestral instruments.

Athletics: Track

Admission : Interview; Entrance Testing

Tuition: (1993-94) $2,311; Second child, $1,629 **Financial Aid** :Available

LINDEN HALL SCHOOL..........(717) 626-8512

212 East Main Street, Lifitz, PA 17543 (near Lancaster, PA)
Moravian, 1746 **Head**: David J. Devey

Grades: K-12, PG **Enrollment**: 80 Girls (65 Boarding; Boarding begins 7th grade)
Faculty: 19 full-, 2 part-time. **Average Class Size**: 10-12

Special Courses: College preparatory with special emphasis on study skills and academic achievement. LD; ESL; Music, Drama.

Athletics: Volleyball, Basketball, Softball, Soccer, Riding. **Community Service**: Students participate in various programs.

Plant: Located in small historic district; Self- contained campus on 46 acres;
Library 10,000 vol.; Gym, Swimming Pool, Outdoor Riding Rink, Stable for 22 horses; Stage. Dormitories with single rooms.

Admission: Application fee, $20; Transcript, 2 Recommendations; Campus visit strongly suggested. Note Rolling admissions until all spaces are filled

Tuition: (1993-94) 7 Day Boarder, $17,100; 5 Day Boarder, $15,600; Day Student, $6,250-$7,400. **Financial Aid**: Some Available

Summer Program: Riding Camp, Basketball Camp, Dance Camp

LINTON HALL..........(703) 368-3157

9535 Linton Hall Road., Bristow, VA. 22013
Catholic 1922. **Head**: Sister Glenna Smith, OSB

Grades: K-8. **Enrollment**: 126 Co-ed **Faculty**: 12 full-, 11 part-time.
Average Class Size: 15.

Special Courses: Standard academic classes as well as instruction in Spanish, Art, Music, Drama, Outdoor Studies, Computer Program. Religion req.; **Extended Day**: 7 a.m.-6:30 p.m.

Athletics: Interscholastic (Basketball, Soccer); Orienteering, **Clubs**: Leo. **Publications**: Yearbook.

Plant: Library 5,000 vol.; Learning Center, Science Lab, Gym/Auditorium, Playing Fields, Tennis Courts, Swimming Pool.

Admission: Personal Interview, Physical exam, good conduct Recommendation from Principal, Transcript, Registration fee $50.

Tuition: (1993-94) K-2, $3,600; 3-5, $3,800; 6-8, $4,050 *Dress Code*: Uniform req.
Scholarship Aid: Some partial available.

Future Plans: Increased student enrollment.

Summer Program: Sports, Recreation, and Enrichment Programs for ages 7-14 and 5-12; Summer Day Camp, 9 one-week sessions.

LITTLE PEOPLE'S PARADISE SCHOOL...,,.......(202) 543-2618

308 15th Street, S.E., Washington, D.C. 20003
Head: Mrs. Dolores Conrad.

Grades: N-6 (N, Ages 2-4). **Enrollment**: 150 Co-ed. **Extended Day** : 6:30 a.m.-6:30 p.m.

Tuition: (1993-94) $75/wk. includes breakfast, lunch and snack, and **Extended Day**.
Grades 1-6, $320/mo.

Summer Program: Year-round program for enrolled students.

LONE OAK MONTESSORI SCHOOL..........(301) 530-4213

10100 Old Georgetown Road, Bethesda, MD. 20814 (ages 2 1/2- 10)
7108 Bradley Boulevard., Bethesda, MD. 20817 (ages 2 1/2 -6)
Head: Patricia Swann

Ungraded: Ages 2 1/2- 10 **Enrollment** : 140 Co-ed

Special Feature: Montessori Program. **Extended Day** : 7:45 a.m.- 5:30 p.m.

Tuition: (1993-94) Half-Day N & K $3,635; full day K-gr.4, $4,435.

LOUDOUN COUNTRY DAY SCHOOL..........(703) 777-3841

237 Fairview Street, Leesburg, VA. 22075
Founded 1953. **Head**: Dr. Randy Hollister

Grades: Pre K-8. **Enrollment**: 182 Co-ed. **Faculty**: 18 full, 2 part-time.
Average Class Size: 18.

Special Courses: Latin 6-8, French K-8; Algebra, Computer as a scheduled class 6-8, other grades with classroom teacher. Gen'l Science 4-8. Civics, American History. Remedial Reading and Math. Note: Resource teacher for LD students. Art & Music. **Extended Day**: 7 a.m. -6:30 p.m.

Athletics: Required all grades. Intramural & Interscholastic: Soccer, Field Hockey, Basketball. Lacrosse, Track. Tennis also available. **Clubs**: Elective courses in photography, computer, jewelry making, chorus, etc. **Community Involvement**: Provide a complete Christmas (includes tree, gifts, and food) for the residents of the Loudoun Abused Women's Shelter.

Plant: Library 5,000 vol., Science Lab, Computer Lab, Playing Fields, Art Studio, Gym, Auditorium.

Admission: Interview, Testing, School Visit, Transcript, Recommendations; $60 Application & Testing fee.

Tuition: (1993-94) Pre-K, $4,350; K- grade 5, $6,650; 6-8: $7,250. **Transportation**: one way: $485-$800; both ways $675-$1,100. *Dress Code*: No jeans or T-shirts; other restrictions involve styles, and colors of dress. **Scholarship Aid**: Available - 24 partial.

Future Plans: New classroom and Library.

LOVE OF LEARNING MONTESSORI SCHOOL.........(301) 596-4412

10840 Little Patuxent Parkway, Columbia, MD 21044
Head C. Awilda Torres

Ungraded : N2-age 12 **Enrollment**: Co-ed

Special Programs: Spanish K4-grade 6; Reading specialist on staff. **Extended Day**: 7 a.m. 6:20 p.m.

Tuition: (1993-94) N2, $580/mo; all other grades, etc. $558

Summer Program : Age 2-12. **Extended Day** : 7 a.m.-6 p.m.

LOWELL SCHOOL.... (202) 726-9153

16th & Kennedy Streets, N.W., Washington, D.C. 20011-4330 (Nursery only)
16th & Decatur Streets, N.W., Washington, D. C. 20011-4330 (K-3)
Founded 1965 **Head**: Abigail B. Wiebenson

Grades: N-3. **Enrollment**: 200 Co-ed **Faculty**: 19 full-, 10 part-time.
Average Class Size: N, 9; K-3, 12-15

Special Programs: Extended Day: ages 5-9, only: 3:00 p.m.-6:00 p.m.

Plant: Library, 3,000 vol.; Science Lab

Admission: Tour for parents; Informal evaluation of child, No Standardized Testing required; Recommendations from current school/ Playgroup.

Tuition : (1993-94) N Half-Day $ 5,400; N Part Days $6,750; N All Day, $8,100; K-3, $ 8,450 Lunch: Bring. **Scholarship Aid:** 30 partial.

Summer Program : Recreational (for ages 3-9), 9 a.m.-12 p.m. or 9 a.m.- 3 p.m. Primary (ages 5-9} 9 a.m.-2:30 p.m.. Includes field trips to area sites; last four weeks spent in waterworks & puppetry.

MacARTHUR SCHOOL..........(202) 965-8700

4460 MacArthur Boulevard N.W, Washington, D. C. 20007
Developmental School Foundation 1975 **Head**: Denese Lombardi, M.A.

Grades : 1-12 (Day School, grades 5-12 only) **Enrollment**: 115 Co-ed: Mostly Boarding at Psychiatric Institute of Washington.

MADEIRA SCHOOL..........(703) 556-8200

8328 Georgetown Pike, McLean, VA. 22102
Founded 1906. **Head**: Dr. Elisabeth Griffith.

Grades: 9-12. **Enrollment**: 279 Girls (132 day, 147 Boarding). **Faculty**: 27 full-, 22 part-time.
Average Class Size: 16

Special Courses: Latin, French, Spanish, 9-12; Biology, Chemistry, Adv. Physics; History - 20th Century, Asian, Ancient, Russian, Medieval, U.S., Modern European; World Religions, Economics. Studio Art, Art History, Computer Science, Word Processing. AP.: All subjects. Broad range offered in Drama, Art, and Music; Driver's Ed., Vocal Performance. Co-Curriculum Program 10-12: all students work Wednesday in community service, on Capitol Hill, or in pre-professional areas. 9th graders participate in study skills and outdoor adventure program.

Athletics: Req. 9-12. Intramural & Interscholastic: Aerobics, Basketball, Cross Country, Field Hockey, Gymnastics, Lacrosse, Life Saving, Modern Dance, Riding, Soccer, Softball, Squash, Swimming, Tennis, , Volleyball, Weight Training.. **Clubs**: Drama, Model U.N., Guides, French, Latin, Debate, Spanish, Math, Science, Student Council, Athletic Assn., Madrigals, Glee Club, Vocal Arts Ensemble. **Publications**: Yearbook, Newspaper, Literary Magazine. **Community Involvement:** (See Co-Curriculum under Special Courses).

Plant: Library 20,000 vol.; 6 Dormitories, 3 Science Labs, Health Center, Art Studio, Gym, Auditorium, Stables, Playing Fields, Outdoor and Indoor Pools, Tennis Courts, Indoor Riding Ring, Note: 400 acre campus with new 28,000 sq. ft. sports center.

Admission: SSAT, Interview, Personal Essays, Teacher & Principal Recommendation, Transcript. Application fee $35. First choice plan application, due December 15.

Tuition: (1993-94) Day $11,350; Boarding $19,000. Lunch included. Books: $350.
Dress Code: Clean, appropriate clothing. **Scholarship Aid**: Available

Future Plans: New Library and Student Center to be completed in 1993

Summer Program: Day camp - Coed ages 6-14; tennis, swimming, crafts, outdoor adventure.

MAHARISHI SCHOOL OF THE AGE OF ENLIGHTENMENT..........(301) 949-8350

12210 Georgia Avenue, Wheaton, MD 20902
Founded 1982 **Head**: Elinor Hall, Principal.

Grades: 2 yrs. to grade 6. **Enrollment**: 90 Co-ed **Faculty**: 5 full-, 7 part-time.
Average Class Size: 12

Special Programs: Art, Music,Transcendental Meditation; Science of Creative Intelligence. **Extended Day**: Available on premises by independent provider.

Athletics: P.E. Note: Additional after school activities organized by parents include Karate and ice skating.

Plant: Library, Playing Field, all purpose room.

Admission: $25 Application fee; Liberal admissions policy. Admission based on Application Review, Interview, and Transcripts: School must determine that the applicant's need can be met.

Tuition: (1993-94) Age 2-K, $1,300- $3,150 plus activities fees ($25-$75 per semester); grades 1-6, $4,950, plus $50 per semester for Books and Material fee. *Dress Code*: Uniform req.

MANOR MONTESSORI SCHOOL..........(301) 299-7400

10500 Oaklyn Drive, Potomac, MD. 20854
11200 Old Georgetown Road, Rockville, MD. 20852 (N & K only)
Founded 1962. **Head**: Katherine Demico

Ungraded: Ages 2-1/2-8. **Enrollment**: 160 Co-ed. **Faculty**: 17 full-time.
Average Class Size: 25.

Special Features: Montessori method, ungraded classes; French, Gifted Children's Program, Computers, Physical Education. **Extended Day**: 7:30 a.m.- 6 p.m.

Main Plant: 3 1/2 acres in Potomac, English Tudor building, All-purpose room, Library, Playgrounds, Gardens.

Admission: Informal Interview with Directress. $50 registration fee. Primary class - not accepted after 4-1/2 unless previously enrolled in Montessori Method. Junior class - (ages 6 to 8) accepted without previous Montessori Training.

Tuition: (1993-94) Half- day $3,550; N-PreK, $4,100; Primary, $4.950; Jr. class (age 7-8) $5,300. **Transportation**: $1,500, one way; $2,000, both ways. **Scholarship Aid**: Available.

Summer Program: Ages 2-1/2-9; swimming lessons, nature studies, hikes, picnics, field trips, arts & crafts. Hours: 7:30 a.m.-6 p.m.(minimum one week)

MARET SCHOOL ....(202) 939-8800

3000 Cathedral Avenue, N.W., Washington, D.C. 20008
Founded 1911. **Head**: Peter Sturtevant.

Grades: K-12. **Enrollment**: 500 Co-ed. Enrollment increases 4, 7, 9. **Faculty**: 75 full-time.
Average Class Size: 12.

Special Courses: Latin 5-12, French K-12, Spanish 4-12; Science: Biology, Chemistry, Physics, Environmental Science; Science & Public Policy, Human Biology, Concepts in Physics;

History: U.S., Mod. European, Ancient, Medieval, Russian, Modern American, West & Non-West; Philosophy, Psychology; History of Film,; Adolescence; Computer Science, Computer Graphics, Pascal Programming; Arts & Crafts, Woodworking, Painting, Sculpture, Graphics, Photography, Music-Chorus, Band, Chamber Choir, Drama. AP.: French, Spanish, Biology, Chemistry, Physics, Calculus, English, History. **Extended Day**: to 6 p.m.

Athletics: Req. K-12. Intramural & Interscholastic: Football, Soccer, Basketball, Volleyball, Softball, Baseball, Skiing, Weights, Aerobics, Wrestling, Tennis, Lacrosse, Track, Cross-Country; **Clubs**: Drama, Enviornment, Math Teams. **Publications**: Yearbook, Literary Arts Magazine Newspaper. **Community Involvement**: 70% of Upper School students do volunteer work on regular or ad hoc basis throughout the year.

Plant: 2 Libraries (12,000 vol.), 6 Science Labs, Fields, 2 Gyms, Auditorium, 5 Art Studios, Math Lab, Music Room, 2 Computer Rooms with 32 computer, all housed in 6 buildings.

Admission: Parent Tour/Interview; child Visits for full day; References & Transcript; SSAT for grades 6-11.

Tuition: (1993-94) $9,450- $11,200 Lunch: $450. Books: $100-$450. *Dress Code*: Neat and appropriate. **Scholarship Aid**: 40 partial.

Future Plans: Renovation of historic Manor House.

Summer Program: Credit, Remedial & enrichment programs for grades 5-12.
Summer Camp ages 4-9. Summer trips to Florida, France and Argentina. (brochure available).

MARTIN BARR ADVENTIST SCHOOL............(301) 261-0078

2365 Bell Branch Road, Gambrills, MD. 21054
Seventh Day Adventist **Head**: Joni Woodruff

Grades: K-8 **Enrollment**: 32 Co-ed

Tuition: (1993-94) $130-$250/mo. Note: discount for siblings and church members. Registration fee $100

MATER AMORIS MONTESSORI SCHOOL..........(301) 774-7468 or (202)362-3279

18501 Mink Hollow Road, Ashton, MD. 20861
36th & Ellicott Streets, N.W., Washington, D.C. 20008
Founded 1968. **Head**: Charlotte Kovach Shea

Ungraded: age 2-1/2 -12. **Enrollment**: 75 (D.C.); 110 (MD) Co-ed. **Faculty**: 11 AMI (Association Montessori International) trained teachers. **Average Class Size**: 25.

Special Courses: Art, Music, General Science, Biology, History, Dance, Drama.
Extended Day: 7:30 a.m.-6 p.m.

Athletics: Softball, Kickball, Field Hockey, Basketball, Soccer, Volleyball.

Plant: Library, Science Lab, Auditorium, Playing Fields, Stables, 13 acre farm in Ashton, Md.

Admission: Parent Visit & Interview, child Visits class.

Tuition: (1993-94) Ages 2-1/2-5, half day $3,100; K, $4,300; Ages 6-12, $4,900- $ 5,200.
Scholarship Aid: Some Available.

MATER DEI SCHOOL..........(301) 365-2700

9600 Seven Locks Road, Bethesda, MD. 20817
Catholic 1960. **Head**: Christopher Abell

Grades: 1-8. **Enrollment**: 220 Boys. **Faculty**: 14 full-,6 part-time. **Average Class Size**: 20.

Special Courses: Latin 8, Art, Music. Substantial Reading requirement. Religious studies req., Typing.

Athletics: Req.; Intramural & Interscholastic 5-8; All sports offered. **Publications**: Newspaper.

Plant: Library 5,500 vol., Chapel, Gym, Art Studio, Swimming Pool, Playing Fields.

Admission: Testing in February, Parent Interview required,

Tuition: (1993-94) $5,225. Bring Lunch. Books: Extra. *Dress Code*: Uniform req.

Summer Program: Day camp for boys, ages 6-12.

McDONOGH SCHOOL..........(301) 363-0600

McDonogh, MD. 21117-0380
Founded 1873. **Head**: Dr. William C. Mules.

Grades: Pre 1-12. **Enrollment**: 1,172 Co-ed Day & Boarding (5 day Boarding begins 9).

McLEAN SCHOOL OF MARYLAND............(301) 299-8277

8224 Lochinver Lane, Potomac, MD. 20854
Founded 1952. **Head**: August Ganzenmuller, III

Grades: K-9. **Enrollment**: 277 Co-ed. **Faculty**: 46 full-, 12 part-time
Average Class Size: 15

Special Program: Basic Traditional, challenging curriculum. Unique Dual Program for Mainstream Students and those with individual learning styles. Special Courses: Spanish 7-9, Art, Music, Drama, Computers/Keyboarding, and Leadership.

Athletics: P.E. classes daily. Interscholastic: Soccer, Softball, Basketball, Field Hockey, Lacrosse. **Publications**: Newspaper, Literary Magazine, Yearbook.
Community Involvement: Ninth Grade Service at Our Lord's Table Soup Kitchen, Recycling Program, Retirement Home and Community Music Programs.

Plant: Library 10,155 vol., Science Lab, Computer Labs, Art Studio, All Purpose Room/Gym, Playing Fields.

Admission: Parent Interview; Student Visits Classroom; Transcript & Test scores, WISC 3, Achievement Testing andTeacher Recommendations. Application fee.

Tuition: (1993-94) $6,975-$10,475 Books: $200-$300. **Transportation**: Available.
Dress Code: Uniform required **Financial Assistance**: Available

MERCERSBURG ACADEMY..........(717) 328-2151

Mercersburg, PA. 17236
United Church of Christ 1836. **Head**: Walter H. Burgin, Jr.

Grades: 9-12, P.G. **Enrollment**: 346 (215 Boys, 131 Girls), 315 Boarding, 31 Day. **Faculty**: 59 full-time. **Average Class Size**: 12-14

Special Courses: Latin, French, Spanish, German,-all 9-12. Math through 2nd yr. Calculus, Computer, Discreet Math. Physical Science, Biology, Chemistry, Physics; term courses in Botany, Genetics, Psychology, Behavioral Science, Anthropology. History - Intro. to World History (9), Introd. to Western Civilization (10), U.S. & European; term courses in Latin America, Sub- Saharan Africa, China & Japan. Economics. Religious Studies-Req.; Art: Drawing, Painting, Sculpture, Art History. Music History, Theory. AP. courses in all academic areas, Art History, and Studio Art. School Year Abroad;-English-Speaking Union; School Farm Trek (Outward Bound Program).

Athletics: Intramural Volleyball, Softball, and Soccer. Interscholastic: Football, Cross Country, Field Hockey, Basketball, Swimming, Diving, Wrestling, Squash, Baseball, Tennis, Golf, Track & Field, Lacrosse, Softball, & Volleyball. **Clubs**: 4 Music groups, 4 Choral groups; Student Council, Drama, Languages, Photography, Debate, Amnesty International, Ecology.

Publications: Weekly Newspaper, Literary Magazine, Yearbook. **Community Involvement**: Tutoring at local elementary school, Youth Club; Helping Senior Citizens; Soup Kitchen.

Plant: New Library/Classroom Bldg.(Jan '93).; 7 new English classrooms,(Ap.'93), 5 Science Labs, Gym, Auditorium, 8 Playing Fields, Swimming Pool, 17 Tennis Courts, All-weather quarter-mile Track, Indoor Track, Outdoor Volleyball court; School Farm, Chapel.

Admission: SSAT, PSAT; Interview, if geographically possible. Recommendations from 3 teachers; Transcripts for the previous 3 years.

Tuition: (1993-94) $11,200 Day, $17,700 Boarding. Books: $500. *Dress Code*: At evening meal: Coat & Tie for boys, skirt for girls. **Financial Aid**: 30% of student body.

Future Plans: New classroom building to be completed Jan. '94.

Summer Program: Individual Camp offerings in June, July, & August. Numerous sports camps including tennis, field hockey, karate, swimming, & soccer camps. Ecology camp 1 week in mid June.

MONTESSORI CHILDREN'S HOUSE (Bowie)..........(301) 262-3566

5004 Randonstone Lane, Bowie, MD. 20715
Founded 1967. **Head**: Anne Riley.

Ungraded: Ages 2 1/2 -14. **Enrollment**: 170 Co-ed. **Faculty**: 5 full-, 4 part-time.
Average Class Size: 30

Special Courses: Montessori method used; Exposure to Music, Art, Dance, Drama (private lessons in art, music, ballet available. Remedial Reading and Math. 22 acre campus used to familiarize children with erosion, forestry, environment and care of animals. Limited **Day Care** 7 a.m.-6 p.m.

Plant: Library 5000 vol., Audio Visual Lab, Stables, Playing Fields, Tennis Courts, Outdoor Amphitheater, 22 acre rustic campus.

Admission: Parent & child Interview. Limited acceptances for children beyond age 5 if not previously enrolled in Montessori program. Special remedial & high aptitude applicants accepted. Those with limited handicaps includes deaf with cued speech and reading disabilities.

Tuition: (1993-94) $3,025-$3,900 **Day Care**: $200/ mo. Books: $15-$50

Summer Program: Rustic Woods Day Camp - (Remedial instruction by special request). Arts & crafts, ecology, primitive construction, riding, sports, swimming, campouts, etc. Continuation of Montessori philosophy for children 6-12 using the out of doors. Late June to late August.

MONTESSORI INTERNATIONAL CHILDREN'S HOUSE..........(410) 757-7789

1641 Winchester Road, Annapolis, MD. 21401
Founded 1977. **Head**: Jean Burgess

Ungraded: Ages 18 mo-9 yr. **Enrollment**: 120 Co-ed. **Faculty**: 6 full-, 5 Montessori Aides.
Average Class Size: 20.

Special Courses: Montessori method. French & Spanish conversation taught, Music, Art, Creative Dramatics, Creative Movements, Cooking. (Infant & Toddlers program) P.E.
Extended Day: 7:30 a.m.-6 p.m.

Plant: Library, new modern facility designed specifically for Montessori Primary & Elementary programs in country setting.

Admission: Interview with parent & child, Testing for Elementary. $25 Application fee.

Tuition: (1993-94) Toddler, $1,738; K Half- Day $2,870; K full-Day, $4,090; Elementary $4,377 (Day Care: Extra) Bring Lunch.

Summer Program: 6 weeks, recreational program for ages 18 months- 5

MONTESSORI SCHOOL OF ALEXANDRIA ....(703) 960-3498

6300 Florence Lane, Alexandria, VA. 22310
Founded 1970. **Head**: Jean Adolphi

Ungraded: Ages 2-1/2-12. **Enrollment:** 99 Co-ed. **Faculty**: 12 full-time.
Average Class Size: 25.

Special Features: Montessori method, ungraded classes. Art, Music, French, Ballet, Piano
Extended Day : 7:30 a.m.-6 p.m.

Admission: Child not accepted after age 3-1/2 unless previously enrolled in Montessori school. Interview.

Tuition: (1993-94) Primary (Age 2-5) $3,150; Age 5, $3,650; Age 6-12 $4,250.
Day Care with Lunch, $205/mo. Hourly Rate: $5.50. *Dress Code*: Uniform Req.
Scholarship Aid: Available.

Summer Program: 11 weeks, includes swimming. Montessori Program Half-day $80/wk, full day (includes hot lunch), $120/wk.

MONTESSORI SCHOOL OF HOLMES RUN..........(703) 573-4652

3527 Gallows Road, Falls Church, VA 22042
Head: Judith Clarke

Ungraded: Ages 2 1/2-12 **Enrollment**: 60 Co-ed

Special Programs: **Extended Day** 8 a.m.- 9 a.m. (School day ends at 2:45 p.m.)

Tuition: (1993-94) Half-day, $2,530; N-K Full-day $2,867; 1-3, $3,360. 4-6, $3,500

MONTESSORI SCHOOL OF McLEAN..........(703) 790-1049

1711 Kirby Road, McLean, VA. 22101
Founded 1973. **Head**: Joan Marie Parasine.

Ungraded: Ages 2 1/2-12. **Enrollment**: 160 Co-ed. **Faculty**: 7 full-, 6 part-time.
Average Class Size: 28.

Special Courses: Ungraded classes. French, (Transition & Elem.); Computers all levels; Art, Drama, Music. P.E. required at all levels. **Clubs** : Bluebirds (if parent leader available)

Plant: Library, 5,500 vol.; Art Studio, Playing Fields

Admission: Interview, Registration fee $80.

Tuition: (1993-94) $3,400-$4,100. Books: $110. **Transportation**: $1,100 one way; $1,400 both ways. **Dress Code**: Neat attire, no jeans in Pre-school & Transition; Uniform required in Elementary grades.

Summer Program: Academic program, Montessori curriculum;
Summer Camp program: cooking, songs, games, field trips, gardening, Ages 2 1/2-7..

MONTESSORI SCHOOL OF NORTHERN VIRGINIA..........(703) 256-9577

6820 Pacific Lane, Annandale, VA. 22003
Founded 1962. **Head**: Betsy Mitchell.

Ungraded: Ages 2-9. **Enrollment**: 129 Co-ed. **Faculty**: 6 full-, 8 part-time.
Average Class Size: 25

Special Courses: Montessori method, French, Orff music program. Art, P.E.; Emphasis on cultural studies. Computer instruction. **Extended Day**: 7 a.m. - 6 p.m.

Plant: Library, well-equipped playground.

Admission: Parents Visit & Observe; Interview. $50 Application fee.

Tuition: (1993-94) $1815-$4,585 includes Books **Transportation**: $70/mo. one way, $130/ mo.both ways. *Dress Code*: Comfortable clothing. **Financial Aid** Limited.

Summer Program: 5 weeks, ages 3-8. Wide range of activities including arts & crafts, water-play, food preparation, nature study.

MONTROSE CHRISTIAN SCHOOL........... (301) 770-5337

5100 Randolph Road, Rockville, MD 20852
Southern Baptist 1977. **Head**: Kenneth Coley

Grades: K-12. **Enrollment**: 610 Co-ed. **Faculty**: 36 full-time. **Average Class Size**: 15-20.

Special Courses: Spanish; Computer. Gen'l Science, Biology, Chemistry, Physics. World History, Civics, Geography. Bible study req. Remedial Reading and Math. Mechanical Drawing, Typing. AP.: English and History. **Extended Day**: 7 a.m.-6 p.m.

Athletics: Req; Soccer, Basketball, Volleyball, Softball, Track. **Clubs**: Student Government. **Publications**: Yearbook. **Community Involvement**: Christmas Baskets.

Plant: Library, Gym, Auditorium, Science Lab.

Admission: Formal Application, Interview, standardized Testing. (Must be able to work at grade level).

Tuition: (1993-94) K, $1,790; 1-6 $2,480; 7-12 $2,740. **Extended Day**: $45-$55/wk..

MUSLIM COMMUNITY SCHOOL, INC.............(301) 340-6713

7917 Montrose Road, Potomac, MD. 20854
Islamic, Non-Sectarian-Multinational 1980 **Head**: Amir Khalili

Grades: Pre K-9 **Enrollment**: 150 Co-ed **Faculty**: 16 full-, 2 part-time.
Average Class Size: 13

Special Courses: Arabic, K-9. Algebra and Computer. General Science. History- World, Islamic, Modern U.S.; Religious Studies, req.; ESOL. Note: All classes except Arabic are taught in English. Art, Science Fairs, Zuramic Competitions, Spelling Bees-annually.

Athletics: Girls: Gymnastics, Volleyball. Boys: Soccer, Martial Arts. **Publications**: Yearbook, Literary Magazine.

Plant: Library, 9,100 vol.; Language Lab, Science Lab, Auditorium, Playing Fields, Tot Lot-Playing Ground, Basketball Court.

Admission: Pre registration June 15th, $50 fee. Transcripts, Personal Interview with Family. Note: Boys and Girls separated at grade 5.

Tuition: (1993-94) $200- $300/mo. Books: $35. **Transportation**: 50-$80/mo. *Dress Code*: Uniform req. **Scholarship Aid**: 11 Available.

Future Plans: New Building for High School to include Gym, Swimming Pool; New separate building for Nursery.

NANNIE HELEN BURROUGHS SCHOOL, INC..........(202) 398-5266

601 50th Street, N.E., Washington, D.C. 20019
Baptist 1909. **Head**: Mattie A. Robinson

Grades: N-6. **Enrollment**: 160 Co-ed. **Faculty**: 9 full-, 5 part-time. **Average Class Size**: 20.

Special Courses: Spanish, Music, Science includes Aerospace and Computer Science; Bible Classes 5 & 6. After school program in cultural arts. Emphasis on Leadership Training. **Extended Day**: 7 a.m.- 5:30 p.m.

Athletics: P.E. Req. - includes kickball. **Publications**: Quarterly newsgram. **Community Involvement**: Share assemblies with public school.

Plant: Library, Auditorium, Gym, Playing Fields.

Admission: Interview (parent & child), Tests. Registration fee $100.

Tuition: (1993-94) $300-$325/ mo. includes **Extended Day**

Summer Program: Enrichment program.

NATIONAL CATHEDRAL SCHOOL..........(202) 537-6300

Mount St. Alban, Washington, D.C. 20016-5000
Episcopal 1900. **Head**: Agnes C. Underwood.

Grades: 4-12. **Enrollment**: 550 Girls, class expands at grade 7. **Faculty**: 67 full-, 17 part-time. **Average Class Size**: 15-18.

Special Courses: Latin & Spanish 7-12, French 4-12, German 10-12; Greek / Russian/ Chinese/Japanese consortium with Sidwell Friends & St. Albans (grades 10-12). English. Math thru Calculus, Computer. Biology, Chemistry, Physics; History-American Gov't American History, Soviet Union, Japan, Islam, Modern European, African-American, DevelopingWorld, Latin American, World, Geography. Economics. Religion Courses req.(grades 4-8 and 2 semesters grades 9-12). Studio Art, Art History. Music - Orchestra & Wind Ensemble; Drama. Some co-ordinate courses & activities with St. Albans. AP.: English, Latin, French

Spanish, Calculus, Computer Science, Biology, Chemistry, Physics, U.S History, Gov't & Politics, European History, Economics, History of Art. **Extended Care**: Available for grades 4-6, until 6 p.m.

Athletics: Req.(except for one season grade 12) Intramural & Interscholastic: Field Hockey, Soccer, Basketball, Volleyball, Tennis, Dance, Gymnastics, Track & Field, Lacrosse, Softball, Swimming, Diving, Cross Country, Aerobics, Weight Training, Voyager, Squash, Fencing. **Clubs**: Foreign Language Seminars, Science, Math, Government, Debate, Drama, Madrigals, Chorale, White Chapel Guild, Black Student Union, Environmental Awareness, Mock Trial, Outing, School Gov't, Service Board, Planning Board, Vestry. **Publications**: Newspaper, Yearbook, Literary magazine. **Community Involvement**: 60 hrs. req. grades 9-12.

Plant: 2 Libraries 20,000 vol., Language Lab, 5 Science Labs, Art Studio, 2 Gyms, 2 Auditoriums, Playing Fields, 8 Tennis Courts, Theater (used jointly with St. Albans) and Experimental Theater, Computer Center, Swimming Pool at St. Albans.

Admission: $60 Application fee, SSAT for grades 7-11, NCS Test for grades 4-7. Interview/ Visit. File application before Feb. 10 for consideration in first group of applicants.

Tuition: (1993-94) $12,020 includes Lunch & Fees; Books: $100-$350 *Uniform*: req. grades 4-6; *Dress Code* gr. 7-12. **Financial Aid**: Full and partial grants available.

Summer Program: Tennis, gymnastics, art, dance, theater, grades 4-9.

NATIONAL CHRISTIAN ACADEMY..........(301) 567-9507

6700 Bock Road, Ft. Washington, MD 20744
Pentecost, 1981 **Head**: Dr. Fred Snowden

Grades: N3-grade 12. **Enrollment**: 506 Co-ed (160 Boys, 250 Girls) **Faculty**: 23 full, 12 part-time aides. **Average Class Size** : 23

Special Courses: Spanish, Gen'l Science, Biology, Chemistry. History- U.S., Gov't, World, and Bible. Computer. Religious Studies req. Typing, Driver's Ed, Band, Drama. **Extended Day**: 6:30 a.m.-6:30 p.m.

Athletics: Girls & Boys Basketball & Volleyball Teams (Jr, & Sr. High)

Plant: Gym, Auditorium, Playing Fields, Science Lab, Computer Lab. Cafeteria, Chapel.

Admission: $50 Registration fee; Parent/Principal Interview; Transcript.

Tuition: (1993-94) N3-N4, $90/wk; K-12, $2,390; Reduction for siblings. Books: Extra. **Transportation**: Available, fees based on distance and numbers of children. *Dress Code*: Uniform req. K5-grade 12.

Summer Program: Day Camp; Call for information.

NATIONAL PRESBYTERIAN SCHOOL...(202) 537-7500

4121 Nebraska Avenue, N.W., Washington, D.C. 20016
Presbyterian 1969. **Head**: Mrs. Jane Harter.

Grades: N3-grade 6. **Enrollment**: 215 Co-ed. **Faculty**: 27 full-, 8 part-time. Note: Reading and Language Specialists (2), Math Specialist on staff. **Average Class Size**: 24, with 2 classroom teachers.

Special Courses: French, Computers, General Science. Religion. Art, Music, P.E.
Extended Day: until 6 p.m.

Athletics: Req. K-6. Intramural Non-competitive program of body movement, skills, and games. **Clubs**: Karate, Computer, After-school Sports, Drama, Art, Science, French, Math, Newspaper. **Publications**: Newsletter, Yearbook

Plant: Library 10,000 vol.; "State of the Art" Macintosh Computer Lab; Science Lab, Art Studio, Gym/Auditorium. School shares 12.5 acre campus with the National Presbyterian Church & Center and shares some of the facilities of the church.

Admission: Parent Visits school; Application and non-refundable application fee; Upon completion of application, child spends day at school; Tests, Transcripts, Recommendations from previous schools; Admissions Committee makes decision and candidate notified after March 1.

Tuition: (1993-94) N & Pre K, $4,500-$6,675; K-6. $8,250 Financial Aid: Some available.

Future Plans: Computerization of Library; increased use of computers in classroom; expansion of physical space to provide for additional resource and specialized teachers; acquisition of additional playing fields.

Summer Camp Program: Early June to early September, variety of summer programs; Ages 4-11; Staff includes professional teachers. Swimming at American University. **Extended Day** Available..

NATIONHOUSE WATOTO SCHOOL.......... (202) 291-5600 FAX (202) 726-5681

770 Park Road, N.W., Washington, D. C. 20010
Head: Mr. Agyei Akoto

Grades: N-12 **Enrollment**: 85 Co-ed

Special Programs : French, Swahili; African Youth Organization and Dance. Drill Team; Computer Club. Adult Education Programs. **Extended Day**: 7:30 a.m.-6 p.m.

Tuition: (1993-94) $200/mo.-$300 /mo. depending on grade, hours, and parent participation.

Summer Program: Academic & Recreational; 8 a.m.-6 p.m.

NATIVITY CATHOLIC ACADEMY..........(202) 723-3322

6008 Georgia Avenue, N.W., Washington, D.C. 20011
Catholic 1925. **Head**: Mrs. Valeri M. Smith.

Grades: PreK-8. **Enrollment**: 250 Co-ed. **Faculty**: Departmentalized small group instruction.

Special Programs: Religion, Reading, Math, Spanish, Language Arts, Social Studies, Science, Music and Art. Education for the whole child: spiritual, intellectual, social and physical; growth i n the knowledge and experience of Jesus as personal Lord, Savior and Brother. Nativity School Band 4-8. **Extended Day**: 7 a.m.-6 p.m.

Athletics: P.E. Girls & boys basketball teams competition (CYO League). **Clubs**: Student Council, Band. **Publications**: Newspaper.

Plant: Library (with large audio/visual sections), Auditorium, Gym, Math Lab, Chapel (at church).

Tuition: (1993-94) $1,750. Registration $30 Books: $100 **Extended Day** Extra

Summer Program: Summer camp for enrolled students

NAYLOR ROAD SCHOOL..........(202) 584-5114

2403 Naylor Road, S.E., Washington, D.C. 20020
Founded 1939. **Head**: Mrs. Patricia Ward.

Grades: N3-grade 6. **Enrollment**: 200 Co-ed. **Faculty**: 22. **Average Class Size**: 18.

Special Courses: Spanish N-6, Art, Music, Shop, Individual Science Program 1-6; Traditional Classes stressing Reading & Language Development. Small groups, individualized instruction. **Extended Day** 6:45 a.m.-6 p.m.

Plant: Library 3,000 vol.; Language Lab, Science Lab, Shop.

Admission: Applications accepted in Feb., Testing 1-6.

Tuition: (1993-94) N, $2,900-$3,000; K, $3,150.; 1-3, $3,450-$3,700.; 4-6 $3,850. Lunch: Bring. Books: Extra. *Dress Code*: K-6, Uniforms.

NEW CITY MONTESSORI SCHOOL..........(301) 559-8488

3120 Nicholson Street, Hyattsville, MD. 20782
Founded 1968. **Head**: Shirley Windsor, Administrator.

Ungraded: Ages 2 1/2-11. **Enrollment**: 80 Coed. **Faculty**: 4 full, 2 part-time, 3 aides.
Average Class Size: 20

Special courses: Montessori method, ungraded. Computers; Spanish; Art.
Extended Day: 7:30 a.m..-6 p.m.

Admission: Application form and $25 fee; Informal Interview with parent & child.

Tuition: (1993-94) $2,500-$3,700. **Extended Day** : Extra; depends on age and number of hours.

NEW HOPE ACADEMY..........(301) 459-7311

7009 Varnum Street, Landover Hills, MD 20784
Non-Denominational Christian **Head** Joy Morrow

Grades: N3-grade 8 **Enrollment**: Co-ed

Special Programs: Korean Language N3-grade 8. Optional after school Dance Program includes Ballet and Ethnic Dance. **Extended Day**: 8 a.m.-6 p.m.

Tuition: (1993-94) $3,200-$3,800; discount for siblings.

NEW LIFE CHRISTIAN SCHOOL ....(301) 663-8418

5913 Jefferson Pike, Frederick, MD 21702
Head: Paul Kemp

Grades: K-12 **Enrollment**: 225 Co-ed

Special Courses: ABEKA; Spanish & French

Plant: Classroom Building and Gym opening in fall of '93

Tuition : (1993-94) K $1,225; 1-5 $1,925; 6-8 $2,065; 9-11, $2,265. Reduction for siblings.

NEWPORT SCHOOLS...........(301) 942-4550

11311 Newport Mill Road, Kensington, MD. 20895
Founded 1930 **Head**: Nina Olin & Andrew Zvara

Grades: N-12 (Note; Town & Country Day School, N-8; Newport Preparatory School, 9-12.)
Enrollment: 290 Co-ed **Faculty**: 45 full & part-time. **Average Class Size**: 15

Special Courses: Latin & French, 7-12; Spanish PreK-12. Biology, Chemistry, Physics, History & Philosophy of Science. History- World, American. Political Theory, Government, Economics. Studio Art & Fundamentals; Fundamentals of Music, Choir, Bell Choir. Study Skills, Drama, Photography. AP.: Biology, Calculus, Computer Science, American History, English Literature & Composition. **Extended Day:** 7 a.m.-6 p.m.

Athletics: P.E. req.; Intramural, Interscholastic. Volleyball, Soccer, Basketball, Track, Softball. **Clubs**: Chess; Variety depending on interest. **Publications**: Year-book **Community Involvement:** Grades 9-12, Community Service.

Plant: Library 11,000 vol., 4 Science Labs, Art Studio, Auditorium/Gym, Playing Fields, Tennis Courts, Weight Room. Computer Lab.

Admission: Rolling Admissions. Pre-school (Interview); K - 11, Tests. Application Fee $35. Student visit.

Tuition: (1993-94) Pre-school $4,900-$ 5,800; K, $5,350-$6,350; 1-4, $6,750-$7,300; 5-7, $7,600; 8-12, $8,100 Lunch $400 Books Extra Uniform: req. grades 1-8; *Dress code* for 9-12. **Financial Aid**: Available for grade 1 and up.

Summer Program: Academic-Math, Language Arts Skills. Computer & Science Camp. Recreational: N-grade 7. Day Camp includes swimming, gymnastics, archery, fencing, dramatics, dance, music, pony rides, arts & crafts. Some special programs for age 8-15 include teen travel, tennis, basketball, gymnastics.

The NEW SCHOOL OF NORTHERN VIRGINIA...........(703) 691-3040

9431 Silver King Court, Fairfax, VA 22031
Founded 1989 **Head**: John Potter

Grades: K-12 **Enrollment:** 60 Co-ed **Faculty**: 7 full-, 6 part- time.
Average Class Size: 8- 10

Special Courses: French & Spanish, K-12. Math through Calculus; Computer. General Science, Biology, Chemistry, Physics. Remedial Reading and Math. Art, Music. Note: Individualized learning co-operative: use written evaluations rather than grades.

Athletics: Required all grades. **Publications**: Yearbook, Newsletter
Community Involvement: Internships req. in high school; visits to S.O. M. E. to serve lunch

to homeless; environmental cleanup and recycling program.

Plant: Playing Field, Basketball Court.

Admission: Application fee, $60; Tuition deposit, $400; Interviews req./ Student Visit req.

Tuition: (1993-94) $6,300-$7,700 **Financial Aid**: Very Limited.

Future Plans: To expand student body to over 130 over next 5 years.

Summer Program: Academic summer school; computer camp.

NORWOOD SCHOOL..........(301) 365-2595

8821 River Road, Bethesda, MD. 20817
Founded 1952. **Head**: Richard Ewing, Jr.

Grades: K-6. **Enrollment**: 308 Co-ed. **Faculty**: 33 full-, 4 part-time. **Class Size Ranges from:** 6-18 students.

Special Courses: Computer at all grade levels. Aural/oral French K & 4-6; Art, Music, Drama, Dance. Variety of after-school enrichment courses have included Piano, Language (French & Spanish), Science, Gymnastics. **Extended Day** : 4-5:45 p.m.

Athletics: P.E. Req. all grades; Skills taught for Hockey, Lacrosse, Basketball, & Soccer. **Clubs**: Brownies, Girl Scouts. **Publications**: Newsletter **Community Involvement**: Each class participates in an outreach project approved by the administration which parents help organize and implement. School participates in various charity drives.

Plant: Library 13,000 vol., 3 Science Classrooms, Computer Lab, 2 Art Classrooms, Gym, Playing Fields, Music/Arts/Drama Bldg.

Admission: Applications taken Sept.-Jan. for following year. Parental Visit req.; Student Visit req. grade 1-5; Testing for 1-6. Transcript and Teacher Recommendations. For K and grade 1, if student tested elsewhere, then visit to school for informal evaluation by K Director. Notification by Mid-March.

Tuition: (1993-94) $8,600-$9,000. *Dress Code*: Simple, serviceable clothes. **Financial Aid**.: Available

Summer Program: "Summer at Norwood" 3 two-week sessions featuring art, music, science, computers, sports & games; Study skills.

NOTRE DAME ACADEMY..........(703) 687-5581

Route l, Box 197, Middleburg, VA. 22117
Catholic 1965. **Head**: Sister Cecilia Liberatore, SND

Grades: 9-12. **Enrollment**: 130 Co-ed **Faculty**: 12 full-,3 part-time.
Average Class Size: 15.

Special Courses: French & Spanish , 9-12; History: World, Russian, U.S., Virginia, Latin American. Sociology, Economics, World Issues, American Gov't.; Psychology, Gen'l Science, Chemistry, Biology, and Physics. Computer Science, Keyboarding. Religious studies req.; Drama, Art-Drawing, Design, Studio Ceramics, Graphics (one credit in Fine Arts Req.) Music-Choral, Instrumental, Orchestra; Photography, AP.: English, Biology, Calculus, American History. Note: Senior Career Internship.

Athletics: Req. to grade 10; Interscholastic: Volleyball, Soccer, Cross-Country, Basketball, Baseball, Tennis. **Clubs**: French, Spanish, Campus Ministry, Admissions Aides, Peer Ministry, Athletic Assn., Choral, Drama. **Publications**: Newspaper, Yearbook. **Community Involvement**: 20 hrs. of Volunteer Service req. each year; Food & Clothing Assistance, Senior Citizens Day; Students may volunteer to teach religion to children in local parish.

Plant: Library 10,000 vol.; Science Labs, Auditorium, Gym, Playing Fields, Tennis Courts, Art Studio. Meeting & Publications Building.

Admission: Interview req.; Application fee $25. Records, Transcripts, References, Applicant must write auto-biography.

Tuition: (1993-94) Day: Catholic $5,025; Non-Catholic $5,675; Boarding: Catholic- $13,780 Non-Catholic $14,430. Lunch: Extra *Dress Code*: Uniform req. **Financial Aid**: Available..

NYSMITH SCHOOL FOR THE GIFTED..........(703) 713-3332

13525 Dulles Technology Drive, Herndon, VA 22071
Founded 1983 **Head:** Carole Nysmith

Grades: N-6 **Enrollment**: 356 Co-ed **Faculty**: 40 full-, 20 part-time.
Average Class Size : 18:2

Special Courses: French daily N-6, Gen'l Science, Science Lab; Poetry, History, Art, Water Color, Jazz Dancing. Computer used daily (30 computers); Individualized Math & Reading.
Extended Day: 6:30 a.m.-6:30 p.m.

Athletics: req.; **Clubs:** Scouts, Art, Gymnastics, French, Poetry, Computer, Math.

Admission: Interview, School visit, IQ Testing 130

Tuition: (1993-94) $6,600-$8,320 includes Books, & **Extended Day** Lunch: Catered or Bring; (milk available). **Transportation**: Available. **Financial Aid**: Some Available

Future Plans : New building, add 7th & 8th grade in 1994

Summer Program: Academic; Swimming, Sports, Crafts, Music daily

OAKCREST SCHOOL..........(202) 686-9736 or 686-5057

4101 Yuma Street, N.W., Washington, D.C. 20016
Founded 1976. **Head**: Barbara Falk

Grades: 7-12. **Enrollment**: 120 girls. **Faculty**: 8 full-, 5 part-time.
Average Class Size: 18.

Special Courses: Latin, French I-IV, Spanish I-V; Biology, Chemistry, Physics, Physical Science, Earth & Life Science. History: U.S/Government, Ancient, Medieval and European, 20th Century, World Geography, Philosophy of Man & Society; Math: Algebra I & II, Geometry, Trig, pre-Calculus and Calculus. Theology: Philosophical Foundations of Theology; Metaphysics : The spiritual doctrinal formation at Oakcrest is entrusted to Opus Dei, a personal prelature of the Catholic Church. Studio Art, Food Technology,. AP.: English, Spanish, Calculus. Note: College preparatory program: Each student meets regularly with her faculty advisor who provides academic, personal and spiritual guidance. Special emphasis on character development: the faculty work closely with the parents who are recognized as primary educators of their children.

Athletics: P.E. PVAC Soccer, Basketball, Softball, Tennis. **Clubs**: Junior & National Honor Society, Service Club, Speech, Right to Life, Performing Arts. **Publications:** Yearbook, Literary Magazine, Newsletter. **Community Involvement**: Help with programs and visits to the Washington Home for the elderly.

Plant: Library, Science Lab, Art Studio, Tennis Court, Basketball Court, Playing Field, Chapel.

Admission: Verbal and Math Aptitude Tests, sample of Writing. $25 fee. Interview, Transcript, Recommendations; Rolling Admission.

Tuition: (1993-94) 7-8, $5,000; 9-12, $5,500. Books: Extra. Lunch: Students bring.
Dress Code: Uniform req. **Financial Aid**: Some partial available.

OAKLAND SCHOOL..........(804) 293-9059

Oakland Farm, Boyd Tavern, VA. 22947 (Near Charlottesville).
Founded 1950. **Head**: Mrs. Joanne Dondero, M.Ed.

Grades : Ages 8-16 (8-14 for admittance **Enrollment** : 84 Co-ed; Boarding 66, Day 18.
Faculty : Residential 13 , Part-time -1. **Average Class Size**: 4-5

Special Features: Ungraded - for children of normal or better intelligence who have not succeeded in regular classroom - many children with learning disabilities. Note: Curriculum through grade 9. Teaching of Reading and Study Skills a specialty; Word Processing taught.

Athletics: Req.; Intramural. Touch Football, Baseball, Basketball. Horseback Riding. **Clubs**: Physical Fitness, Jogging, Rocket models, Cooking,etc. **Community Involvement**: Participate in special community events.

Plant: Library, Large farm, Swimming Pool, Tennis Courts, Horseback Riding Trails & Ring, Gymnasium and Recreation Building. New Dining Room and Kitchen. Note: Computers: one for every four students.

Admission: Application, Transcripts including Educational & Psychological Evaluations; Interview with Visit to school.

Tuition: (1993-94) Day, $9,890; Boarding, $20,760; includes Books

Summer Program: 7 week summer camp & school. Academic Reading, Math, and English for 4 hrs.daily during week; Recreational instruction includes horseback riding, swimming, tennis, golf, archery, arts & crafts, and nature. .

OAKWOOD SCHOOL/CHILDREN'S ACHIEVEMENT CENTER..........(703) 941-5788
FAX (703) 941-4186

7210 Braddock Road, Annandale, VA. 22003
Founded 1971. **Head**: Robert C. McIntyre.

Grades: K-9. **Enrollment**: 95 Co-ed. **Faculty**: 25 full-time.
Average Class Size: 8-10

Special Courses: General Science, Biology, Earth Science; History - U.S. and World; Geography. Reading/Language arts; Math. Music Appreciation; Perception Art; P.E. (regular & adaptive) Speech/Language Therapy. Occupational Therapy. All subjects taught remedially for the bright learning disabled child as needed.

Athletics Req.; Volleyball, Football, Softball, Soccer, Hockey, Gymnastics, Weights, Trampoline. All taught as part of the Physical Education program for all students.

Plant: Library 3,000 vol.; Large bright class rooms; Science & Math Labs; Computer Lab; Reading Lab, Speech/Language Therapy Clinic; P.E. Room; Weight room; Athletic field, custom designed playground.

Admission: Interview with parents or referring professional. Parents complete confidential history . Transcripts of other evaluations and school records. Oakwood "short form" educational evaluation. Conference with parents at which placement recommendation is made. Students who are LD, Gifted LD, Speech/ Language Disfunctions-mild to moderate range of disabilities. Oakwood is not appropriate for MR, ED, seriously physically handicapped.

Tuition: (1993-94) $ 11,400 **Transportation**: Privately arranged. *Dress Code*: Appropriate, modest, and clean. **Financial Aid** : Partial grants available based exclusively on need.

ODENTON CHRISTIAN SCHOOL.......... (410) 674-5625 or (301) 621-9469

8410 Piney Orchard Parkway, Odenton, MD. 21113
Head: Mr. T.E. Pike

Grades: K3-grade 10. **Enrollment**: 515 Co-ed **Faculty**: 31 full-time.

Special Program: Music, Art, Gym, Computers and Foreign Languages. ABEKA Curriculum Open year 'round, including summer school program. DIFFERENT ON PURPOSE: Different in "purpose, belief, goals, discipline, emphasis, academics, and results."
Extended Day: 6 a.m.-6 p.m.

Plant : New gym

Admission: Test(s) and Interview. Admit qualified students of any race, color, national or ethnic origin.

Tuition: (1993-94) $1,500. Books & Activity Fees: K, $195; 1-8, $205. Registration $75, Testing $35. *Dress Code*: Uniform req.

Future Plans: Expand Music program, Band, Art, Computer, Athletic and Foreign Language Programs.

OLDFIELDS SCHOOL...(410) 472-4800

1500 Glencoe Road, Glencoe, MD. 21152
Founded 1867. **Head**: Hawley Rogers.

Grades: 8-12. **Enrollment**: 180 Girls (36 Day, 144 Boarding). **Faculty**: 37 full-, 13 part-time. **Average Class Size**: 10; Student/Teacher ratio, 5:1.

Special Courses: Latin, French, Spanish, 8-12; Math thru Calculus, Computer. General Science, Biology, Chemistry, Physics, Astronomy, Human Physiology; Electives in Psychology and in Child Development. History- Ancient History, Western Civilization, American History (req.), Holocaust/WWII, Comparative Systems, America and the World, Women in Modern America, Civil Rights Movement & the Vietnam War, Life on the Frontier. Art: Studio, Portfolio, Photography, Ceramics, Art History (Modern Art 1800-1980 & American Art), Performing Arts: Acting, Stagecraft, Introd. to Musical Theatre, Advanced Dance, Music Theory, Singers. Note: Small ESL program; Tutoring and extensive teacher help available but no LD program per se. AP.: In all disciplines.

Athletics: Req.; Intramural & Interscholastic: Field Hockey, Basketball, Tennis, Lacrosse, Softball, Soccer, Volleyball, Cross-Country, Badminton, Riding, Dance: Jazz, Ballet; Aerobics,

Weight Training. **Clubs**: Art, Current Issues Forum, Dance Co., Dubious Dozen, Environmental Awareness, Focus, International, Outing, Tour Guides, Volunteer Action. **Publications**: Literary Magazine, Yearbook, Newspaper. **Community Involvement**: Volunteer program-projects include Day Care & Nursing Home Visits, Shelters, etc.

Plant: Library 10,000 vol., Science Labs, New Fine Arts Wing (includes studios for Graphics, Sculpture, Drawing & Painting; Library extension for expanded Art History collection). Gym, Computer Center; 6 Dorms, 3 Dark Rooms, Choral Arts Center with 4 practice rooms; Playing Fields, Tennis Courts, Outdoor Pool, Stables, Indoor Riding Arena, Outdoor Riding Rings, David Niven Theater, Dance Studio.

Admission: Application fee $35; SSAT or WISC, Interview, 2 Teacher Evaluations, Transcripts. Early decision: Dec. l; Regular decision March 10.

Tuition: (1993-94) $10,900, Day; $19,600 Boarding, Books: $400 per semester. *Dress Code*: No jeans, T-shirts or sweatshirts; otherwise, clothing in good repair. **Scholarship Aid:** Some Available.

OLD MILL CHRISTIAN ACADEMY........... (410) 987-4744

649 Old Mill Boulevard., Millersville, MD 21108
Christian non-denominational 1979 **Head**; Rev. Darryl Hare
(Formerly Calvary Temple Christian) Principal: Mary E. Rodgers

Grades: PreK-12 **Enrollment**: 100 Co-ed **Faculty**: 6 full-, 3 part-time.
Average Class Size: 15-20

Special Courses; Video Spanish 9-12. Computer Basics and Basic Programming. General Science, Biology, Chemistry. U.S. and World History, Constitutional History, Geography. Remedial Reading and Math. Religious Studies req. Typing, Home Ec., Auto Mechanics. Music, Chorus. P.E. req.

Plant: Library , Multi-purpose Room, Sanctuary

Admission: Testing throughout the year.

Tuition: (1993-94) K-12, $170/mo.; Note; all rates are for church members. Books: Extra Lunch: Bring *Dress Code*: No blue jeans, no tennis shoes; some rules relating to color of clothing.

ONENESS-FAMILY SCHOOL..........(301) 652-7751

6701 Wisconsin Avenue, Chevy Chase, MD 20815
Founded 1988 **Head**: Andrew Kutt

Grades: PreK3- grade 6. **Enrollment**: 50 Co-ed **Faculty**: 4 full-time **Average Class Size**: 15

Special Courses: Spanish, Pre K-6. Computer. General Science. History- Creation Stories, Earth History, Ancient History to Present including American. Human Values Education, Health, World Religions, World Cultures. Art, Music, Drama, Creative Movement. Note: Pre-school can be 3 full or 5 half days. **Extended Day** : 7:30 a.m.-6 p.m.

Athletics: Not Required. Intramural: Soccer, Basketball, Running; Many non- competitive and cooperative games. **Clubs**: Ecology, Peace. **Publications**: Newspaper. **Community Involvement**: Performances at Nursing homes and at cultural events which fosters international harmony and communication. Cleaning local parks and streams; Recycling and Conservation.

Plant: Library 3,500 Vol., Language Lab, Science Lab, Art Studio, Auditorium. Use Norwood Park for many activities.

Admission: Application, $50 fee; Interview and Visit, Recommendations. March 15th deadline; other spaces open on an individual basis and occasionally open up during school year.

Tuition: (1993-94) $5,500- 5,900 includes Books. Bring Lunch **Transportation**: one way, $500; both ways, $800. **Extended Day** : Extra **Financial Aid**: Some Available

Summer Program: Camp-3 sessions. Peace studies, creative arts, environmental science.

OPEN DOOR CHRISTIAN SCHOOL..........(410) 969-0121

7300 Ridge Road, Hanover, MD 21076-1417
Head: Jack Constable

Grades: N3-grade 7 **Enrollment**: 130 Co-ed

Special Program: Quality traditional education. ABEKA Program.
Extended Day : 6:15 a.m.-6 p.m.

Tuition : (1993-94) 8 a.m.-3 p.m; N & K, $1,900; grades 1-7, $1,500
Extended Day: Extra

OUR LADY OF PERPETUAL HELP..........(202)678-0211; K-4, (202)896-1662

1409 V Street, S. E., Washington, D. C. 20020 (K-4)
1604 Morris Road, S. E., Washington, D. C. 20020 (5-8)
Catholic **Head**: Sister Mary Elizabeth Semmelmayer, SSND (Upper School)

Grades: K4-8 **Enrollment**: Co-ed

Special Programs: Freedom Academy, independent program after school at Morris Road until 8 p.m. **Extended Day** 6:30 a.m.-6 p.m., at V Street;

Tuition: (1993-94) $2,000 **Financial Aid** : Available

OUR LADY OF SORROWS SCHOOL..........(301) 891-2555

1010 Larch Avenue, Takoma Park, MD 20912
Catholic **Head**: Ms. Melodie Woodruff

Grades : K4-8 **Enrollment** : Co-ed

Special Programs: Spanish 6-8; Computers, K-8; Performing Arts program with emphasis on drama and dance. **Extended Day** : 7 a.m.-6 p.m.

Tuition: (1993-94) $2,000

OUR LADY OF VICTORY SCHOOL...........(202) 337-1421

4755 Whitehaven Parkway, N.W., Washington, D.C. 20007
Catholic 1954. **Head**: Miss Susan Milloy, Principal

Grades: N3-grade 8. **Enrollment**: 110 Co-ed. **Faculty**: 10 full-, 4 part-time.
Average Class Size: 12.

Special Courses: Spanish, Computer, Art, Study Skills, Library Skills, Algebra, General Science. Band, Choir. **Extended Day**: 7:30 a.m.- 6 p.m.

Athletics: P.E.: After school, Soccer, Softball, Basketball, T-Ball.

Plant: Library, Computer Lab, Auditorium.

Admission: Interview with Principal; Visit school for day; Placement test.

Tuition: (1993-94) $3,000, in parish; $4,000 out of parish. Books: $180. Lunch: Bring.
Dress Code: Uniform req.

Summer Program : Re-enforcement programs for Math and Language Arts.

OUR LADY QUEEN OF PEACE SCHOOL..........(202) 584-4278

33740 Ely Place S. E., Washington, D. C. 20019
Catholic **Head**: Sister Ellen Marie Hagar, DC

Grades: K4-8 **Enrollment**: Co-ed

Special Programs: Learning Disabled program. **Extended Day**: 6:30 a.m.-6 p.m.

Tuition: In Parish, $1,100; Out of Parish, $1,850 **Extended Day** Extra

OUR SAVIOR LUTHERAN SCHOOL..........(703) 892-4846

825 South Taylor Street, Arlington, VA. 22204
Lutheran 1953. **Head**: Charles Fischer.

Grades: K-8. **Enrollment**: 135 Co-ed. **Faculty**: 6 full-, 3 part-time.
Average Class Size: 20.

Special Courses: Gen'l Science K-8. Christian Education, strong phonics program, self-contained classrooms. Religious Studies req.; Outdoor camping trip in Spring for upper grades; Music, Band.

Plant: Library 2,400 vol.

Admission: Interview, Testing if needed. $100 Registration fee.

Tuition: (1993-94) $2,200. Limited **Transportation**: $800. (contact school for further fee schedules.) *Dress Code*: Traditional school clothes.

OWL SCHOOLS..........(202) 462-4034

1328 16th Street, N.W., Washington, D.C. 20036
Founded 1971. **Head**: Margaret Harris.

Grades: N-6. **Enrollment**: 115 Co-ed. **Faculty**: 6 full-, 4 part-time.
Average Class Size: 12.

Special Courses: French N-6, Remedial Reading. Math, Art, Music, P.E. Note: Special classes for advanced students, Reading Enrichment. **Extended Day**: 7:45 a.m.-6 p.m.

Community Involvement: Foster grandparent program at Rock Creek Manor Nursing Home.

Plant: Library, Gym/Auditorium

Admission: Child Visits school for a day; Placement Tests. Application Fee $60.

Tuition: (1993-94) $4,200 Fees $150 **Extended Day** $1,200 Development Fund Fee $250

Summer Program: All day Camp Program: Academic program in morning, afternoon focus is on arts & crafts, recreational, swimming, etc.

PAINT BRANCH MONTESSORI SCHOOL..........(301) 937-2244

3215 Powder Mill Road, Adelphi, MD. 20783
Head: Patricia Barshay

Ungraded: Ages 3-12. **Enrollment**: 100 Co-ed.

Special Features: Art & Music; full day for age 3; Before and After School, Students attend Fairland Athletic Complex for P.E. **Extended Day:** 8 a.m.-5 p.m.

Tuition: (1993-94) Half-Day, $2,648; Full Day, $4,142- $4,315. Before & After School, $1,530.

PARKMONT SCHOOL..........(202) 726-0740

4842 16th Street N.W., Washington, D. C. 20011
Founded 1972. **Head**: Ron McClain.

Grades: 6-12 (ungraded). **Enrollment**: 65 Co-ed. **Faculty**: 7 full-, 7 part-time. **Average Class Size**: 8-12.

Special Courses: Small classes allow for individualized programs. Schedule permits students to select from diverse course offerings. Staff makes considerable use of local city resources for field trips and student projects. All courses are voluntary, no requirements (to graduate students complete D.C. Board of Education minimum requirements in addition to their own individual course of study). School focuses on all dimensions of personal growth-social, emotional, physical and intellectual. It seeks to have its students independent and sensitive thinkers and forces for constructive change in society. Humanistically oriented, the school is run by faculty & students (1 vote each) in weekly meeting which determines rules and their enforcement.

Athletics: Complete Soccer Program, Marathon Training, Tennis, Volleyball, Softball, Canoeing and Camping, Climbing, Dance.

Plant: Science Lab, Art Room, All Purpose Room, Ceramics Room., Photo Lab. New Hampshire Campus.

Admission: Selection to maintain heterogeneous student body. Family Interview at school and at home. Student Visits school for full day. Application fee $50.

Tuition: (1993-94) $9,750.

PAUL VI HIGH SCHOOL..........(703) 352-0925

10675 Lee Highway, Fairfax, VA 22030
Catholic **Head**: Father Mulligan

Grades: 9-12 **Enrollment**: 1,100 co-ed

Special Courses : Broad Computer curriculum; 11 AP Courses.

Athletics: Diverse program, Boys and Girls Jr. Varsity and Varsity Teams.

Tuition: (1993-94) In parish, $3,985; Non-parish $4,385; Non-Catholic $5,185

PHELPS SCHOOL..........(215) 644-1754

Sugartown Road, P.O. Box 476, Malvern, PA 19355 (22 miles west of Philadelphia)
Founded 1946 **Head**: Norman T. Phelps, Jr.

Grades: 7-12, PG. **Enrollment**: 140 Boys, all Boarding **Faculty**: 22 full-. 6 part-time.
Average Class Size: 8

Special Courses: Traditional curriculum with remedial and developmental programs available. Strong program for underachievers; LD, ADD. Reading, ESL; Instrumental Music, Computers. Art, Photography, Framing, Woodworking, Drama, Publications..

Athletics: Soccer, Cross-Country, Basketball, Baseball, Lacrosse, Riding, Golf, Tennis, Weight Training, Wrestling.

Plant: 110 acre campus; Library, Science Lab, Computer Lab, Student Center, Dark Room, Music Studio, Gym, Auditorium with Stage, 4 all-weather Tennis Courts, Indoor and Outdoor Equestrian facilities, 8 Dormitories.

Admission: Interview, References.

Tuition: (1993-94) $14,420. **Financial Aid**: Some Available
Future Plans: New Dormitory, Additional Faculty

Summer Program: 5 week, Remedial: Reading, Language Arts, Math & Study Skills.

PINECREST SCHOOL..........(703) 354-3446

4015 Annandale Road, Annandale, VA. 22003
Founded 1957. **Head**: Mrs. Elaine Alger

Grades: N-3. **Enrollment**: 90 Co-ed. **Faculty**: 8 full-, 4 part-time. **Average Class Size**: 12.
Special Courses: French, Music, P.E.

Plant: Library

Admission: Interview, Registration fee $75.

Tuition: (1993-94) Half-day N, $280/mo.; Half-day K $310/mo.; K-1, $430/mo.; grades 2-3, $455/mo.; **Financial Aid**: Available

POTOMAC HEIGHTS CHRISTIAN ACADEMY..........(301) 753-9350

37 Glymont Road, (P,O.Box 149) Indian Head, MD. 20640
Head: Gilbert Bailey.

Grades: K3-grade 8. **Enrollment**: 95 Co-ed.

Special Courses: ABEKA curriculum.

Tuition (1993-94) Half-day K, $924; Full day K, $1,355; 1-8, $2,218 **Transportation** : Public School Bus

Future Plans: **Extended Day** Program.

POTOMAC SCHOOL..........(703) 356-4101

1301 Potomac School Road, McLean, VA. 22101
Founded 1904. **Head**: Brian R. Wright, Ph. D.

Grades: Pre K-12. **Enrollment**: 870 Co-ed. **Faculty**: 140 full-, 39 part-time.
Average Class Size: 16-18.

Special Courses: Latin, French and Spanish, all 7-12; Japanese, 9-12. Math thru Calculus, Computer (2 Labs). General Science, Biology, Chemistry, Physics, Astronomy, Marine Biology History: Ancient & Medieval, Modern Western, U.S., American Gov't, Russian, Chinese, Japanese; World Religions. Economics, Art, Music, Drama. AP.: American History, French, Latin, Spanish, Biology, Chemistry, Physics, Art History, Computer Science and Calculus. Note: Ethics Course, grade 10; Month long Senior Project.

Athletics: Req.; Intramural & Interscholastic. Football, Cross Country, Soccer, Baseball, Lacrosse, Track, Field Hockey, Basketball, Golf, Wrestling, Softball. **Clubs**: Chorus, Madrigal Singing group, Band, Student Gov't, Math team, Chess, Environmental, Model Senate, Model U.N., Peer Support Group. **Publications**: Newspaper, Yearbook, Literary Magazine of the Arts . **Community Involvement**: Community Service Program PreK-12.

Plant: 3 Libraries, 32,000 vol.,; 11 Science Labs, 5 Art Studios, 2 Gyms, Auditorium, Playing Fields, Nature Trails, Swimming Pool, Tennis Courts; 75 acre campus.

Admission: Applications by Jan. 15, Fee $60; Testing in Jan. & Feb.; Acceptance March. Visits by parents requested. School seeks broad ethnic, geographic and socio-economic student body.

Tuition: (1993-94) $6,235-$11,080 Lunch Bring, PreK-grade 8; $590, grade 9-12.
Books: Extra **Transportation**: $750 one way; $1,200 both ways. Uniform: Req. grade 4-8

only; *Dress Code*, Grades 9- 12. **Financial Aid**: partial and/or full Available.

Summer Program: Academic: Co-ed, Grades 7-12. Writing Workshop, French, Spanish, Algebra, Geometry, Physics, Biology, Chemistry, Study Skills, Computer Skills. Camp for age 3-17, Co-ed: Computer, Weight Training, Wilderness Adventure, Counselor Apprentice, Theater. Discovery Camp, Science Camp, Out for Fun Camp, Day Camp, Jr. Day Camp,

POWHATAN SCHOOL.......... (703) 837-1009

Route 2 A, P.O. Box 177A, Boyce VA.22620
Founded 1948 **Head**: John Lathrop

Grades: K-8 **Enrollment**: 173 Co-ed **Faculty**: 20 full-, 4 part-time. **Average Class Size** : 18

Special Courses: Latin 7-8, French K-3, 7-8; Algebra, Geometry, Computer. General Science, Biology. History- U.S., American. Remedial Reading and Math. Art, Music.

Athletics: Req.; Soccer, Field Hockey, Lacrosse, Basketball, Track, Skiing, Skating, Gymnastics.
Community Involvement: Nursing Home Project; African Literacy Project; Salvation Army Food Drive; Adopt a Family at Christmas, and Christmas Toy Drive.

Plant: Library 9,000 vol., Science Lab & Art Studio; Auditorium, Gym, Playing Fields, Music and Dance Facility.

Admission: $25 Registration fee. Testing in Spring. Classroom visits encouraged.

Tuition: (1993-94) $6,325-$7,570. Books : up to $200. **Transportation**: $250-$550 both ways
Dress Code : yes **Financial Aid** : Available.

Summer Program: Summer Sports Camp/ General Summer Camp.

THE PRIMARY DAY SCHOOL..........(301) 365-4355

7300 River Road, Bethesda, MD. 20817
Founded 1944. **Head**: Mrs. Carter-Ann Nadonley.

Grades: Pre K-2. **Enrollment**: 175 Co-ed **Faculty**: 20 full-, 7 part-time.
Average Class Size: 20 - 24

Special Courses: Curriculum includes all subjects appropriate to well-rounded primary program. The Phonovisual Method, a multi-sensory phonics based system, is the foundation for the language arts subjects. Resource teachers, working with small groups, allow for individual attention. Weekly assembly programs, presented by the students, help develop poise and self-confidence in appearing before an audience. In addition to literature, art, music, and physical activities included in the curriculum, children may pursue extra classes in these subjects. Second Graders enjoy hands-on science, computers, a special course in Creative Writing, and French..

Community Involvement: Children participate in MS Readathon, UNICEF, Christmas gifts to children in the Handicapped Children's ward at D.C. General Hospital.

Plant: Library, 5,500 vol., Auditorium, Playing Fields, Science Room, Art Room.

Admission: Parent and child Interview in Jan. & Feb. for following fall. Age, maturity level, & average intelligence are criteria for admission & placement. $40 fee.

Tuition: (1993-94) $4,3,00-$6,300, includes books. Lunch: Brown bag. **Scholarship Aid**: Available.

PURITAN CHRISTIAN SCHOOL...........(301) 253-4357

6325 Griffith Road, (P.O. Box 5039) Laytonsville, MD. 20882
Orthodox Presbyterian 1977 **Head**: Dr. Barry M. Whitcomb

Grades: N3-grade 12 **Enrollment**: 130 Co-ed. **Faculty**: 11 full-, 3 part-time.
Average Class Size: 15.

Special Courses: French 7-8, Spanish, Latin, & Greek, all 9-12. Computer K-12; Math includes Trig & Calculus. General Science, Biology, Chemistry, Physics. Various History and Social Science Courses. Religious Studies required. Art & Music K-8.

Athletics: P.E. req. all grades; Basketball, Soccer, Volleyball. **Publications**: Yearbook

Plant: Science Lab, Playing Fields.

Admission: Fee $60; Interview, Recommendations, Standardized Test Scores, Transcript.

Tuition: (1993-94) N3-K, $2,150; 1-9, $2,900; 9-12, $3,000; Reduced rate for siblings.
Transportation: $850 round trip,. *Dress Code*: Uniform req.

QUEEN ANNE SCHOOL.........(301) 249-5000

14111 Oak Grove Road, Upper Marlboro, MD. 20772
Episcopal 1965. **Head**: J. Temple Blackwood

Grades: 7-12. **Enrollment**: 183 Co-ed. **Faculty**: 17 full-, 9 part-time.
Average Class Size: 15.

Special Courses: French & Spanish, 8-12; Math includes Calculus & Computer. General Science, Biology, Chemistry, Physics, Ecology, Biology of Chesapeake Bay, Physiology; History- Geography, U.S., American Gov't, World, Contemporary Issues, Gov't & Politics, American History and Culture. Introduction to the Principle of Economics, Psychology. Religious studies req. Studio Art, Art History. Chorus, Madrigal Singers, Symphonic Band,

Religious studies req. Studio Art, Art History. Chorus, Madrigal Singers, Symphonic Band, MS Band. Beginning & Advanced Acting. AP.: Calculus, Biology, Chemistry, English, French, Spanish, Art, History. **Extended Day** 3:30-5 p.m.

Athletics: Req. through Grade 10. Intramural & Inter-scholastic: Soccer, Lacrosse, Basketball, Softball, Track & Field, Baseball, Tennis. **Clubs**: Minority Awareness, SADD, Spirit. **Publications**: Yearbook, Literary Magazine, Newspaper. **Community Involvement**: Nursing home volunteers, Community outreach.

Plant: Library 10,000 vol., 3 Science Labs, Art Studio, Auditorium, Gym, Playing Fields, Tennis Courts, Computer Lab.

Admission: Student & Parent Interview, Tests(ERB), Application fee $25; Recommendations, Transcript. Full or half-day Visit by student (optional). Writing sample.

Tuition: (1993-94) Grades 7 & 8, $7,500; 9-12, $7,700. **Transportation**: $960- $1,575 depending on distance. Books: $150. *Dress Code*: Moderate **Financial Aid**: Some Available..

Summer Program: "EXCEL 2000" intensive science and math curriculum. Summer classes offered are Language Skills; Mathematics- Basic Math & Algebra; English-Creative Writing. Study Skills, Tutoring. Art, Photography. Soccer & Basketball camps.

RANDOLPH MACON ACADEMY....(703) 636-5200 or 1-800-272-1172

Front Royal, VA 22630
Methodist 1892 **Head**: Col. Trevor D. Turner, USA Ret.

Grades: 7-12, PG **Enrollment**: 370 Co-ed,(265 Boys) 60 Day students, rest Boarding

RESTON MONTESSORI SCHOOL SCHOOL.........(703) 481-2922

1928 Issac Newton Square West. Reston, VA 22090
1625 Weihle Avenue, Reston, VA 22090 (N & K only)
Head: Eilene Minarik & Kathleen Lamfear

Grades: N 2 1/2- grade 2.

Special Programs: Bilingual French immersion program for grades 1 & 2; (all subjects taught in English and French) **Extended Day** 7 a.m.-6:30 p.m.

Tuition: (1993-94) N & K, $2,290-$5,800; 1 & 2, $5,900

Future Plans: to add grade 3 in 1994

RIVENDELL SCHOOL.........(703) 525-3860

1031 North Vermont Street, Arlington, VA 22201
Non-Denominational, Christ Centered 1989 **Head**: Mr. Steve Larson

Grades: K-8 **Enrollment**: 90 Co-ed **Faculty**: 6 full-, 1 part-time.
Average Class Size: 15

Special Courses: All academic subjects areas are taught within 4-8 week unit themes. French, Art, & Music K-8. Paedeia seminar discussions are conducted weekly at all grade levels. Non-denominational, Christ centered school.

Athletics: P.E. req. 1-8. Instruction in Soccer, Volleyball, Basketball, Softball, Fitness.
Publications: Weekly newspaper. **Community Involvement**: Students visit Nursing Homes, assist in Salvation Army feeding and toy distribution programs.

Plant: Library, 9,500 vol.; Music Room, Art Room, Chapel, Auditorium, Playing Field, Playground.

Admission: Applications accepted all year, Fee $25. March 15th notification date for following year admission. Possible Testing. Students are admitted on basis of Transcript, Recommendation Form, and Family Interview.

Tuition: (1993-94) K, $2,900; 1-8, $3,750; includes Books, Fees, Activities, Field Trips, and $100 Uniform allowance. Bring Lunch. *Dress Code*: Uniform req., **Scholarship Aid**: 20% of school's operating budget is used to provide aid (based on need).

Future Plans: To add a class a year (15 students) until school has student body of 120-150, grades K-8.

RIVERDALE BAPTIST SCHOOL..........(301) 249-7000

1133 Largo Road, Upper Marlboro, MD. 20772
Baptist 1971. **Head**: Rev. James Hockenberry

Grades: K4-12. **Enrollment**: 1,000 Co-ed. **Faculty**: 52 full-time. **Average Class Size**: 26.

Special Courses: Spanish grades K5-12; Math: Algebra, Geometry, Trig & Calculus, Math Analysis, Accounting. Computer: College Keyboard, Basic Computing, Cobol/Pascal; Science : General Science, Physical Science, Anatomy, Enviornmental Science, Biology, Chemistry, Physics, Psychology. History: Geography, U.S., World, Modern, European, American Government. English: includes Creative Writing, Journalism. Fine Arts: Art, Mechanical Drawing, Choir, Band (grades 5-12).Speech, Drama. Driver's Ed. **Extended Day**: 7 a.m.-6 p.m.

Athletics: Not required. Interscholastic: Boys Football, Wrestling, Soccer, Basketball, Tennis, Baseball, Track. Girls Volleyball, Soccer, Basketball, Softball. Cheerleading, Track, Tennis..

Clubs: Nat'l Honor Society, Student Council. **Publications**: Yearbook.

Plant: Library 15,000 vol.; Computer Lab, Science Lab, Gym, Auditorium, Playing Fields.

Admission: Achievement Test Scores; Transcript; Personal Evaluation Form, Interview.

Tuition: (1993-94) $2,893-$3,575. Books: $80-$225. **Transportation** : $645-$900 one way, $970-$1,355 both. *Dress Code*: Uniform req. **Financial Aid**: By application

Summer Program: Camp for Elementary Grades

ROCK CREEK INTERNATIONAL SCHOOL..........(202) 387-0387

2200 California Street, N.W., Washington, D.C. 20008
Founded 1988 **Head**: J. Daniel Hollinger, Ph.D.

Grades: N-3 **Enrollment**: 100 Co-ed **Faculty** : 14 full, 3 part-time
Average Class Size: 12

Special Programs: Beginning in Kindergarten, students take a core curriculum of Language Arts and Math in two languages. Other subjects of Science, World Studies, Music, Art, Computer, and Theatrical Arts are taught in English, French or Spanish. Instrumental Music, Sewing, and Cooking. **Extended Day**: 8 a.m.- 6 p.m.

Athletics: P.E.; Soccer, Dance. **Clubs**: Science

Plant: Science Lab, Art Studio, Gym, Auditorium, Playing Fields.

Admission: Parent Visit, Child Visit; Current school record

Tuition: (1993-94) Pre-School $7,510; K-3, $8,285 includes Books. Lunch, Bring.
Extended Day: Extra. **Transportation**: $1,000 one way, $1,400 both. **Financial Aid:** Some

Future Plans: To add a grades through grade 12

Summer Program: Merry-Go-Round the World Summer Camp: in English, French or Spanish; includes Swimming, Art, Music, Sports, Games, Theatrical Arts, Camping Trip and Computers.

ROOTS ACTIVITY LEARNING CENTER.........(202) 882-5155

6222 N. Capitol Street, N.W., Washington, D.C. 20011
Founded 1977. **Head**: Bernida Thompson.

Grades: N3 - grade 8. **Enrollment**: 100 Co-ed. **Faculty**: 11 full-time.
Average Class Size: 15.

Special Courses: Spanish & French; Full academic curriculum, Computer. Specialize in African-American History & Culture. P.E. **Extended Day**: 7 a.m.-6 p.m.

Admission: Interview with parent, $10 Application fee.

Tuition: (1993-94) Pre-school $346/mo. includes Breakfast, Lunch and **Extended Day**. 1-4 $320/mo.; 5-8 ,$300/mo. Breakfast & Lunch Extra.

Summer Program: Day Camp 7 a.m.-6 p.m. Swimming, arts & crafts, field trips. Academic program for grades 1-8.

SACRED HEART SCHOOL..........(202) 265-4828

1625 Park Road, N. W., Washington, D. C. 20010
Catholic **Head** : Reynaldo Almeida

Grades : K4-8 **Enrollment**: Co-ed **Extended Day** : 6:30 a.m.-6 p.m.

Tuition: (1993-94) Registration fee, $175. K, $179/mo.; 1-8, $169/mo.; Reduction for siblings. **Extended Day**: Extra.

ST. AGNES SCHOOL......(See St. Stephen's School)

ST. ALBANS SCHOOL..........(202) 537-6440

Wisconsin & Massachusetts Avenues, N.W., Washington., D.C. 20016
Episcopalian 1909. **Head**: The Rev. Mark H. Mullin.

Grades: 4-12. **Enrollment**: 550 Boys (25 Boarding). Boarding begins 9th grade.
Faculty: 65 full-, 8 part-time. **Average Class Size**: 15.

Special Courses: Latin, French, Spanish: all 8-12; Russian, Japanese, 9-12; Chinese & Greek. Math thru Calculus. Science Biology, Chemistry, Physics, Earth Science. History- Ancient Rome, Ancient Greece, Omnibus-American & European History, History & Culture of Islam. Fine Arts Painting and Drawing, Graphics, 3-Dimensional Art, Studio; Music-Survey of Western Music, Music Theory, Instrumental-Orchestra. Computer. Religious studies req.; The Bible, Question of God. Drama, Film-Making. AP: English, Languages, Math, Computer, History Science.
Note: Coordinate classes with National Cathedral School for Girls; Boys in both the Boys Choir and the Men's Choir at the Cathedral often attend St. Albans. Student Exchange program with Russia & Japan. **Extended Day** ; Grades 4-8 only, 3:30 p.m.-6 p.m.

Athletics: Req.; Intramural & Interscholastic (13 Varsity Sports): Basketball, Soccer, Swimming, Wrestling, Track, Lacrosse, Weight Training, Football, Baseball, Tennis, Cross

Country, Golf, Rock Climbing, Kayaking. **Clubs**: Glee, Madrigals, Orchestra, Press, Drama, Service, Government, Art, Band.. **Publications**: Newspaper, Yearbook, Literary Magazine. **Community Involvement:** 60 hours of Social Service prior to senior year are required for graduation.

Plant: Library 24,000 vol., (A computer system now links the libraries of St. Albans with those at National Cathedral School for Girls.) 3 Science Labs, 3 Art Studios, 2 Gyms, Auditorium, Playing Fields, Swimming Pool, 8 Tennis Courts, Computers, Music Room.

Admission: SSAT Dec.- Jan.; Interview, Transcript, teacher Recommendations. Fee $60. Lower School (4-8) has own testing in January.

Tuition: (1993-94) Day $11,250; Boarding $17,090 Books: Extra. Lunch : $740 (Day students) *Dress Code*: Coat & tie. **Scholarship Aid**: Both full and partial available.

Summer Program: Academic. Summer Camp: Tennis, Soccer, Basketball, Baseball, Sports Clinics; Early June Program; Late afternoon program 3 -6 p.m., ages 6 -12.

ST. ANDREW'S ELEMENTARY SCHOOL..........(410) 266-0952

4 Wallace Manor Road, Edgewater, MD 21037
Methodist 1985 **Head**: Donald Backe

Grades: N-5 **Enrollment**: 150 Co-ed

Special Programs: Spanish, K-5 **Extended Day**: 6:30 a.m.-6 :30 p.m.

Tuition: (1993-94) N, $3,480; K-5, $3,480 **Extended Day** Extra

Summer Camp: N-grade 5, 7 a.m.-6 p.m.

ST. ANDREW'S EPISCOPAL SCHOOL.........(301) 530-4900

8935 Bradmoor Drive, Bethesda, MD 20817
Episcopal 1978. **Head**: Dr. James Cantwell

Grades: 6-12. **Enrollment**: 385 Co-ed. **Faculty**: 55 full-, 3 part-time
Average Class Size: 15

Special Features: Latin, French, & Spanish, all 7- 12; Spanish for native speakers. Math thru Calculus; Computer-Basic, Pascal, C-Language. Earth Science, Life Science, Physical Science, Biology, Chemistry I & II, Physics I & II. History: World and American, Africa's History, Geography-Area Studies, Modern Opperession & Resistance, History Consortia (Middle Eastern Studies & Modern Day Issues/Science & Technology). Religious Studies: one trimester req.

each year. Visual Art: one tri-mester per year of Painting, Film Making, Sculpture; Performing Arts: Music, Drama, Public Speaking, Dance, one trimester req. each year. AP., English, Biology, Math, Latin, French, Spanish, History.

Athletics: Req. Interscholastic. Soccer, Basketball, Volleyball, Tennis, Baseball, Softball, Lacrosse, Weight Lifting, Wrestling, Track & Field, Cross Country. **Clubs**: Outing, Hiking, Camping, Chorus, SADD, Model U.N., International Club, Band. **Publications**: Yearbook, Literary Magazine, Newspaper. **Community Involvement**: Grades 6-11, 20 hrs. a year req.; Grade 12, 60 hrs.

Plant: Library 14,000 vol.; Language Lab, 5 Science Labs, 4 Art Studios, Gym, Auditorium, Playing Fields, 4 Tennis Courts, 3 Computer Labs.

Admission: $50 Application fee, student and parent Interviews, SSAT, 2 teacher Recommendations, Transcript, Writing sample. Feb. 15 deadline for application, Rolling Admission after deadline if space available.

Tuition: (1993-94) $10,450-$10,650 Books: extra Lunch: Cafeteria service or bring from home. *Dress Code*: Neat and tidy. **Scholarship Aid**: 40 partial

Summer Program: Word Processing, Study Skills, Typing.

ST. ANN'S ACADEMY..........(202) 363-4460

4404 Wisconsin Avenue, N. W., Washington, D. C. 20016
Catholic **Head** : Mrs. Barbara A. Kelly

Grades: K-8 **Enrollment**: Co-ed

Special Programs: Spanish, 1-8; Art, Music. Computers K-8. P.E. **Extended Day**: 7 a.m.- 6 p.m.

Tuition : (1993-94) $2,530; Reduction for siblings. **Extended Day** : Extra

ST. ANNE'S-BELFIELD SCHOOL............(804) 296-5106

2132 Ivy Road, Charlottesville, VA 22903
Episcopal 1910, merged 1970 **Head**: The Reverend George E. Conway

Grades: PreK-12 **Enrollment**: 795 Co-ed (45 Boarding; 5 day Boarding begins 7th grade)
Faculty: 67 full-, 5 part-time. **Average Class Size**: 14

Special Courses: Latin 7-12, French & Spanish 8-12. Math includes Calculus, Computer. Biology, Chemistry, Physics, Honors Chemistry, Honors Physics, Independent Research; History- Medieval & Early Modern, Modern World, U.S., American Gov't, History of Russia & USSR, Global Change: The Developing World. Economics, Humanities, Public Speaking.

Religious Studies- one semester each of Old and New Testament req.; Art History, Ceramics, Studio Art; Applied Music, Music Appreciation; Drama, Theatre History, Photography. AP: English, Calculus, Computer Science, U.S. History, Biology, Latin, French, Spanish.

Athletics: req. all grades. Intramural: Tennis. Interscholastic: Field Hockey, Lacrosse, Cross Country, Football, Basketball, Golf, Tennis, Soccer, Wrestling. Also offered: Weight Lifting, Aerobics. **Clubs**: Student Gov't, Ski, Drama, Video Update, Pop Quiz Team, Yearbook, Newspaper, Foreign Language Clubs, Art Forum, Gold Key Society. **Publications**: Newspaper, Literary Magazine, Yearbook. **Community Service**: 60 hrs. req. for graduation.

Plant: Library 10,000 vol., 6 Science labs, Art Studios, Gym, 2 Auditoriums, 5 Playing Fields, 5 Tennis Courts, Weight & Aerobics Rooms, New Fine Arts facility, New Academic building grades 5-8, IBM & Apple Computer Lab, and New Environmental Science Center, grades 5- 12.

Admission: Application fee $25. Required: Interview, Teacher Recommendations, Transcript, SSAT, ERB, or ISEE Test. Rolling admissions begin Jan. 1.

Tuition: (1993-94) Day $4,400-$7,500; Boarding $13,600-$14,700. Lunch: $1.50-$2.00 daily Books: $150-$225 *Dress Code*: Shirts must have collars and be tucked in, no T-shirts or cut-offs. **Scholarship Aid** : 51 full, 104 partial.

Summer Program: Academic: 6 weeks : Algebra and pre-Algebra, Basic English Writing Skills, Biology, Chemistry, Computer Skills/Typing, SAT Preparatory (2 wk), Spanish Review, Upper Level Writing Competency. Summer Camp: ages 3-5 or ages 5-12, 9 one week sessions. Adventure Camp: grades 1-8; Summer Stock Theater, age 7-15 and 16 to adult programs. One week camps: Boys' Lacrosse, Girls' Lacrosse & Field Hockey; Boys', Girls', Fathers & Sons Basketball Camps.

ST. ANSELM'S ABBEY SCHOOL..........(202) 269-2350

P

4501 S. Dakota Avenue, N.E., Washington, D.C. 20017
Catholic 1942. **Head**: Rev. Peter Weigand, OSB, M.T.S.

?

Grades: 6-12. **Enrollment**: 183 Boys. **Faculty**: 22 full-, 16 part-time.
Average Class Size: 15.

Special Courses: Latin 7-12, French & Spanish, 8-12, German, 10-12, Greek 11-12. Math includes Calculus and Computer. Gen'l Science, Biology, Chemistry, Physics. History- U.S., Western Civilization, Economics. Religious Studies, req.; Art, Music. AP. English Literature, Composition, American Literature, Latin, French Literature & Conversation, Physics, Chemistry, Biology, U.S. History, European History, Comparative Governments, U.S. Politics and Government, and Calculus.

Athletics: Req. thru grade 10: All students 6-10 are req. to participate weekly in intramural sports; Basketball, Softball, Soccer, Volleyball, Stickball. Note: Students in grades 11-12, req. to participate in a sport; optional co-ed recreational program offered 9-12. Interscholastic: Soccer, Basketball, Baseball, Tennis, Cross-Country, Wrestling **Clubs**: Newman, Forensic,

Soccer, Basketball, Baseball, Tennis, Cross-Country, Wrestling **Clubs**: Newman, Forensic, Priory Players, Latin Bowl, Cultural Student Organization, Math Counts, Knowledge Master, "It's Academic," Theater, Film, Science. **Publications**: Yearbook, Newspaper, Literary Magazine. **Community Involvement**: 2 1/2 hours a week of community service to various off-campus agencies in the metro area req. for all students in grades 11-12.

Plant: Library 12,500 vol., 3 Science Labs, Art Studio, Gym, Auditorium, Green House, 2 Playing Fields, 4 Tennis Courts, Chapel, 35 acres of land.

Admission: Rolling Admission, Tests in Jan. & Feb. or until classes filled. Interview follows testing. Limited openings for transfer into gr. 8, 10, 11. $35 Application & Testing fee.

Tuition: (1993-94) 6, $7,950; 7 & 8, $8,000; 9-12, $8,200; plus fees ($350-$600). **Transportation**: school accessible by Red & Green Metro lines. *Dress Code*: Jacket & tie, no jeans or athletic shoes. **Scholarship Aid**: 40 partial.

Future Plans: New gym, new Library; expand athletic program & facilities.

Summer Program: Remedial courses in Math, Languages; Enrichment courses in Science Math, English, Study skills.

ST. ANTHONY SCHOOL..........(202) 526-4657

12th & Lawrence Streets N.E., Washington, D. C. 20017
Catholic **Head**: Sister Francene Van Eck, OSB

Grades: K-8 **Enrollment**: Co-ed **Extended Day** : until 6 p.m.

Tuition: (1993-94) In parish, $1,525; Out of parish, $1,995; Reduction for siblings. Books: $75

ST. AUGUSTINE SCHOOL..........(202) 667-2608

1421 V Street, N. W., Washington, D. C. 20009
Catholic **Head**: Ms. Adela Acosta

Grades: K4-8 **Enrollment**: Co-ed **Extended Day**: 7 a.m.-6 p.m.

Tuition: (1993-94) $1,600; Reduction for siblings. **Extended Day**: Extra.

ST. BARTHOLOMEW'S SCHOOL...........(301) 229-5586

6900 River Road, Bethesda, MD 20817
Catholic 1962 **Head**: Sister Rose McCully, CSC

Grades: K-8 **Enrollment**: 215 Co-ed **Faculty**: 15 full-, 5 part-time.

Special Courses: Spanish. Algebra, Computer. General Science. U.S. & World History, World Regions, U.S. Geography, Civics. Religious Studies req.; Ability Grouping in Reading & Math which allows acceleration in both disciplines. Art, Music. **Extended Day**: 3 p.m.- 6 p.m.

Athletics: Req.; CYO Basketball, Baseball, Soccer. **Clubs**: Yearbook, Newspaper. **Publications**: Newspaper, Yearbook, Literary Magazine. **Community Involvement**: Students are encouraged to participate in service projects.

Plant: Library, 3,000 vol.; Science Lab, Playing Fields, Church Hall Auditorium.

Admission: Testing (fee) Math, Reading ; Transcript; School Visit

Tuition: (1993-94) In parish, $2.045; Out of parish, $3,495. Reduction for siblings. Books: $200. *Dress Code*: Uniform req **Scholarship Aid**: Limited, full and partial.

Summer Program: Academic Enrichment.

ST. BENEDICT THE MOOR SCHOOL..........(202) 397-3897

330 Twenty-first Street N. E., Washington, D. C. 20002
Catholic **Head**: Sister Brenda Cherry, OSP

Grades: K-8 **Enrollment**: Co-ed

Special Programs: Remedial Reading & Math; P.E., Art, Music, Choir. Computer
Extended Day: 7 a.m.-6 p.m.

Tuition: (1993-94) $1,750; Reduction for siblings. **Extended Day** Extra

ST. CATHERINE'S SCHOOL..........(804) 288-2804 FAX (804) 285-8169

6001 Grove Avenue, Richmond, VA 23226
Episcopal, 1890 **Head** : Auguste J. Bannard

Grades: Jr.K-12 **Enrollment**: 704 Girls (Boarding, 79, begins grade 9)
Faculty: 76 full-28 part-time. **Average Class Size**: 15-17

Special Courses: 20 credits required for graduation: English 4; Foreign Language 3 (Languages offered include Mandarin Chinese and Russian); History 3; Math 3; Lab Science 2; Religion 1 1/3; Fine Arts 1; Computer Literacy and P.E.; Co-ed Classes with St. Christopher's at all levels. Tri-mesters. AFS ; Mini-mester(2 wk. mid-winter program) Concentrated study in specific areas encourages internships, travel-study trips. Honors and AP Courses.
Extended Day: 7 a.m.-6 p.m., year round for Jr.K-7, including holidays.

Athletics: P.E. all levels; 24 Teams in 12 Sports, JV and Varsity; Horseback Riding, Tennis, Wilderness Program, Waterman Program (Camping, Canoeing, etc.) **Clubs and extra-**

curricular activities: Choir, Band, String Ensembles, Performing Dance Groups, Drama Group, Student Council, Altar Guild, Multicultural Awareness Group; **Publications**: Newspaper, Yearbook, Literary Magazine.

Plant: 16 acre campus; 2 Libraries.; Science, Fine Art, Music, and Theater Buildings; Gym, Tennis Courts, Playing fields.

Admission: $25 fee; Transcript; SSAT Math & English; Recommendations; Rolling Admission.

Tuition: (1993-94) Upper School: Day, $7,895; Boarding, $17,250 **Financial Aid**: Available

Future Plans: Lower School Addition, Theater renovations; Additional Computer Labs

Summer Program: Creative Arts Program for ages 3-12.

ST. FRANCIS EPISCOPAL DAY SCHOOL..........(301) 365-2642

10033 River Road, Potomac, MD 20854
Episcopal 1988 **Head**: Carol R. Shabe, Director

Grades: N2-grade 3. **Enrollment**: 210 Co-ed. **Faculty**: 19 full-, 11 part-time.
Average Class Size: 12 (small classes, low pupil teacher ratio 6:1).

Special Courses: Spanish, 1-3. Computer, Pre School-grade 3. Reading, Whole Language/ Creative Writing. Hands on Science. Chapel. Art. Music, all classes twice a week. Cultural Arts Enrichment Program, Field Trips integrated into the curriculum. Nurturing, self-esteem building environment; Developmentally appropriate curriculum in all subject areas.

Athletics: req. grades 1 & 2. Sports Skills program. Note: Pre-school, Creative Movement.
Community Involvement: MANA- Feed the hungry program.

Plant: Library, Multi-purpose room, Creative Playground.

Admission: Application Fee, $40, Apply Sept. through Jan. Children, applying for Pre-school participate in play-session evaluations. Primary grades spend a day at school. Parents tour school, meet with Director. Siblings and children of St. Francis church members given priority.

Tuition: (1993-94) $1,600-$5,150; includes Books. Lunch: Bring

ST. FRANCIS deSALES SCHOOL..........(202) 529-5394

2019 Rhode Island Avenue, N. E., Washington, D. C. 20018
Catholic **Head**: Sister Vicki Staub, SSJ

Grades : K4-8 **Enrollment**: Co-ed **Extended Day**: 7 a.m.-6 p.m.

Tuition: (1993-94) In parish, $1, 675; Out of parish, $1,780; Reduction for siblings. Registration fee $80. Books $90 PreK supplies. $150. **Extended Day** $42/wk;, Reduction for siblings.

ST. FRANCIS XAVIER SCHOOL..........(202) 581-2010

2700 O Street. S. E., Washington, D. C. 20020
Catholic **Head**: Mrs. Therese Leeke

Grades: K-8 **Enrollment** Co-ed
Special Courses: Spanish, Computer, Music, Art, P.E. **Extended Day**: 6:30 a.m.-6 p.m.

Tuition (1993-94) In parish, $1,320; Out of parish, $1.980. Reduction for siblings.
Extended Day: Extra

ST. GABRIEL'S SCHOOL..........(202) 726-9212

510 Webster Street. N. W., Washington, D. C. 20011
Catholic **Head**: Sister Janet Stolba, RJM

Grades : K-8 **Enrollment** : Co-ed **Extended Day**: until 6 p.m.

Tuition (1993-94) $1,800. Reduction for siblings.

ST. JAMES SCHOOL ....(301) 733-9330 Fax (301) 739 1310

St. James, MD. 21781
Episcopal 1842. **Head**: Rev. D. Stuart Dunnan, Ph. D.

Grades: 7-12. **Enrollment**: 150 Co-ed, Boarding & Day, Boarding begins 7th.
Faculty: 25 full-time. **Average Class Size**: 10.

Special Courses: French & Spanish 9-12, Latin 7&8; Math thru Calculus; Biology, Chemistry, Physics; History: English, American, Modern European, Ancient, Russian. Geography. Religion, Philosophy, Economics. Word Processing, Drama, Art, Music, Study Skills. AP.: Calculus, American History, Biology, Chemistry, Physics.

Athletics: Req.; Interscholastic: Football, Baseball, Basketball, Soccer, Track, Tennis, Cross Country, Squash, Aerobics, Wrestling, Field Hockey, Golf, Weight Lifting, Lacrosse. **Clubs**: Ski, Chess, Irving Society(literary), Mummers Society (Drama), Orpheus Society (Music), Library Committee, Varsity Club, Photography, Choir. **Publications**: Yearbook, Newspaper, Literary Magazine.

Plant: Library 10,000 vol., 3 Science Labs, Art Studio, 2 Gyms, 6 Playing Fields, 10 Tennis Courts (4 indoor), Squash Courts, Pottery Shed, Chapel, 8 Dormitories, Computer Room.

Admission: SSAT or SCAT (latter administered on campus during visit) Interview/campus tour; $35 Application fee; Transcript, Recommendations.

Tuition: (1993-94) Day $8,600; Boarding $15,300. Books: $200. *Dress Code*: Boys: coat & tie; Girls: Skirt or Dress, & Blazer. **Scholarship Aid**: 4 full, 24 partial.

Future Plans: New Fine Arts Center; new and expanded Library.

ST. JOHN'S COLLEGE HIGH SCHOOL..........(202) 363-2316

2607 Military Road, N.W., Washington, D.C. 20015
Catholic 1851. **Head**: (President) Brother D. Luke Maher, FSC
(Principal) Brother Ed Gallagher, FSC

Grades: 7-12. **Enrollment**: 550 Co-ed **Faculty**: 50 full-, 4 part-time.
Average Class Size: 16

Special Courses: College Preparatory with AP and Honor Courses in all areas. Grades 9-12: required Leadership Development Program (JROTC or Lead).

Athletics: Athletic Program participates in all Girls and Boys Sports under the new Washington Catholic League. **Clubs**: Numerous. **Publications**: Yearbook, Newspaper.

Plant: Library 13,000 vol., 4 Science Labs, Computer Lab, Chapel, Auditorium, Gym, Football/Baseball Stadium, Soccer/Lacrosse Field, Softball Field, 4 Tennis Courts, Rifle Range-28 acre campus.

Admission: Archdiocese Admission Tests; Interview, Transcript, Recommendations; $25 Application fee.

Tuition: (1993-94) 7 & 8, $5,200; 9-12, $5,700 Books: $200. *Dress Code*: Uniform (military) req. **Financial Aid:** Available.

Summer Program: Review & makeup courses in most major subjects. Enrichment courses in Writing and Computer Literacy. Reviews of elementary Math, English, Reading, Study Skills, and Keyboarding.

ST. JOHN'S EPISCOPAL SCHOOL...........(301) 774-6804

3427 Olney-Laytonsville Road, Olney, MD. 20832
Episcopal 1961. **Head**: Mr. John H. Zurn

Grades: K-8. **Enrollment**: 155 Co-ed. **Faculty**: 8 full-, 14 part-time.
Average Class Size: 17, max. 18

Special Courses: Spanish K-8, Latin 7-8, Algebra, General Science. Religious studies req.; Art, Music, Drama. **Extended Day**: 3:15 p.m.- 6 p.m.

Athletics: Req.; Intramural: Field Hockey, Soccer, Lacrosse, Track, Volleyball, Gymnastics, Wrestling, Aerobics, Basketball. **Publications**: Yearbook, Literary Magazine. **Community Involvement**: Visit nursing home, food & clothing collections; Thanksgiving baskets for needy;, MS Read-a-Thon; Work at soup kitchen;

Plant: Library 6,000 vol., Science Lab, Art Studio, Playing Fields.

Admission: Parent Interview, Classroom Visits; Application Fee $50. Students may be admitted during school year, if space available.

Tuition: (1993-94) $3,900-$4,900. Lunch: Bring. Books: Approx. $100. *Dress Code*: Uniform req. **Scholarship Aid**: Based on need.

Summer Program: Reading Enrichment program and Soccer Camp.

ST. JOHN'S LITERARY INSTITUTION AT PROSPECT HALL..........(301) 662-4210

FAX (301) 662-5166

889 Butterfly Lane, Frederick, MD. 21702
Roman Catholic 1829. **Head**: Mr. Edward Hoffman

Grades: 9-12. **Enrollment**: 155 Co-ed. **Faculty**: 17 full-, and part-time. **Average Class Size**: 14.

Special Courses: French, Spanish; Math through Calculus; Science includes Physics. Epochs in History & Philosophy, Religion req. ; Art, Computer Science. Note: Honors Courses 9-12 with children placed according to testing. In connection with the county, courses are offered for the gifted child in Art & Music or any specific subject.

Athletics: Intramural & Interscholastic. Soccer, Volleyball, Basketball, Baseball, Softball, Golf, Tennis. **Clubs**: Ski, Cheerleaders, Science, Nat'l Honor Societies, Student Council, Afro-American, Drama, Mock Trial, SADD. **Publications**: Yearbook, Student-Alumni Newsletter. **Community Involvement**: Nursing Home; Soup Kitchen in Washington monthly; Each grade involved in on-going projects.

Plant: Main Bldg. nominated to Nat'l Historic Trust. Library, Computer Lab, Chapel, Gym, Playing Fields, Science Labs, Tennis (nearby).

Admission: Interview upon request. Placement Testing, Transcript. Two letters of Recommendation.

Tuition: (1993-94) $3,820. Lunch: Cafeteria optional. Activity Fee: $125. Books: Extra. **Transportation**: Available to Montgomery County. *Dress Code*: Uniform req. **Financial Aid**: Available

Summer Program: Stu Vetter's Basketball Camp; Baseball program.

ST. JOHN THE EVANGELIST SCHOOL..........(410) 647-2283

669 Ritchie Highway, Severna Park, MD. 21146
Catholic **Head**: Sister Linda Larsen

Grades: K-8. **Enrollment**: 445 Co-ed

Tuition: (1993-94) Half-day K $1,615; K-8 $2,310; Reduction for siblings.

ST. JOSEPH'S SCHOOL..........(301) 937-7154

11011 Montgomery Road, Beltsville, MD 20705
Catholic **Head** : Mr. Thomas F. Moran

Grades: K-8 **Enrollment** : Co-ed

Special Courses: Religion req.; Language Arts, Science, Social Studies, Art, Computer 1-8. Remedial Reading. Advanced Math 7 & 8. Extensive vocal and instrumental music program. **Extended Day** : until 6 p.m.

Athletics: Basketball, Softball, Soccer, Baseball, T-ball, etc. **Clubs**: Altar Service, Safety Patrol, Brownies, Girl Scouts, Boy Scouts, Band.

Tuition: (1993-94) In parish, $1,692; Out of parish, $2,358. **Extended Day**: Extra
Financial Aid: Available

ST. LUKE'S CATHOLIC SCHOOL..........(703) 356-1508

7005 Georgetown Pike, McLean, VA 22101
Catholic **Head:** Margaret Cahill

Grades: K-8 **Enrollment**: 236 Co-ed

Special Programs: Seton Center for Learning Disabled. Computer, French, Art, Music, P.E. Religious Studies are an integral part of academic program. **Extended Day**: to 6 p.m.

Tuition: (1993-94) In Parish, $2,285; Out of Parish, $4,315; **Extended Day**: Extra

ST. MARGARARET'S SCHOOL..........(804) 443-3357

P.O. Box 158, Tappahanock, VA. 22560
Episcopal 1921 **Head**: Margaret R. Broad

Grades: 8-12 **Enrollment**: 130 Girls (95 Boarding) **Faculty**: 30 full-time.
Average Class Size: 10

Special Courses: Latin 8-12, French & Spanish, 9 -12. Physical Science, Biology, Chemistry, Physics. History- U.S., Virginia, History & Gov't, Modern European, Ancient & Medieval, American Civilization, World Issues. Religious Studies Req.; Intro. to Bible (Ethics- elective) Art History, Studio Art; Glee Club & Piano. Microcomputer. Word Processing, Driver's Ed, Drama, SAT Preparation, Study Skills. AP.: Biology, Math, Language, English.

Athletics: Req.: 2 yrs. of P.E. and 1/2 yr. of Health. Interscholastic- Field Hockey, Tennis, Soccer, Basketball, Softball ,Volleyball, Lacrosse. **Clubs**: Dance, Walking, Drama, Chapel, French, Spanish, Latin. **Publications**: Yearbook, Newspaper, Literary Magazine. **Community Involvement**: Sponsor parties for underprivileged; Volunteer in Soup Kitchen, at Children's Center, Nursing Home, Hospital.

Plant: Library, 2 Science Labs, Art Studio, New Student Center, Gym, Auditorium, Playing Field, 2 Residence Halls, Swimming Pool, Tennis Courts. Riverfront Location -(school owns sailboats, wind-surfers, & canoes).

Admission: Recommendations (Math, English, personal); Interview, Testing, Transcript. Application fee $30.

Tuition: (1993-94) Day, $7,200 (includes Lunch) Boarding $17,200. Books & other incidentals: $600 *Dress Code*: No Jeans. **Financial Aid** : 28% of student body receive assistance.

Future Plans: New Dorms 1995

Summer Program : Summer school offers academic enrichment courses; also English as a Second Language. Afternoon activities program includes sailing, canoeing, windsurfing, tennis, drama & art.

ST. MARIA GORETTI REGIONAL HIGH SCHOOL..........(301) 739-4266

1535 Oak Hill Avenue, Hagerstown, MD. 21742
Catholic 1930. **Head**: Sister Susan Albert

Grades: 9-12. **Enrollment**: 195 Co-ed. **Faculty**: 11 full-, 3 part-time.
Average Class Size: 23.

Special Courses: French I-IV, Spanish I-IV, Latin. Math-5 yr., Computer Science, Key boarding. Biology, Chemistry, Physics, Psychology. World Cultures, U.S. History. Shakespeare,

Athletics: Req. 9-12. Intramural & Interscholastic. Soccer, Tennis, Swimming, Golf, Volleyball, Basketball, Baseball, Softball. **Clubs**: Drama, Folk Music, Cheerleading. **Publications**: Yearbook, Newspaper, Literary Magazine. **Community Involvement**: Tutoring elementary pupils, and helping handicapped and elderly in nursing homes.

Plant: Library, 2 Science Labs, Art Studio, Gym/Auditorium, Playing Fields.

Admission: Admission is open. Interviews conducted.

Tuition: (1993-94) $3,768 includes lab fees. Books & Fees: $100- $200 *Dress Code*: Uniform req. **Scholarship Aid**: Some partial tuition assistance available.

Summer Camp: Basketball, Soccer, Volleyball Camp for boys & girls.

ST. MARTIN'S EVANGELICAL LUTHERAN CHURCH SCHOOL..........(410) 269-1955

1120 Spa Road, Annapolis, MD. 21403
Founded 1965. **Head**: Margaret Wolfe

Grades: Pre K-6. **Enrollment**: 174 Co-ed. **Faculty**: 6 full-, 9 part-time.
Average Class Size: 22.

Special Courses: Music, Art, Library, Computer Program. Religion req., Remedial Reading & Math. P.E. Req.

Plant: Library, All-Purpose room.

Admission: Interview parent/child. Testing K-6. Registration fee $100.

Tuition: (1993-94) grades l-6 $3,113 Lunch: Hot lunch 3 days, Bring 2 days/wk; fee for milk

ST. MARY'S RYKEN HIGH SCHOOL..........(301) 475-2814, or 932-4422

Camp Calvert Road, Leonardtown, MD. 20650
Catholic 1981. Sponsored by Xaverian Bros. **Head**: Mr. Harry L. Swaney

Grades: 9-12. **Enrollment**: 500 Co-ed. **Faculty**: 26 full-time **Average Class Size**: 25.

Special Courses: Latin, French, & Spanish all 9-12. Computer. Physical Science, Biology, Chemistry, Physics, Earth Science, Physiology, Psychology, Child Development; Electronics. World & U.S. History, Contemporary Issues, World Geography, World Cultures - Third World, Russia Since 1917, The Civil War. Religious Studies: req. Art, Music, Typing, Orchestra, Band, Mechanical Drawing, Drama. Remedial Reading & Math. All students take a Life Skills ` Program. AP.: English, History, Chemistry, Math, Music, Art.

Athletics: Not req. Interscholastic. Basketball, Baseball, Cross County, Soccer, Track, Wrestling, Field Hockey, Softball, Golf, Tennis, Cheerleading. **Clubs**: Science, Forensics, Foreign Language, Religious Activities. **Publications:** Newspaper, Yearbook, **Community Involvement**: 30 hrs. of community service req. for graduation.

Plant: Library 20,000 vol., Science Labs, Art Studio, Gym, Playing Fields, 110 acre campus.

Admission: 8th grade, Entrance/Placement Test - others submit Transcript.

Tuition: (1993-94) $3,525 and fees. Books: $150. Lunch: purchase **Transportation**: Some Available - extra charge *Dress Code*: specific regulations.

ST. MARY'S SCHOOL...........(301) 263-3294 (H.S.) 263-2869 (Lower)

Duke of Glouster Street, Annapolis, MD. 21401-2599
Catholic. **Head**: Sister Phyllis McNally (H.S.)

Grades: K-12. **Enrollment**: Co-ed: High School, 540; Lower School, 900.

Special Features: **Extended Day** in Lower School: until 5:30 p.m.

Tuition: (1993-94) Half-Day K, $1,500; K, $2,400 ; grades 1-8, $2,128-$2,224; High School, $3,330-$3,830 Note: Lower tuition for in parish family.

ST. MARY'S STAR OF THE SEA SCHOOL..........(301) 283-6151

Bryans Road, Accokeek, MD.
Note: Mailing: Route 2, Box 157, Indianhead, MD 20640
Head: Ms. Sheila Tomlinson

Grades: K-8 **Enrollment**: 250 Co-ed **Extended Day**: 6:30 a.m.-6:30 p.m.

Tuition: (1993-94) K, $81/mo.; 1-8,$143/mo. Note: Higher fees for out of parish family; reduced fees for siblings.

Summer Program: Recreational. **Extended Day**: 6:30 a.m.-6:30 p.m.

ST. PATRICK'S EPISCOPAL DAY SCHOOL..........(202) 342-2805

4700 Whitehaven Parkway, N.W., Washington, D.C. 20007
Episcopal 1956. **Head**: Robert R. Peterson.

Grades: N-6. **Enrollment**: 428 Co-ed. **Faculty**: 35 full-, 15 part-time.

Special Courses: French K-6, Latin 5-6. Gen'l Science. Remedial Reading & Math. Computer. Religious Studies req. Art; Music, Choir, Bellringers. Video classes 4-6.
Extended Day: to 6 p.m.

Athletics: Req. Low structure games & activities K-l; 2-6 Soccer, Basketball, Volleyball, Gymnastics, Softball, Dance, Wrestling. **Publications**: Yearbook. **Community Involvement**: Outreach program in partnership with St. Phillip's in Anacostia and Haiti, American Indians in Idaho, and St. Patrick's Senior Center.

Plant: Library 15,000 vol., Computer/Video Production Center, Amphitheater, 2 Science Labs, Art Studio, Gym, Auditorium, 2 acre Playing field, 4 Playgrounds..

Admission: Parent/child interview, call school by Nov.; testing fee $90, application fee $40. Seek diverse student body but preference given to siblings and parish children.

Tuition: (1993-94) N Half-Day $5,420; N Full Day $8,475; K-6 $8,550. includes Books. Bring Lunch. *Dress Code*: Conservative. **Scholarship Aid**: 40 partial, 3 full

Summer Program: Day Camp, Ages 2-12; Swimming, sports, arts, drama and video. Residential Science Camp, grades 3-6.

ST. PETER CATHOLIC SCHOOL...........(301) 774-9112

2900 Sandy Spring Road, Olney, MD 20832
Head: Carol A. Mikone

Grades: K -8 **Enrollment**: 300 Co-ed

Special Features: Spanish 1-8. **Extended Day** : until 6 p.m.

Tuition: (1993-94) Half-day K, $1,070; Full-day K, $1,890; 1-8 (in parish) $1,355 +$800 parish contribution.; 1-8 (non-parish) $2,330 Reduced rate for siblings. **Extended Day**: Extra *Dress Code:* Uniform req. **Transportation**: Limited

Summer Program: Call for information.

ST. PETER'S INTERPARISH SCHOOL..........(202) 544-1618

422 Third Street, S. E., Washington, D. C. 20003
Catholic **Head**: Mrs. Mary M. Randolph

Grades: K4-8 **Enrollment**: Co-ed

Special Courses: French 1-8, Computer, Art, Music, P.E. **Extended Day**: 7:30 a.m.-6 p.m.

Tuition: (1993-94) In Parish, $2,240; Out of Parish, Catholic, $2,560; Non-Catholic, $2,660; Reduction for siblings. **Extended Day**: Extra

ST. STEPHEN'S & ST. AGNES SCHOOL...(703) 549-3542 (K-8)
(703) 751-2700 (9-12)

P

400 Fontaine Street, Alexandria, VA. 22302 (K-8)
1000 St. Stephen's Road, Alexandria, VA. 22304 (9-12)
Episcopal, St. Agnes 1924, St. Stephens 1944. **Head**: Joan G. Ogilvy Holden

Grades: K-12. **Enrollment**: 990 Co-ed **Faculty**: 118 full-, 20 part-time.
Average Class Size: 15.

Special Courses: Latin 6-12, French & Spanish 4-12; Algebra I-III, Geometry, Trig., Calculus, Finite Math; Computer Science, K-12. General Science K-9, Biology, Chemistry, Physics, Field Studies. History: 9-12 Ages of Humanity-(4 yrs. req.) Interdisciplinary, Multicultural History course; Medieval History (gr.6), Twentieth Century World History (gr.7) Interdisciplinary Science/Geography (gr.8). Religious Studies req.; Studio Art; Music: K-6 Orff Music Program, 7-12 Chorus, Band, Orchestra, Guitar, Chamber Music, Jazz Band. Photography, Drama, Dance. AP.: English, Calculus AB, Calculus BC, Art, Pascal, Latin, Spanish, French, History, Biology, Chemistry, Physics. **Extended Day**: 7 a.m.-6 p.m.

Athletics: Req. to grade 11. Intramural & Interscholastic. Basketball, Football, Softball, Baseball, Tennis, Field Hockey, Soccer, Lacrosse, Track & Field, Wrestling, Volleyball, Cross Country. **Clubs**: In Middle School, generated by student; Upper School: Language, Debate, Model O.A.S. & U.N., Library, SADD, Service Unity. **Publications**: Yearbook, Newspaper, Literary Magazines. **Community Involvement**: Service Projects at all grade levels. Required Service Project, 60 hrs. for Upper School students.

Plant: 3 Libraries, Language Lab, 11 Science Labs, 6 Art Studios, 2 Gyms, 6 Playing Fields, 6 Tennis Courts, Large Multi-purpose Room, 3 Performing Arts Studios.

Admission: Tour & Interview & Campus Visit. Testing- SSAT 6-12. Transcripts, Essay, 2 Teacher Recommendations. $50 Application & Testing Fee. Students generally fall into above average to superior range of ability.

Tuition: (1993-94) K- 8, $9,280. 9-12, $10,320. Lunch: $415-$575 Books: $125-$275. **Transportation**: Available. *Dress Code*: Appropriate attire expected at all times- specific rules for Lower, Middle & Upper School. **Financial Aid**: 200 partial.

Future Plans: Renovate classrooms, expand P.E. and Performing Arts facilities on Upper School campus.

Summer Program: Courses for credit, enrichment and remedial work; for all grades, Adults welcome. Classes daily early June - early August. Also SAT Prep. Course. Note: For rising Seniors: Internships in area businesses, Oxford Study Program in England.

Summer Camp: Day Camp early June - early August, Co-ed, Ages 3-11: Sports, computer, swimming, arts & crafts, music/drama, field trips. All Sports Camps: Boys & Girls: Lacrosse, Soccer, Basketball, Softball, Tennis, Football, Weight Training; New '93: World Cultures, Adventures in Spanish, Flight Camp, Music Academy, Computer Camp.

ST. TIMOTHY'S SCHOOL..........(410) 486-7400 FAX (410) 484-5910

Stevenson, MD. 21153
Episcopal 1882. **Head**: Deborah Cook.

Grades: 9-12. **Enrollment**: 73 Girls (57 Boarding) **Faculty**: 20 full-, 2 part-time.
Average Class Size: 7

Special Courses: French I-V, Latin I-II, Spanish I-IV; Science: Physical Science, Biology, Chemistry, Physics. History: World History I & II, American, Women in American History; Religious Studies (req. one year)--Intro. to World Religion. Studio Art, Ceramics, Photography, Music Theory, Piano, Modern Dance, Ballet, Drama. AP.: English, French, Calculus, History of Art, Biology. Note: Special Programs; English Speaking Union; Independent Senior Project..

Athletics: Req.; Intramural & Interscholastic. Field Hockey, Cross-Country, Lacrosse, Soccer, Tennis, Aerobic Dance, Basketball, Riding, Badminton **Clubs**: Choir, Handbell Choir, Madrigals, Dramatics, Spanish, French, Science, Social Activities, Current Events. **Publications**: Yearbook, Literary Magazine. **Community Involvement**: Social Service, Tutoring, Special Games Day.

Plant: Library 20,000 vol., 3 Science Labs, Language Lab, Art Studio, Gym, Auditorium, Theater, Stables & Indoor Riding Arena, Cross Country Equestrian Course, Playing Fields, Swimming Pool, 10 Tennis Courts, Music & Dance Studios, Chapel, Dormitories, Infirmary, Faculty Homes, Darkroom.

Admission: $30 fee; Transcript, Interview, SSAT, English, Math; Applicant Essay; Principal and Personal Recommendations. Notification: Rolling with reply by April 10.

Tuition: (1993-94) Day $9,800; Boarding $18,900. Books: $400-$500 *Dress Code*: Uniform req. for classes. **Scholarship Aid**: 33% of student body receives aid.

ST. THOMAS MORE CATHOLIC SCHOOL..........(202) 561-1189

4265 Fourth Street, S. E., Washington, D.C. 20032
Catholic **Head**: Ms. Roberta Taylor

Grades : K4-8 **Enrollment**: Co-ed

Special Programs: Spanish K-8, Computer K-8; Art. Music, P.E. **Extended Day** : 6:30 a.m. -6 p.m.

Tuition: Out of parish $180/mo; Reduced rate for in parish students and siblings.
Extended Day: Extra

ST. VINCENT PALLOTTI HIGH SCHOOL..........(301) 725-3228

113 Eighth Street, Laurel, MD. 20707
Catholic 1921 **Principal**: Mr. Paul Leonarczyk

Grades : 9-12. **Enrollment**: 450 Co-ed. **Faculty**: 30 full-, 11 part-time.
Average Class Size: 20-25.

Special Programs : Student Internships; Student Exchange with Foreign Countries; Req. Christian Service Projects; University Program.

Special Courses: Sculpture, Mechanical Drawing, Photography, Quattro, Cable TV, Creative Writing; Economics; Pascal I & II, Word Processing, Desk Top Publishing; Sociology, Psychology. AP Courses in Math, Science, History, English.

Athletics: Pom Pons, Cheerleading, Football, Basketball, Baseball, Track, Swimming, Soccer, Lacrosse. Tennis, Softball, Volleyball. **Clubs**: Language, Computer, Ski, Photography, Mock Trial, Odyssey of the Mind, Multi-cultural, Art, Drama, Chorus. **Publications**: Yearbook, Literary Magazine, Newspaper. **Community Involvement**: Christian Service Class, Interact, Partnership with Laurel-Beltsville Hospital.

Plant: Library 10,000 vol., 3 Science Labs, Playing Field, Gym, Cafeteria, 2 Resource Centers.

Admission: Interviews, Tests, Recommendations. $100 Tuition deposit.

Tuition: (1993-94) $4,150 for first child, reduced rate for siblings. Books : included *Dress Code*: Uniform req. **Financial Aid**: Some Available

Future Plans: Building expansion due to increased enrollment.

Summer Program: Academic : Remedial, to complete credits in most subjects.

SANDY SPRING FRIENDS SCHOOL..........(301) 774-7455 P

16923 Norwood Road, Sandy Spring, MD. 20860
Quaker 1961. **Head**: Stephen Gessner, Ph.D.

Grades: PreK-12. (Note: July, 1993, Friends Elementary merged with Sandy Spring Friends)
Enrollment: 375 Co-ed; 45 Boarding (begins at 9th grade); **Faculty**: 48 full-, 5 part-time.
Average Class Size: 15.

Special Courses: French 6-12, Spanish 1-12, ESL. Math thru Calculus; Gen'l Science, Biology I and II, Chemistry, Physics; English Literature Survey Courses, Writing, Tri-mester length English Electives; World History, 20th Century Courses; Visual Arts & Performing Arts at all levels. 9th Grade Experience with Outdoor Exploration Program and Activities in community building, Community Service and Drama; Weekly meeting for worship-period emphasizing reflection and values; Intersession (one week experimental learning).

Athletics: Req.; Intramural & Interscholastic: Tennis, Cross Country, Ultimate Frisbee, Gym Games, Soccer, Lacrosse, Basketball, Gymnastics, Jogging, Hiking, Biking. **Clubs**: Multi-Cultural Committee, Yearbook, Ecology, Amnesty Internat'l, Recycling, Computer. . **Publications**: Literary Magazine, Weekly Newspaper, Yearbook. **Community Involvement**: Required at all levels.

Plant: New Library 17,000 vol.; Observatory /Gym ; New Elementary facility, Renovated Middle School, Science Labs, Photography Lab, Shop, 3 Art Studios, Shop, Theater, 6 Classroom Buildings, Dormitory, Print Shop, 4 Soccer and Lacrosse Fields, Tennis Courts.

Admission: Interview and Visit; Application, $50 fee; Suggest applying by Feb. 15th for consideration in first round of decisions. References, Transcript. SSAT, Middle School placement Test. Fee $30.

Tuition: (1993-94) Elementary, $4,000-$6,400; Middle, $7,725-$8,150; Upper, (Day) $10,250; (Boarding) $17,650; Enrollment Fees $400, $500, $700 (depending on grade). **Transportation**: Available, one way or round trip $1,000. *Dress Code*: Clean, neat, simple & appropriate. **Financial Aid**: Approximately 25% of the student body receives aid.

Summer Program: Summer Friends: Numerous sports, arts, and trip camps available.

SEVERN SCHOOL.........(410) 647-7700

Water Street, Severna Park, MD. 21146
Founded 1914. **Head**: William J. Creeden

Grades: 6-12. **Enrollment**: 465 Co-ed. **Faculty**: 40 full-, 15 part-time.
Average Class Size: 15

Special Courses: Latin, French, & Spanish, all 6-12. Study Skills, Art, Music, Math through Calculus, Business Math, Computer Programming. Biology, Chemistry, Physics, Ecology, Marine Biology. History: Third World Cultures, Ancient History, European Civilization, Sociology, Economics, American Philosophy, Local Government. Typing, Driver's Ed, Drama, Mechanical Drawing, Sculpture, Ceramics, Painting & Drawing, Music Appreciation Choir, Theater. AP.: English, History, Physics, Biology, Languages, Math.

Athletics: Req.; Intramural 6-8, Interscholastic 8-12; Lacrosse, Football, Soccer, Tennis, Golf, Wrestling, Swimming, Basketball, Field Hockey, Baseball. **Clubs**: French, Latin, Spanish, Radio, Ecology, Sailing, SADD, etc. **Publications**: Yearbook, Newspaper, Literary Review.

Plant: Library 16,000 vol.; Language Labs, Science Labs, Art Studios, Gym, Playing Fields, Tennis Courts, Use of Golf Course & Swimming Pool.

Admission: Testing; Transcripts. Interview, Recommendations; $30 fee.

Tuition: (1993-94) $8,250. Lunch: Extra. Books: Approx. $200. **Transportation** Bus available *Dress Code*: Uniform- Boys, shirt & tie; Girls, dresses or pants. **Financial Aid** Available.

Summer Program.: Summer School; Day camp; Field Hockey, Lacrosse, & Soccer camps.

SHERIDAN SCHOOL..........(202) 362-7900

4400 36th Street, N. W., Washington, D. C. 20009
Founded 1927. **Head**: Hugh C. Riddleberger.

Grades: K-8. **Enrollment**: 200 Co-ed. **Faculty**: 26 full-, 3 part-time
Average Class Size: Student/teacher ratio, 7:1

Special Courses: Strong academic emphasis with much time also given to Art, Music, and Sports. French 4-8. Computers K-8. General Science; Unique Mountain campus in Blue Ridge provides outdoor and environmental education including ropes course, rock-climbing and caving. History : includes Colonial, Greek, Medieval, and American Black Studies; Anthropology. Spring Musical 6-8. **Extended Day** 7:30 a.m.-6 p.m..

Athletics: Req.; Intramural Basketball; Interscholastic: Soccer, Basketball, Softball, Track. **Clubs**: Science, Computer, Photography, Art. **Publications**: Yearbook, Newspaper, Literary Magazine. **Community Involvement**: All classes participate in at least one community service project per year.

Plant: Library 8,400 vol., Science Lab, Art Studio, Auditorium/Gym, Playing Fields, Mountain Campus - 130 acres in Lurray, VA.

Admission: Parent Interview, Student Visits School; Tests for K-8. Fee $50. Notification mid-March.

Tuition: (1993-94) $9,400-$11,025, includes Lunch & Books *Dress Code*: Uniform req. Fridays only, grades 4-8 **Financial Aid**: Available.

Future Plans: New building for Gym, Music & Art rooms, and additional Science Labs.

Summer Program: Discovery Camp at Mountain Campus; Town campus, Computer Camp; Gap Camp- Day camp, June & August, Co-ed, ages 6-12.

SIDWELL FRIENDS SCHOOL..........(202) 537-8100

3825 Wisconsin Avenue, N.W., Washington, D.C. 20016
(Lower School: Pre K-grade 4, 5100 Edgemoor Lane, Bethesda, MD.)
Quaker 1883. **Head**: Earl Harrison, Jr.

Grades: Pre K-12. **Enrollment**: 1,034 Co-ed (increases K, 3, 5, 7, 9). **Faculty**: 105 full-, 35 part-time. **Class Size**: 15-24

Special Courses: Latin, French, Spanish - all 7-12; Chinese 9-12. (l yr. study in Art req.; 2 yrs. of Science) Environmental Science, Philosophy, Physical Science, Scientific Writing, Physics; Math thru Calculus. History - Global, Ancient, Medieval, Modern European, English, American; American & Chinese studies program. Typing, Drama, Outdoor Leadership, Technical Theater, Sculpture, Music. AP.: Physics, Biology, Chemistry, Math, Languages and Computer Science. **Extended Day**: 3-6 p.m.

Athletics: P.E. Req. Intramural & Interscholastic: Baseball, Basketball, Cross Country, Field Hockey, Golf, Indoor Soccer, Lacrosse, Gymnastics, Soccer, Tennis, Track & Field, Volleyball, Swimming, Diving.. **Clubs**: Over 20 special interest - including Language, Debate, Chess, Computers, Model U.N. **Community Service**: Required.

Plant: Library 35,000 vol., Language Lab, Science Labs, Computer Labs, Auditorium, Gym, Playing Fields, 6 Lane Track, Tennis Courts, Arts Center, Quaker Meeting Room.

Admission: Applications, Sept.- Jan. 15, $40 + Testing fee.

Tuition: (1993-94) $9,947-$11,587. Lunch: included. **Transportation**: To grade 6, $600 one way; $1,000 both ways. Books: $150-$350. *Dress Code*: Cleanliness, neatness, simplicity. **Financial Aid**: Available.

Summer Program: Word Processing, Photography; Summer Camps: Baseball, Basketball, Lacrosse, Soccer, Tennis, Volleyball, Arts, Dance, Drama, Pottery; Summer in the City. Residential Summer Camp-Corsica.

SILVER SPRING CHRISTIAN ACADEMY.......(301) 445-1033

7201 Sixteenth Place, Hyattsville, MD. 20783-4399
Presbyterian 1986 **Head**: Mrs. Janice Adams, Principal

Grades: 9-12 **Enrollment**: 15 Co-ed **Faculty**: 12 part-time **Average Class Size**: 8-10

Special Courses: German; Math thru Calculus; Computer. Biology, Chemistry, Physics. History: American, European, Government. Religious Studies Req.; Art, Typing. AP: European History, Government- courses to be added as student interest demands.

Athletics: req.; Intramural: Soccer, Basketball, Volleyball. **Publications**: Yearbook
Community Involvement: Christian service projects available.

Plant: Library, 5,000 vol.; Science Lab, Auditorium; Basketball court outside.

Admission: Parent Application, Student Questionnaire, Transcript, Possible Testing; Parent & Student Interview Note: Student and one or both parents should be members in good standing in an evangelical church OR Board approval for non-church applicants. Registration fee $100

Tuition: (1993-94) $2,850 Lunch: Bag *Dress Code*: Students are expected to dress with modesty and decency. **Scholarship Aid**: Available.

Future Plans: To expand school to 30 students at present location; curriculum to continue to be college preparatory and to expand as school grows.

SISTER CLARA MUHAMMAD ELEMENTARY SCHOOL...........(202) 610-1090

2313-15 Martin Luther King, Jr. Avenue, S.E., Washington, D. C. 20020
Islamic **Head**: Mrs. Zakiyyah Abdus-Salaam, Principal

Grades: N-8 (N ages 2-4) **Enrollment**: 85 Co-ed **Faculty**: 13 full-, 1 part-time
Average Class Size: 9

Special Courses: Islamic Studies, Arabic Language, Quranic recitation; discipline and moral conduct stressed. **Extended Day**: 7 a.m.-6 p.m.

Tuition: (1993-94) $175/mo; reduction for siblings. $25 Application fee.

Future Plans: To expand to grade 9.

SLIGO ADVENTIST ELEMENTARY SCHOOL..........(301) 434-1417

8300 Carroll Avenue, Takoma Park, MD. 20912
Seventh Day Adventist 1929. **Head**: Dr. Eugene Brewer.

Grades: N3-8. **Enrollment**: 400 Co-ed. **Faculty**: 23.

Special Courses: Remedial Reading, French, Art, Music, General Science; Bible req.
Extended Day : 9:45 a.m.-6 p.m. Note: Full Day Care program for 3 & 4 yr. olds, year-round 7:30 a.m.-6 p.m.

Athletics: Req. 5-8. **Clubs**: Drama, Pathfinders (church sponsored -like Scouts).
Publications: Weekly newspaper.

Plant: Library, Auditorium/Gym, Playing Fields.

Admission: Testing, Recommendations; Admission Board approves application.

Tuition: (1993-94) K-8, $3,120. Activity Fee $25 **Transportation**: $39-$118/mo. depending on zone. Books: $85-$100 *Dress Code*: Modest apparel. **Day Care** (3 & 4 yr. olds) $85/wk

SOUTHERN MARYLAND CHRISTIAN ACADEMY..........(301) 870 -2550,
934-3655, 753-8148

Route 2, P.0. Box 548 D, White Plains, MD 20695
Head: Mrs. Colleen Gaines

Grades: K3-12 **Enrollment**: 180 Co-ed

Special Programs: Regular Academic Program; Foreign Language, Sign Language, Computers. Typing, Drafting; Music, Band, Art. **Extended Day** 6 a.m.-6:30 p.m.

Athletics : P.E.; Jr. & Sr. High play sports in conference play league.

Tuition: (1993-94) $2,250; Reduced rate for siblings. High School Fee $300, Registration $250.

Summer Camp: 5-12 yrs. Field trips, swimming, etc. $90 wk.($73/wk. for second child. $59 for other siblings). Hours- 6 a.m.-6:30 p.m.

SPENCERVILLE JUNIOR ACADEMY..........(301) 421-9101

15930 Good Hope Road, Silver Spring, MD. 20905
Seventh Day Adventist 1946. **Head**: Harold Grosboll

Grades: K-10. **Enrollment**: 183 Co-ed. **Faculty**: 11 full-time.
Average Class Size: 19.

Special Courses: Algebra, Geometry, Physical Science, Biology, Typing, Band, Choir; Religious studies req. **Extended Day**: Mon.-Thurs. 3-6 p.m.

Athletics: Req.; Intramural: Volleyball, Floor Hockey, Soccer, Softball, Basketball, Tennis, Flagball, Badminton. **Publications**: Yearbook.

Plant: Library 9600 vol., Science Lab, Auditorium, Gym, Playing Fields, Lab.

Admission: Interview, Test, Registration fee.

Tuition: (1993-94) $1,575-$3,500 depending on grade level & whether student is member of sponsoring church, Adventist but non constituent, or non-Adventist. Books: Extra. Lunch: Bring. *Dress Code*: Neat, no jeans or T-shirts.

Future Plans: Expand after-school program

Summer Program: Band Camp

SPRINGFIELD ACADEMY..........(703) 256-3773

5236 Backlick Road, Springfield, VA. 22151
Founded 1958. **Head**: Jack Merritt.

Grades: age 6 wks.-grade 3. **Enrollment**: 135 Co-ed. **Faculty**: 12 full-, 5 part-time.
Average Class Size: (K-2) 15.

Special Courses: Remedial Reading & Math,; Ballet, Art, Music.
Extended Day: 6:30 a.m.-6:30 p.m.

Plant: Library 100+ vol., 5 acre campus.

Admission: Parent & child interviews; registration fee N and K $45, and lst & 2nd, $75.

Tuition : (1993-94) Infant Care (6 wks-age 2), 117/wk.-$145 wk; N-grade 3, $105 wk.. includes **Extended Day &** Lunch. *Dress Code*: Moderate.

Summer Program: Camp 6:30 a.m.-6:30 p.m., arts & crafts, swimming, films, field trips, outdoor activities. Registration fee $25.

STONE RIDGE COUNTRY DAY SCHOOL..........(301) 657-4322

9101 Rockville Pike, Bethesda, MD. 20814
Catholic 1923. **Head**: Sister Anne Dyer, RSCJ

Grades: Jr.K-12. **Enrollment**: 576 Girls (13 Boys Jr.K-K only), Expands at grades l, 6, 9.
Faculty: 54 full-, 11 part-time. **Average Class Size**: 16-18. Student/teacher 9:1

Special Courses: College Preparatory. Advanced & accelerated preparation for AP exams in History, Biology, Chemistry, English, Art, French, Spanish; Math, and Computer Science. Independent Study; Career Internship. Exchange program through Network of Sacred Heart schools in U.S. and abroad. Middle School: Choice of French or Spanish, (5-8) Latin req. grade 8. Communications Lab provides training in effective leadership and group process skills.

Athletics: Req.; Intramural & Interscholastic: Field Hockey, Tennis, Basketball, Volleyball, Softball, Soccer, Lacrosse, Swimming, Diving, Cross Country, Track. **Clubs**: 20 including Model U.N., SADD, Ethnic Awareness, etc. **Publications**: Yearbook, Literary Magazine, Newspaper. **Community Involvement**: Jr.K-8: Develop. of social awareness. Grade 9: Training program for service in Education/Geriatrics/ Social Justice. Instruction in Proposal Writing. Grade 10-12: Community Service required.

Plant: Chapel, 3 Libraries, 2 Language Labs, 5 Science Labs, 3 Art Studios, Auditorium, 3 Gyms, 3 Playing Fields, 4 Tennis Courts, Photography Lab, Playgrounds..

Admission: $50 Application Testing fee Jr.K-12. Rolling admission. Applicants should apply by Feb. l. Test and Interview required. Will accept SSAT, gr. 6-12, then application fee $35.

Tuition: (1993-94) Half- day Jr.K. & K., $4,750; K-6, $7,875; 7-12, $8,525- $9,050. Books: $150-$200. *Dress Code*: Uniform req. **Transportation**: Metro- Medical Center **Scholarship Aid**: Need based grants available.

Summer Programs: Art; Reading Skills.

STUART HALL..........(703) 885-0356

P.O. Box 210, 235 West Frederick Street, Staunton, VA. 24401
Episcopal 1831. Head: Rev. J. Kevin Fox

Grades: 6-12. **Enrollment**: 113 (107 Girls; 6 Boys in middle school only); 80 Boarding, begins grade 8. **Faculty**: 18 full-, 3 part-time. **Average Class Size**: 8

Special Courses: Latin, French, Spanish, & German, all 9-12. Math includes Pre-Algebra thru Calculus; Computer Processing. Gen'l Science, Biology, Chemistry, Physics, Earth Science, Physical Science. History- Geography, World, U.S./Government I & II. Religious Studies involves Ethics and Volunteer Work. Art: all media including Stained Glass and Ceramics. Music: Appreciation, Voice, Piano. Drama. Note: LRC-Learning Resource Center and ESL (English as a Second Language). AP. at Mary Baldwin College.

Athletics: P.E. Req. Intramural: Field Hockey, Volleyball, Aerobics, Tennis, Swimming. Interscholastic: Member Blue Ridge Conference: Volleyball, Field Hockey, Soccer, Basketball, Tennis, Softball, and Riding (all year), Cross-Country, Cycling, Lacrosse, Skiing, Dance: Ballet, Tap, Modern. **Clubs**: Ecology, World Affairs, Student Gov't, Art. Drama, Pop Quiz Team. **Publications**: Literary Magazine, Newspaper, Yearbook. **Community Involvement**: All Seniors participate in Volunteer work: Tutoring at local elementary school; Hospitals, Ride with Pride; Special Olympics, Friendship Club.

Plant: Library, Gym 14,000 vol.; Science Labs, Art Studio, Gym, Auditorium, 3 Tennis Courts, Indoor Pool, Darkroom, Playing Fields, Riding at nearby stables.

Admission: SSAT, Personal Interview; Rolling Admission. Note: Seek motivated college-bound individual who is an average to above average student.:

Tuition: (1993-94) Day, $5,500; 5 Day Boarding, $12,550 (includes Lunch) Full- time Boarding, $15,475. Books, Fees, etc.: $500. *Dress Code*: Class Dress- Skirts, Dresses, Bermuda Shorts, Dress Pants, Collared Shirts. **Scholarship Aid**: Available; 25% of student body receives need-based aid.

Future Plans: New Labs, Athletic Fields and Gym in next few years.

Summer Program: Co-ed Summer School for new credit or enrichment work in ESL, English, Math, Science, History, French, Spanish, SAT prep.

SUDLEY MONTESSORI SCHOOL..........(703) 257 1203

10391 Sudley Manor Drive, Manassas, VA 22110
Founded 1990 **Head**: Rose Wade

Grades N-3 **Enrollment**: 35 Co-ed **Faculty**: 2 full-, 3 part-time. **Average Class Size**: 15

Special Programs: Classes mixed in age; Music, Dance, Drama, Piano. **Extended Day:** Available.

Admission: Interview, Transcripts.

Tuition: (1993-94) $2,000-$4,500

Summer Program: Call for information.

SUMMIT SCHOOL...........(301) 880-4256; 952-0787; 741-1242

4205 S. Crain Highway, Upper Marlboro, MD 20711
Founded 1989 **Head**: Dr. Jane Snider

Grades: 1-8 **Enrollment** 55 Co-ed **Faculty**: 14 Full-, 3 part- time. **Average Class Size**: 8

Special Courses: Pre-Algebra, 8; Computer. Gen'l Science 1-6, Life Science, 7, Earth Science 8. Remedial Reading and Math. Note: Ungraded, dyslexic type of learning problems, classes of 8-9, individualized reading. Art, Music, Workshop.

Athletics: Not req. **Clubs**: Different clubs offered on a rotating basis: Pioneering, Puppet making, Sports, Gardening, Newspaper, Art, Sewing, Cooking, Drama, Signing, Chorus. **Publications**: Yearbook, Newspaper. **Community Involvement**: 8th grade class involved in service project, visiting local convalescent home or schools for handicapped.

Plant: Library, 3,000 vol. Science Lab, Shop, Art Studio, Auditorium, Playing Field, Swimming Pool, Fishing Pond, Stream.

Admission: Application fee $50. Diagnostic testing (WISCR) and Achievement testing, followed by a Visit for a day. Must be of average to gifted intelligence, Reading and Spelling problems only.

Tuition: (1993-94) $13,900 Lunch: Bring *Dress Code*: Boys: solid color trousers and shirt; must have collar on shirt; navy/ Khaki camp shorts. Girls: solid shirts/ jumpers/ skirts/pants. Shorts same as Boys. **Scholarship Aid:** 1 full, 9 partial.

Future Plans: Gym and new wing.

Summer Program: Tutoring in Reading; Summer Reading Camp

SYDENSTRICKER SCHOOL.........(703) 451-4141

7001 Sydenstricker Road, Springfield, VA. 22152
1965. **Head**: Mrs. Lore Araujo.

Grades: N-grade 2. **Enrollment**: 120 Co-ed. **Faculty**: 4 full-, 2 part-time.
Average Class Size: 15.

Special Courses: German l-2. Remedial Reading & Math, Developmental Reading, Study Skills; Computer. General Science. Music, Art, Dancing. Note: Program is designed to provide stimulating atmosphere in which child is relaxed, develops enthusiasm for learning and gains self-confidence, enabling him to make a smooth transition into other school systems. (Psychologist on call.) **Extended Day** : 7 a.m.-6 p.m.

Plant: Library 2000 vol., Computer Lab, Art Studio, 5 acres, Nature Trail.

Admission: Application, Interview, Transcript or Tests for K-2; Primary Mental Abilities test.

Tuition: (1993-94) $100-$430/mo. depending on age and hours in school.

TAKOMA ACADEMY..........(301) 434-4700

8120 Carroll Avenue, Takoma Park, MD. 20912
Seventh Day Adventist 1904. **Head**: Larry Blacklemer

Grades: 9-12. **Enrollment**: 336 Co-ed. **Faculty**: 19 full-, 2 part-time.
Average Class Size: 21.

Special Courses: French I-II, Spanish I -III. Math includes honors courses in Algebra, Geometry, Trig, Calculus; Word Processing. Science includes honors courses in Biology and Chemistry; Physics. History: World, U.S., and American Government. Religious Studies req. Remedial Reading and Math; ESL program. Note: TALL-Takoma Academy Learning Laboratory is set up to help any student with study skills, gap learning, organization, etc. Art: Drawing & Design, Color & Methods. Music: Choir, Bell Choir, Orchestra, Sax Quartet. Drama. AP.: English, American Government.

Athletics: Req. 9-10; Intramural Basketball, Volleyball, Football, Softball; Interscholastic: Basketball, Cross-Country, Track. **Clubs:** Biota, TA Magazine. **Publications**: Newspaper, Yearbook. **Community Involvement**: TALK- program to adopt a kid at Christmas. Community Service Day: student body spends a day cleaning up regional parks and communities.

Plant: Library 16,000 vol., Science Lab, Art Room, Shop, Auditorium, Gym, Tennis Courts, Playing Fields. 400 meter track.

Admission: Application fee $10; Placement Test, Interview, Transcript Recommendations. Registration starts in July.

Tuition: (1993-94) $3,600 - $4,600. Lunch: Purchase Books: $150. *Dress Code*: Clean, tidy clothes which are modest.

TALENT HOUSE PRIVATE SCHOOL..........(703) 273-8000

9211 Arlington Boulevard., Fairfax, VA. 22031
Founded 1963. **Head**: Administrator- Lisa Turissini

Grades: N (6 weeks)-grade 6. **Enrollment**: 330 Co-ed. **Average Class Size**: 10-18.

Special Programs: Spanish, Music, Computer Lab, P.E., Dance; Values curriculum; Gymnastics, Intergenerational activities, Field Trips. **Extended Day** : 6:45 a.m.-6:30 p.m..

Plant: Extensive Playground, Swimming Pool 7 acres of grounds.

Admission: Parent/child Interview, Registration fee.

Tuition: (1993-94) $75-$170 wkly. Lunch K-6, $2.50 daily **Transportation:** Available upon request.

Future Plans: Construct new classroom space & expand to grade 8.

Summer Program: Recreational - games, arts & crafts, swimming lessons, field trips, picnics.

TARA-RESTON CHRISTIAN SCHOOL..........(703) 438-8444

10742 Sunset Hills Road, Reston, VA. 22090
Bible oriented, non-denominational 1972. **Head**: Mrs. Jane A. Rogers.

Grades: PreK-12. **Enrollment**: 300 Co-ed. **Average Class Size**: 25

Special Courses: French K-3 and High School, Latin 4-6 and High School. Computer. Bible req. Strong academic program, students generally 2 years ahead of average public school grade. ESL program and Federal Gov't approval for I-20 students.

Tuition: (1993-94) K-6, $1,710; 7-12, $2,016. **Transportation**: Limited

TERESA HOME SCHOOL..........(703) 524-7677

813 N. Cleveland Street, Arlington, VA. 22201 (grade 1-5)
2401 N. Ninth Street, Arlington, VA. 22201 (age 2-6 yrs)
1835 N. Nash Street, Arlington, VA. 22209 (age 2-6 yrs.)
Christian 1928. **Head**: Pamela Lassell, Principal.

Grades: N-5 **Enrollment**: 65 (grades 1-5), Co-ed. **Faculty**: 6 full-, l part-time. **Average Class Size**: 10-15.

Special Courses: Art, Music, Dance, Math, Computers, General Science; Advanced Reading Program. Informal Christian education offered, accelerated academic program for all grades. Piano lessons available. **Extended Day** 7 a.m.-6 p.m.

Athletics: Req. - Soccer available.

Plant: Library, Auditorium.

Admission: Parent/child interview; summer school may be req. Registration in March for following year.

Tuition: (1993-94) K-5, $375/mo. includes **Extended Day** (Nursery Day Care Extra)

Summer Program: Academic & camp programs include swimming, field trips, arts & crafts, and Bible School.

THORNTON FRIENDS SCHOOL..........(301) 384-0320

13925 New Hampshire Avenue, Silver Spring, MD. 20904
Quaker, 1973. **Head**: Douglas R. Price.

Grades: 9-12 & PG (somewhat ungraded). **Enrollment**: 54 Co-ed. **Faculty**: 8 full-time, 4 part-time. **Average Class Size**: 10.

Special Courses: College Preparatory (95%); Communication skills emphasized (writing, speaking, thinking); Development of strong inner self taught/learned; Socratic teaching method; Computer Applications.

Athletics: Not required. Interscholastic: Soccer, Basketball, Softball. **Publications**: Yearbook, Literary Magazine, Newspaper **Clubs:** Drama. **Community Involvement**: 40 hrs. per year required per student.

Plant: Library 8000 vol., Science Labs, Auditorium, Tennis Court, Playing Field. Use of nearby Gym, Pool, and Stables.

Admission: Transcript & Recommendations. Interview with parents & student - student may visit class. Rolling Admission. We are looking for students who are curious, alert, lively, interesting, persuasive, kind.

Tuition: (1993-94) $8,745 Lunch: Bring. Books: $300 *Dress Code*: Students dress may not advertise drugs, alcohol, smoking violence, or sex. **Financial Aid**: Available

TOWN & COUNTRY SCHOOL OF VIENNA...(703) 759-3000

9525 Leesburg Pike, Vienna, VA. 22182
Founded 1970. **Head:** Barbara Katz

Grades: N-3. **Enrollment**: 200 Co-ed. **Faculty**: 13 full-, 10 part-time.

Special Courses: French, Music, P.E., Library, Computers. **Extended Day Care** 7 a.m.-6 p.m.

Athletics: Trampoline, Tumbling, Softball, Kickball, Gymnastics, Soccer, Basketball. Regular P.E. program,

Plant: 6 acres, Swimming pool, Fields and Playground, Library.

Admission: Parent/child interview, transcripts, registration fee.

Tuition (1993-94) Half- day $310/mo.; Full day $558/mo. **Extended Day** Extra.
Transportation: Available.

Summer Program: Day Camp - age 2-l/2-grade 5. Extended hours, **Day Care** available. Swimming instruction, arts & crafts, sports, over-nights for older children, field trips.

TREE OF LIFE CHRISTIAN ACADEMY..........(410) 761-6102

1406 B Crain Highway, Suite 102, Glen Burnie, MD 21061
Head : Janet Giles

Grades: K-12 **Enrollment**: 40 Co-ed

Special Programs: ACE; Art, Music, P.E.

Tuition: (1993-94) $140/mo.

TRINITY CHRISTIAN SCHOOL..........(703) 273-8787

10520 Main Street, Fairfax, VA 22030
Interdenominational, 1987 **Head**: Mr. James L. Beavers

Grades: 1-8 **Enrollment**: 175 Co-ed **Faculty**: 10 full-, 3 part-time.
Average Class Size: 15

Special Courses: Latin, French, Spanish, in a Language Survey course, Grades 6-8. Art, Music, weekly; Religious Studies, req.: Bible classes daily, all grades, Chapel twice monthly.

Clubs : Some Athletic Clubs. **Publications**: Yearbook, Newsletter, Literary Magazine.

Admission: Apply after mid February. Registration fee $75. Interview required; Assessment Testing; References.

Tuition: (1993-94) $2,850. Books: $200-$300. *Dress Code*: Uniform req. **Scholarship Aid**: 10 partial.

Future Plans: Long range plans include the addition of High School grades; Search is underway for expanded school site.

TRUTH FOR YOUTH SCHOOL.........(301) 733-0712

41 Bryan Circle, Hagerstown, MD. 21740
Church of God (Universal). **Head**: Miss Lucille Marquiss.

Grades: K-8. **Enrollment**: 53 Co-ed. **Faculty**: 5 full-, 3 part-time.

Tuition: Donations -no tuition charge.

VIENNA JUNIOR ACADEMY..........(703) 938-6200

340 Courthouse Road, Vienna, VA. 22180
Seventh Day Adventist 1930. **Head**: Mr. Tim Boundy

Grades: K-9. **Enrollment**: 70 Co-ed. **Faculty**: 5 full-time.

Special Programs: English Handbells, Choir. **Extended Day**: 7:15 a.m.- 6 p.m.

Athletics: Baseball

Tuition: (1993-94) Call for information; Reduction for siblings.

WAKEFIELD SCHOOL..........(703) 364-4111

P.O. Box 869, Marshall, VA 22115
Founded 1971. **Head**: Tony Rex Wilson, Acting Headmaster

Grades: Pre K-12. **Enrollment**: 200 Co-ed., 6 Boarding (begins at 8th grade). **Faculty**: 30 full-, 2 part-time. **Average Class Size**: 18.

Special Courses: Latin 7-12, French 1-12, Spanish, German 7-12, & Homeric Greek 7-12. Math thru Calculus, Computer. General Science, Biology, Chemistry and Physics. History: British, U.S., World Civilizations, Philosophy of History, Geography, Political Science, Economics, Geopolitics. Studio Art, Art History; Music Theory & Literature, Instruments. Calligraphy. AP.: French, Spanish, German, Latin, English Composition and Literature, Calculus, Biology, Physics, Chemistry. Note: Trips to foreign countries, JCL convention, Model U.N. &

Harvard Model Congress participants; Hiking, Nature Study, Sightseeing, & Theater opportunities. **Extended Day** : PreK & K only, 2-4 p.m.

Athletics: Req. to grade 10. Intramural & Interscholastic: Volleyball, Soccer, Basketball, Field Hockey, Skiing, Tennis, Golf. **Clubs**: Math (including Chess, Checkers, etc.), Ski, Publications, Debate. **Publications**: Newspaper, Literary Magazine, Science Journal, Yearbook . **Community Involvement** : Scout Troops, Adopt a Highway Program; Provide food for needy at holidays; Work with elderly residents of assisted care facility; Environmental Club.

Plant: Library 7,000 vol.; 2 Science Labs, Art Studio; Leased facilities include auditorium and gym, playing fields, tennis courts.

Admission: SSAT, Wakefield Placement Test (March, and as needed) Transcripts, Recommendations, Interview. Note: Will not accept students expelled from other schools or those with serious learning disabilities.

Tuition: (1993-94) Day $3,000-$5,250. Boarding: Additional Charge. Lunch: Extra Books: $100-$250. **Transportation**: $270-$420 one way, $540-$890 both ways (varies according to distance). *Dress Code* Uniform req. **Scholarship Aid**: 20 full, 25 partial.

Summer Program: Review courses in Latin, Greek and English; Preparation for SSAT, Math, as well as other subjects as need indicates.

WALKERSVILLE CHRISTIAN FAMILY SCHOOLS...........(301) 662-0022

One, West Second Street, Frederick, MD 21701
Head: Gary Cox

Grades: K-12 **Enrollment**: All students enrolled in a home schooling program to be taught by parents.

Special Programs: Fully accredited Bible based Christian education. Individually structured curriculum based on child's test results, discernment of the child's nature, talents, and needs. Individual testing done at regular intervals. Six different high school diploma programs are available: Basic, College Preparatory, Vocational Tech., Christian Service, Business, Home Maker.

Admission: $75 Application fee, Interview, and Placement Tests.

Tuition: 1st child, $720; 2 children $900; 3 children $1,020; 4 or more children $1,080; (May be paid in monthly installments).Other low income reductions available. Books: $50-$150.

WASHINGTON ACADEMY..........(202) 686-5617

4301 Connecticut Avenue, N. W. (Van Ness Center, Suite 147) Washington, D.C. 20008
Founded 1981. **Head**: Dr. David Martin; Marcel Rocca(President)

Grades: 9-13. **Enrollment**: 30 Co-ed. **Faculty**: 5 full-, 10 part-time.
Average Class Size: 5-7.

Special Courses: Latin, Ancient Greek, French, Spanish, German, ESL; U.S., British, & World Literature; Gen'l Science, Biology, Chemistry, Physics, Ecology. Environmental Science; Computer Theory . Ancient, World, and U.S. History; History of Art. Government, Sociology, Anthropology, Economics, Philosophy, Psychology, Sociology; Speech. Note: Accelerated Programs; Independent study; College texts used in most classes. Concurrent enrollment with local universities- Faculty teach college majors only. Languages taught by native speakers.

In connection with the International Language Institute, a year round program of English and Academic Preparation for International Students who wish to enter U. S. High Schools is also available; usually very small classes with a high degree of personal attention.

Athletics: Not req.; Intramural Tennis, Interscholastic Soccer, Basketball, Softball. **Clubs:** National Honor Society, Drama, Camping. **Publications**: Newsletter, Yearbook.
Community Involvement: Community Service Program

Plant: Language Lab, Science Lab at a local college; Computer Lab.

Admission: Interview, School Visit. Biographical sketch; $50 fee with Transcripts & Standardized Tests.

Tuition: (1993-94) $6.300 Books: $150. *Dress Code*: Good taste.

Future Plans To expand facilities

WASHINGTON CHRISTIAN SCHOOL......... (301) 649 1070

1820 Franwall Avenue, Silver Spring, MD 20902
Protestant-Interdenominational 1960 **Head**: Jeff Doll

Grades: N3-8 **Enrollment**: 265 Co-ed **Faculty**: 12 full, 8 part-time
Average Class Size: 20; except Pre-school, 15.

Special Courses: Spanish 5-8; Art, Music; Bible; Science, Computer; **Extended Day**: Available

Athletics : P. E. Req.; Intramurals.

Plant: Library, Playing Fields, Science Lab.

Admission: Principal Interview. Registration fee $100 - applies to tuition (per family).

Tuition: (1993-94) K-grade 5, $3,144; 6-8, $3,348 (if paid in one payment); discount for siblings *Dress Code*: Appropriate and decent. **Scholarship Aid**: Some partial.

WASHINGTON EPISCOPAL SCHOOL..........(301) 652-7878 FAX (301) 652-7255

5161 River Road, Bethesda, MD 20816
Episcopal 1986 **Head**: Mrs. Isabelle Schuessler

Grades: N3-grade 6. **Enrollment**: 230 Co-ed **Average Class Size**: 16; Pupil/teacher ratio 1:8

Special Courses: French N4-6, Latin 5-6. Computer skills taught & used in relation to all curriculum areas. Music, Art, Chapel. Note: After school Enrichment Classes in Art, Sports, Music, Crafts, etc. **Extended Day**: until 6 p.m.

Athletics; P.E. req.

Admission: Applications accepted Sept.-Feb.1 (later if space available). Testing generally scheduled Nov.- Jan.,; Transcript & Independent School Recommendation Form; school visit by applicant req .

Tuition: (1993-94) N3, $4,900; N4 -grade 6, $9,100. *Dress Code*: Uniform req. grades 1-6. **Scholarship Aid**: Based solely on financial need.

Summer Program: Summer Camps, on and off campus, ages 4-13.

WASHINGTON ETHICAL HIGH SCHOOL..........(202) 829-0088

7750 16th Street, N.W., Washington, D.C. 20012
Founded 1964 (as Eberhard School). **Head**: David Mullen.

Grades: 9-12. **Enrollment**: 40 Co-ed. **Faculty**: 8 full-, 6 part-time. **Average Class Size**: 6

Special Courses: French I, II; Math: Algebra, Geometry, Trig, Pre-Calculus. Biology, Chemistry, Physics, Ecology, Contemporary Issues in Science. History and Social Science- Becoming Equal: Studies in civil Rights & The Holocaust; World Culture through Literature (English and Social Studies), Shakespeare, British Literature; Leadership; Street Law; Ethics. Remedial Reading & Math (Independent Study) Art, Crafts, Music. Advanced studies in Genre; Writing Seminar. Note: Untimed SAT's given to qualifying students; On site tutoring; Small classes and individual attention.

Athletics: Not req.; Informal Basketball & Volleyball; Involved in Washington Small Schools Association League for Interscholastic Soccer, Basketball, Softball. **Clubs**: Student Government, Fairness Committee, Yearbook, Community Action Committee. **Publications**: Literary Magazine, Newsletter, Yearbook. **Community Service**: All-school participation in social action project to be decided on by student committee. Students & Faculty work on such topics as hunger (working in soup kitchens and/or food banks, etc.) or the environment. Assemblies often have speakers who will address the topic.

Plant: Campus close to Rock Creek Park; Science Lab, Art Studio, Auditorium, Volleyball Court.

Admission: Parent/Child Interview with Director, Students generally visit school for one day. $40 Application Fee $50.

Tuition: (1993-94) $8,500 Books $50 deposit *Dress Code*: Appropriate dress is expected. **Financial Aid**: Some Available.

WASHINGTON INTERNATIONAL SCHOOL......(202) 364-1800

3100 Macomb Street N.W., Washington, D.C. 20008
Founded 1966 **Head**: Anne-Marie Pierce

Grades: N-12 **Enrollment** : 655 Co-ed **Faculty** : 65 full-, 12 part-time.
Average Class Size: 16

Special Courses: French & Spanish immersion in N & K. Bilingual curriculum req. in 1-3; offered in 4-8. In Intermediate and Upper Schools, History, Geography, & Literature are taught from a world perspective. All Upper School students take Biology, Chemistry, & Physics. In grades 11-12, all students follow the International Baccalaureate Diploma Program, which is the equivalent of an Honors or AP schedule. **Extended Day** : 8 am-6 p.m. through grade 6.

Athletics: PE Req. to grade 10. Intramural & Interscholastic. Track, Basketball, Soccer, Softball, Volleyball, & Tennis. **Publications**: Yearbook, Newspaper, Literary Magazine. **Community Involvement** 60 hrs. of community service req. in grade 11 & 12; some involvement at younger levels.

Plant: 2 campuses(8 buildings on 7 acres); 3 Libraries, 16,000 vol.; 7 Science Labs, 2 Art Studios, Darkroom, Auditorium, Basketball Court, Playing Field.

Admission : Applicant Visit, Interview, Recommendation, Transcript; Parent Interview. No standardized testing req. but achievement testing is done at time of interview. Apply before Feb. 1.

Tuition: (1993-94) $9,050-$10,500. Bring Lunch Books $50 deposit **Transportation**: Limited. **Financial Aid**: Available

Future Plans: New Gym/Theater complex within 8 yrs; 6 Science Labs to be renovated in summer of '94.

Summer Program: Academic review on a tutorial basis when needed. Summer Camp: Bi-lingual, ages 3-12. General camp activities. Summer Language Institute: French, Spanish, and ESL intensive courses for 9-12 yrs. old.

WASHINGTON-MCLAUGHLIN CHRISTIAN SCHOOL..........(301) 270-2760

6500 Poplar Avenue, Takoma Park, MD. 20912
Interdenominational 1983 **Head**: Dr. Pauline P. Washington

Grades: N-8 **Enrollment**: 160 Co-ed **Faculty:** 7 full-, 7 part-time.
Average Class Size: N-20; K-6, 27.

Special Courses: Art, Music. Computer grade 2-6. Religious Studies req.
Extended Day: 7 a.m.-6 p.m.

Athletics: P.E. req. **Clubs**: Glee, Ballet.

Plant: Library, Auditorium, Playing Fields, Computers.

Admission: Interview, Transcript; Grades 3-5, California Achievement Test.

Tuition : (1993-94) $2,500 for all grades including **Extended Day**. Lunch: Purchased on weekly basis. Books: $27-$146. *Dress Code:* Uniform req.

WASHINGTON NEW CHURCH SCHOOL...........(301) 464-5602

11914 Chantilly Lane, Mitchellville, MD 20721
Swedenborgian 1970 **Head**: Rev. Thomas H. Rose

Grades: K-10 **Enrollment**: 36 Co-ed

Tuition: (1993-94) K $800; Grades 1-10, 1st child $1,100, Reduced rate for siblings

WASHINGTON WALDORF SCHOOL....(301) 229-6107 (Lower School)
(301) 229-1040 (High School)

4800 Sangamore Road, Bethesda, MD. 20816
Founded 1969 Faculty Directed

Grades: N-12. **Enrollment**: 295 Co-ed. **Faculty**: 27 full-,13 part-time.
Average Class Size: 26 Lower, 16 High School.

Special Courses: An international educational movement with 500 Waldorf Schools world-wide. Waldorf Schools (Rudolph Steiner Education) offer a developmental approach balancing the academic, artistic, and practical to educate the whole child. Two foreign languages in Grades 1-12; Greek, 5; Latin, 6. History includes Ancient, Medieval, Renaissance, American, Modern. Social Studies and Geography. Art is an integral part of the curriculum, 1-12, and includes Painting, Drawing, Sculpture, Woodwork, Handwork. Music, Drama, and Eurythmy (movement to speech and music) throughout. Recorder and Strings, middle and high school Orchestra and Chorus. HS Math includes Trig, Calculus, and Computer. Four years of HS Science: Biology, Chemistry, Physics, and Earth Science. HS Typing, Driver's Ed.

Athletics: Full school program. Interscholastic: Member of Potomac Valley Athletic Conference. Interscholastic: Baseball, Soccer, Basketball, Cross Country, Softball, Track and Field, Volleyball.. Hiking and Camping in both Lower and Upper School. **Publications**: Yearbook, Literary Magazine. .**Community Involvement**: Class Service Projects.

Plant: Library 10,000 vol.; Computer Lab, 2 Science Labs, Art Studio, Music Room, Multi-purpose Room, Music Room, Wood Working Shop, Sewing room, Eurythmy Room. Tennis Courts, Playing Fields.

Admission: Lower School: Parent/child Interview with appropriate class teacher; Child visits class 2-3 days. High School: Parent /child Interview with class advisors; student visits HS for 2-3 days. $35 Application fee. Transcript ; Evaluation of Math and Language Skills.

Tuition: (1993-94) N (Half-day) $3,600; N (full day) $7,300; gr. 1-8, $7,300 9-12, $7,600 Lunch: Bring Supply Fees: $275-$400 *Dress Code*: Clean, neat & practical; no shirts with writing on them. **Financial Aid**: 41 partial.

Future Plans: Build an Auditorium/ Gym.

WAY OF FAITH CHRISTIAN ACADEMY..........(703) 573-7221

8800 Arlington Boulevard., Fairfax, VA. 22031
Founded 1975. **Head**: Rev. Ellen Blackwell.

Grades: K4-12. **Enrollment**: 125 Co-ed. **Faculty**: 12 full-, 6 part-time.
Average Class Size: 12-15.

Special Courses: Spanish 9-12. Computer, Word Processor. General Science, Biology, Physics; History: U.S., World, U.S. Gov't.; Religious Studies req.; Music-Vocal & Instrumental. Typing, Bookkeeping.

Athletics: Req. 1-10. Basketball, Softball, Soccer, Parallel Bars, Volleyball, Tennis. **Clubs**: Spanish. **Publications**: Yearbook, Newsletter.

Plant: Library, Science Lab, Chapel, Recording Studio, Tennis Courts, Playing Fields, Auditorium.

Admission: Parent/child Interview, $50 Registration fee. Enrollment, April lst - August 25th.

Tuition: (1993-94) Half-day K $1,200; K-12 $l,950 Books per semester: K4-3 $100; grade 4-12, $150. *Dress Code:* Uniform Req. for elementary grades.

WESTMINSTER SCHOOL..........(703) 256-3620

3819 Gallows Road, Annandale, VA. 22003
Founded 1962. **Head**: Ellis H. Glover, Jr.

Grades: K-8. **Enrollment**: 249 Co-ed. **Faculty**: 21 full-, 4 part-time.
Average Class Size: 13-14.

Special Courses: French K-8, Latin 6-8, Art & Music K-8, Study Skills, Drama. Teacher-centered instruction; disciplined learning environment; homework; early mastery of English grammar, spelling, etc.; strong History & Classical Studies program; frequent subject related field trips, all grades, including performing arts performances.

Athletics: Req. 1-8. Interscholastic: Basketball, Soccer, Track, Softball, 6-8. **Publications**: Newsletter, Literary Magazine, Yearbook.

Plant: Library 5,000 vol., Gym/Auditorium, Playing Fields, Outdoor Basketball Court. Note: 23 classrooms, carpeted, paneled, air-conditioned.

Admission: Placement Testing K-8, Jan.-March; Parent & child Interview. Registration new families March to May. Enrollment Contract.

Tuition: (1993-94) $5,100 Full-day K; $5,200-$6,200 (grades.1-8). **Transportation**: 10 bus routes, cost varies by zone. *Dress Code*: Uniform req.
Future Plans: Little Theater building, Camp site.

Summer Program: Academic Review (Reading, English, Math, etc.); Enrichment Courses (Science, History, Drama; French Grammar, Conversation, Culture, and Cooking) Basketball Camp; Tutoring (singly or group), mainly for lateral entry to middle grades up to 7.

WEST NOTTINGHAM ACADEMY.............(301) 658-5556

Colora, MD. 21917
Non-Denominational 1744 **Head**: Edward Baker

Grades: 9-12, P.G. **Enrollment**: 115 Co-ed, 20 Day. **Faculty**: 16 full-, 6 part-time.
Average Class Size: 6-8.

Special Programs: Remedial Reading & Math-Chesapeake Learning Center Program: for Dyslexic students; ESL.

WILLOWBROOK MONTESSORI SCHOOL.......... (301) 445-1563

8151 15th Avenue, Hyattsville, MD. 20783
Head: Mrs. Harvey

Ungraded: Ages 2 -9. **Enrollment**: 82 Co-ed **Faculty**: 4 full-time, 4 aides, 2 part-time aides.

Special Courses: Montessori program, Spanish, French. Creative Movement.
Extended Day: 7 a.m.-6 p.m.

Admission: Interview parent/child. Registration fee $25.

Tuition: (1993-94) N, $330/mo.; K-3, $350/mo. including **Extended Day**

Summer Program: Arts & Crafts, Sports. **Extended Day**: 7 a.m.-6 p.m.

THE WINCHESTER SCHOOL ....(301) 598-2266

3223 Bel Pre Road, Silver Spring, MD. 20906
Founded 1970 **Head**: Mary L. Rhim

Grades: N-1 **Enrollment**: 70 Co-ed **Faculty**: 3 full-time, 1 part-time; 4 full-, 3 part-time.
Average Class Size: 8-10.

Special Courses: Art, Music, Cooking, Baking. **Extended Day**: 7:30 a.m-6 p.m.

Plant: Libraries 500-800 vol.; Playing Fields.

Admission: Parent Visit, Interview. $24 Application fee. No Testing. Open to all children who are not severely handicapped, emotionally disturbed, or retarded.

Tuition: (1993-94) Half-day $310/mo.; Full-day $525/mo., (reduction for less than 5 days) includes **Extended Day** Bring Lunch

Summer Program: Organized play program with art, music, stories, water play, field trips

WOODBERRY FOREST SCHOOL...........(703) 672-3900

Woodberry Forest, VA 22989
Founded 1889 **Head**: John S. Grinalds

Grades: 9-12 **Enrollment**: 365 Boys, Boarding, 1 Day **Faculty**: 60 full-3 part-time.
Average Class Size: 12

Special Courses: Latin, French, Spanish, Japanese- all I-IV. Science : Biology, Chemistry, Physics, Physical Science: various electives include Relativity, Physiology, Microbiology, Human Genetics, Animal Behavior, Ecology. History- Ancient, European, U.S.-also electives including The Eisenhower Presidency, Winston Churchill & 19th Century Engineers (both studied through biographies)., Latin American Civilization. Principles of Business Management and Economics. Religious Studies req. for one semester-Sunday evening Chapel. Art-Painting,

Drawing, Sculpture, Architectural Drawing. Music, Typing, Driver's Ed, Drama Speech. AP.: History, Biology, Chemistry, Physics, English, European History, Languages, Math, Science, Computer Science.
Note: Each year 14 Seniors spend a trimester living in Cambridgeshire, England studying British Literature, History, Contemporary Britain and the Fine Arts.

Athletics: Req.; Intramural & Interscholastic. Football, Soccer, & Cross-Country, Indoor Track, Basketball, Wrestling, Swimming , Diving, Squash, Outdoor Track, Baseball, Lacrosse, Golf, Tennis. Also Weight Training, and Rapidan: an outdoor program of Kayaking, Rock-climbing, and Conditioning on a ropes/obstacle course. **Clubs**: Chapel Council, Civil War, Choir, Math, Model U.N., Literary Society, Outing, Rod & Gun, Science. **Publications**: Literary Magazine, Newspaper, Yearbook. **Community Involvement:** 60 hrs. of Community Service is req. for graduation.

Plant: Library 49,000 vol. with Audio-visual center & 3 viewing rooms; 5 Science Labs, Shop, Art Studio, Theater, 8 Dormitories, & Computer Lab., 3 Gyms, Auditorium, 11 Playing Fields, Both Indoor & Outdoor Pool, 3 Indoor and 14 Outdoor Tennis Courts, 1 Racquetball Court, 4 Basketball Courts, 8 Dormitories, 9 hole Golf Course, Indoor Track, 3 Squash Courts, Computer Lab.

Admission: SSAT, Interview at school. For consideration in first round acceptances, complete Application by Feb. 15. School seeks boys with proven academic success, desire to learn, good character, active involvement in extra curricular activities. $50 Application fee.

Tuition: (1993-94) Boarding, $15,800. Books & Supplies : $500 *Dress Code*: Neat attire- Long pants, collared shirt. **Scholarship Aid**: awarded to 25% of student body in '92.

Future Plans: Presently involved in fund drive to construct additional Faculty Housing, renovation of Dormitories and Classroom facilities.

Summer Program: 6 week Co-ed (boarding) Enrichment or Remediation program in major academic fields. Courses also in Art History, Computer, ESL; Language study programs abroad in France, Japan, Spain. Summer Camp: 4 week all sports camp, Boys 10-13. Includes weekend field trips to nearby activities, i.e. Baltimore Orioles baseball game.

WOODBRIDGE CHRISTIAN SCHOOL............(703) 670-0200

5023 Davis Ford Road, Woodbridge, VA 22192
Head: Rev. Dean Kennedy

Grades: K-11 **Enrollment**: 220 Co-ed **Faculty**: 10 full-, 4 part-time.
Average Class Size: 21

Special Programs: French 7-9; Algebra, Geometry, Computer. General Science, Biology. Virginia, American, & World History. Religious Studies required. Remedial Reading & Math. Art, Music. **Extended Day**: 6 a.m.-6:30 p.m.

Athletics: Not required. Girls Volleyball & Basketball; Boys: Volleyball, Basketball, Baseball, and Track. **Publications**: Yearbook

Plant: Gym, Auditorium, Playground, Soccer Field..

Admission: Interview

Tuition: (1993-94) $2,190; Books : Extra **Extended Day**: Extra *Dress Code*: Described in handbook. **Financial Aid**: Some available

Summer Program: Remedial and advanced academic program. General recreational activity program.

THE WOODS ACADEMY..........(301) 365-3080

6801 Greentree Road, Bethesda, MD. 20817
Catholic 1977. **Head**: Miss Madeleine S. Ortman.

Grades: Montessori Pre-school ages 3-5; Traditional class-room 1-8. **Enrollment** : 196 Co-ed. **Faculty**: 19 full-, 7 part-time. **Average Class Size**: 18.

Special Courses: French K-8; Computer 1-8; Kumon Math; Hands on & Lab Science 4-8;. Drama 7-8; Fine Art, Music, Religion. **Extended Day**: 7 a.m.-6 p.m.

Athletics: P.E. req. Intramural & Interscholastic. Basketball, Field Hockey, Softball, Soccer, Track & Field. **Clubs**: Computer Club; Cooking. **Publications**: Yearbook, Newspaper. **Community Service**: Committee on Caring works closely with Student Council to heighten their awareness and encourage helping others throughout the community.

Plant: Library 5,300 vol.; Science Lab, Garden (ties in with Science program); Computer Lab, Art Studio, Auditorium, Gym, Playing Fields, Tennis Courts.

Admission: School visit by applicant. Testing; Recommendations.

Tuition: (1993-94) $3,775-$5,775; Reduction for 3rd child. **Transportation**: Available. *Dress Code*: Uniform req. **Scholarship Aid**: Available

Summer Programs: Mid-June-mid July; Co-ed, Ages 4-11, 9 a.m.-1 p.m. Daily activities divided into Creative Writing/Computer, Sports and Games, Creative Arts, Hands on Science, Dramatic Art. $135/wk or $495 for 4 weeks. **Transportation & Extended Care**: Available.

WORD OF LIFE ACADEMY...........(703) 354 4222

5225 Backlick Road, Springfield, VA.22151
Head; Ralph Southerland

Grades: N-12 **Enrollment**: 300 Co-ed

Special Courses: All academic courses; Spanish I & II. Computer, Typing, Introduction to Business; Home Economics, Family Living; Art. Religious Studies. **Extended Day** 6:30 a.m. -6 p.m.

Athletics: P.E. req. Competitive (for Boys and Girls) Basketball, Soccer, Volleyball, and Cross Country.

Admission: Registration Fee $65 Pre school; $100 grades 1-12

Tuition: (1993-94) Half-day N, $235/mo.; N with **Extended Day** $380/mo.; Grades 1-6, $255/mo.(with **Extended Day** $380/mo.) Grades 7-12, $265/mo. Books: Extra. Note: Reduction in all areas for siblings.

Summer Program: Day camp, N-6; Day care available. Academic Enrichment program 6-12.

YESHIVA HIGH SCHOOL..........(301) 649-6996

1216 Arcola Avenue, Silver Spring, MD.20902 (Boys)
1910 University Boulevard, West, Silver Spring, MD. 20902 (Girls)
Jewish Orthodox 1963. **Head**: Rabbi Irving Merkin.

Grades: 7-12. **Enrollment**: 236 (111 Boys, 125 Girls) Note Boarding for out of town students
Faculty: 19 full-, 20 part-time.

Special Courses: French 10-12; Hebrew. Remedial Math. Art, Music. Math through Calculus, Biology, Chemistry. Religious studies req.; Typing, Drama, Family Living. AP.: English, Biology, Chemistry.

Athletics: Req. P.E. **Clubs**: Drama, Chorus. **Publications**: Yearbook. **Community Involvement**: Work at Hebrew Home for Aged.

Plant: Library 5000 vol., Science Lab, Art Studio, Gym, Playing Fields, Tennis Court.

Admission: Students admitted on basis of previous academic record and interviews; must come ` from Jewish religious background.

Tuition: (1993-94) grades 7-8 $5,500; grades 9-12 $6,300. **Financial Aid**: Available

Future Plans: To build new facility at 315 University Boulevard West for girls.

EDUCATIONAL SPECIALISTS

CENTER FOR APPLIED MOTIVATION, INC..................(301) 468-1200; FAX (301) 469-0708

6208 Montrose Road
Rockville, MD 29852

Director: Peter A. Spevak, Ph.D

Services: Established in 1984, the Cenrter for Applied Motivation specializes in motivating underachievers. We are a private organizaton whose professional staff are licesed psychologists who work full-time at the Center. Our success in treating underachievers is based on a developmental approach which addresses the problems of underachievement psychologically. Significant improvement in both attitude and performance can be achieved as a result of this approach. In addition to our Applied Motivation program for underachievers, we offer psychological assessment, career and vocational testing, and consultation and workshops to community, school, and parent groups.

As a piublic service, our newsletter, Issues in Development, Education, Achievement and Success (IDEAS), is available without charge.

Offices are conveniently located in Rockville, Maryland and Annandale, Virginia.

CENTER FOR UNIQUE LEARNERS........(301) 231-0115

5705 Arundel Avenue,
Rockville, MD. 20852

Executive Director: Patricia E. Williams, M.ED.

The Center for Unique Learners offers an environment where persons of all ages with learning difficulties can experience success. The Center's programs provide growth opportunities in a flexible, caring, and individualized manner.

All students begin by discovering how they learn best and are taught to use this information to help with weaker areas. Many students who come to the Center due to academic difficulties also suffer from low self-esteem and problems with peer relationships. Others have completed school but may still live with family unaware of how to develop skills for success at independent living. Most young adults benefit from career exploration as well. Because of these diverse needs, the Center offers assistance in all of these areas- academic, emotional, career, independent living and social skills, allowing each person to utilize only the services needed for their growth and success.

CERTIFIED LEARNING CENTERS, INC...................(301) 593-3700

11309 Classical Lane,
Silver Spring, MD 20901 (additional locations in Bethesda and Olney)

Director: Patricia Marie Felton, B.S., M. Ed.*

Services: CLC operates the largest centers in the Metro area offering complete educational, psychological, testing, psychotherapy, one-on-one remediation in most subjects and Scholastic Aptitude Test (SAT) and (PSAT) Preparation, as well as most other prep courses (i.e. LSAT, GMAT, GED, ASVAB, ACT, etc.) Career and College Counseling, Study Skills, reading, math workshops, speed reading, ESOL, and writing classes. Through an affiliation with Indiana University's Independent Study programs, high school and college credits can be awarded for make-up at our centers. Full support for home instruction is provided to parents educating their children at home.

CLC staff consists of certified teachers, with advanced degrees in subject specialties, including learning disabilities. Services are available in the student's home, at school or in our centers. Clientele served include pre-schoolers through adult students. Contractual arrangements are available to private and public schools for applicant screening, resource support and all services provided at the centers.

The Centers are open from 9 a,.m. to 9 p.m., seven days a week. The Director is State certified at the Advanced Professional level. She has been in practice for over fifteen years.

*Patricia Marie Felton Biography B.S. Elementary Education, West Chester University, West Chester, PA (cum laude); M.Ed., Special Education and Learning Disabilities, George Mason University. MD state certification at the Advanced Professional level. LD resource and self-contained classroom teacher for Fairfax County Public Schools. Elementary school teacher for Prince George's County Public Schools Pre-school instructor at the Accotink Academy in Springfield, VA. Established the Certified Learning Centers, Inc. in 1981.

COLLEGE BOUND...................(301) 468-6668

6809 Breezewoood Terrace
Rockville, MD 20852

Educational Counselor: Shirley Levin, M.A.

Services: Comprehensive college and career counseling for high school students and adults. Evaluation of academic credentials and extracurricular activities, advice on high school curriculum, summer activities, scheduling of SAT, ACH, AP, GRE, MCAT tests, etc. Assistance with all aspects of undergraduate and graduate college selection and application procedures, including planning college visits, interview preparation, essay evaluation.

Biography: B.A. (Honours), M.A., University of Toronto, Psychology; President, College Bound, Inc. 12 years; career/educational counselor, 24 years; College Programs Coordinator, Jewish Community Center. Published books: Summer on Campus: College Programs for High School Students; What to do Until the Counselor Comes , Member: ACCESS, WISER, PCACAC. Listed in Who's Who in the East.

EDUCATIONAL ASSESSMENT ASSOCIATES ....(202) 775-7443

1129 20th Street, N. W., Suite 400
Washington, D. C. 20036

President: June A. Wagner

Educational Assessment Associates was founded in January 1993 by the assessment staff of the former George Washington University Reading Center. The team of twelve educational specialists continues to offer a full range of diagnostic testing and consulting services to the Washington metropolitan community. Many years of testing at all levels, as well as teaching, research and review in the field of assessment, have kept the staff in the forefront of current educational philosophy and practice.

We believe that a person's cognitive ability or academic achievement cannot be expressed simply in numerical terms. Accordingly, our assessments are individually designed to identify and provide a thorough understanding of the client's learning patterns, significant strengths, and areas which need further development.

We also believe that the assessment process should be interactive; that is, the client's observations of his or her learning styles, problem-solving approaches and reactions to the assessments need to be discussed with the clinician and made an integral part of the evaluation.

Following the completion of the assessment session, the examiner analyzes the results of the valuation and prepares a written report, which is reviewed by members of the assessment team. The findings are presented to the client at a conference and recommendations and plans for their implementation are discussed. Follow-up consultation with school personnel, tutors, employers, or other concerned individuals can be arranged when appropriate

EDUCATIONAL ASSESSMENT AND CONSULTATION......................(703) 764-0222

5284 Lyngate Court, Suite 100,
Burke, VA 22015

Director: Dr. Constance Anderson   Co-Director: Susan W. Cole, M. Ed................ (202) 387-3126

Assessment: Comprehensive educational and cognitive assessment for children, adolescents, and adults. Evaluations are carefully planned to obtain a profile of an individual's functioning and processing in many different areas which may affect achievement.

Consultation: Dr. Anderson works closely with parents, school personnel, and/or the students to make provisions, identify resources, and discuss strategies to help students achieve their maximum potential. Appropriate school placement (public or private) is researched and recommended.

Instruction: Individual instruction is available for children, adolescents, and adults. Tutorials are tailored to the unique needs of each student; whether it be support in specific academic areas; organizational and study skills strategies; reading and writing; adapting learning styles for Learning Disabled students, or enrichment for the creative and gifted child.

Biography: Dr. Anderson: Doctorate in Special Education with support fields in Psychology and Human Development, George Washington University.

Susan W. Cole, M. Ed., M.A. in Special Education with a support field in Educational Psychology from U.C.L.A., and is currently a Doctoral student in the Reading Department at George Washington University.

EDUCATIONAL AND GUARDIANSHIP SERVICES....................(301) 530-6944

P.O. Box 2561
Rockville, MD 20847

Educational Specialist: Jeanette Simpson

Educational and Guardianship Services provides counseling by professionals with extensive knowledge and expertise on the U. S, educational system and experience working with foreign and diplomatic families. These professionals have a commitment to provide the best possible academic guidance and personal counseling to students of all ages and backgrounds.

Educational and Guardianship Services is ably headed by Mrs. Jeanette Simpson. She has over fifteen years of experiences as an Academic Counselor for private and public primary, secondary, and college level students. She has worked extensively with foreign students studying at U. S. institutions and has a comprehensive knowledge of the financial aid programs available for all age groups in the U. S. and abroad. Her other experience includes working for international organizations in the U. S., the United Kingdom, and the Middle East.

EDUCATIONAL GUIDANCE SERVICE....................(301) 652-1003

9213 Farnsworth Drive
Potomac, MD 20854

Director: Virginia Vogel Co-Director: Judith Reidy

Educational Guidance Service was founded to assist students and parents in their search for an appropriate school or college choice. Our complete counseling process begins with an evaluation of the student's developmental and academic needs, leading to a presentation of selected school or college programs. Assistance is given with interviewing skills, application materials, and curriculum decisions.

Virginia Vogel, Ed.S. and Judith Reidy, B.A. present backgrounds of extensive graduate work in counseling with higher education administration, experience in college admissions and high school college counseling. Virginia Vogel is a member of National Association of College Admissions Counselors and Independent Educational Consultants Association.

JANE ERVIN, P.P.D., Ed.D. ....(202) 337-1132

3604 Fulton Street, N. W.
Washington, D. C. 20007

Dr. Ervin has practiced in Washington, D. C. for over 20 years. She is particularly known for her concentrated programs for children with learning problems. As well as tutoring, she does educational testing and counseling for parents and children.

Jane Ervin also teaches study skills and reading comprehension courses to small groups based on her books published by Scholastic and Educators Publishing Service, which are used in schools throughout the nation.

Jane Ervin has authored over twenty educational books for children, parents, and teachers. She has appeared on television and radio and is a popular speaker at a wide variety of parent, teacher, librarian and volunteer groups. She received a post doctorate diploma and doctorate in education from U.C.L.A.

PATRICE B.F. GARVER, Ph.D. ....(703) 281-6058

2915 Hunter Mill Road, Suite 21
Oakton, VA 22124

Psycho Educational Diagnostician: Patrice B.F. Garver, Ph.D.

Dr. Patrice B.F. Garver's practice focuses primarily on working with Gifted, Learning Disabled, and ADHD students, including psychological and psycho-educational evaluation, psycho-educational consultation, therapy with children, parent and school consultation and home or school intervention programs. Prior to beginning her private practice, her experience included working as a special educator, a learning disabilities specialist, a psychometrician, and a school psychologist.

Dr. Garver was awarded her Ph.D. in developmental psychology specializing in assessment and treatment of children with learning and behavior problems. She also has Masters Degrees in the areas of special education and clinical/developmental psychology.

Normal office hours are Monday through Friday. Limited evening hours are available.

RUTH C. HEITIN, Ph.D....................(703) 519-7181

Educational Consulting Services of Northern Virginia
100 West Howell Avenue
Alexandria, VA 22301

Dr. Heitin has more than 20 years experience as a teacher and/or administrator in educational settings ranging from the preschool to the university level. Her hands-on approach includes holding certification as a regular and special education teacher in elementary and middle schools and as an Elementary Principal in Virginia. Dr. Heitin is also proficient in sign language. (PSE)

Dr. Heitin is an enthusiastic and powerful advocate for the educational rights of all children. Her practice includes psychoeducational assessment, support for identification of Attention-Deficit Disorder, diagnosis of learning disabilities, support for the Gifted/Learning Disabled student, advocacy, and assistance in the special education process.

ETHNA HOPPER ASSOCIATES.....(202) 686-1774

3925 Ingomar Street, N.W.,
Washington, D.C. 20015-1916

Director: Ethna Hopper College Consultant: Geraldine Fryer

Ethna Hopper works with families who are concerned about their child's school or college placement. Experienced in understanding the educational and emotional needs of young people, they visit and evaluate schools and colleges throughout the country. A consultant meets with the family to determine the goals of all concerned, and to help identify those schools or other sources of assistance which are appropriate. (see ad back cover)

GEORGIA K. IRVIN AND ASSOCIATES, INC....................(301) 951-0131 FAX (301)951-1024

4701 Willard Avenue, Suite 227
Chevy Chase, MD 20815

Director: Georgia K. Irvin

Georgia K. Irvin is nationally recognized for her personal knowledge of a broad range of schools that can meet unique needs of children entering nursery through post-graduate high school in day schools in the greater Washington area and boarding schools nationwide. Believing that understanding a child's strengths, interests and learning style is the key to selecting a school where the child will flourish, we meet with both the child and the parents before making specific recommendations. We work with local families, those moving into the area, and families from all over the country and abroad who are seeking boarding schools. Hallmarks of the firm are personal involvement with each child, commitment to each family and close personall contact with admissions officers.

Georgia Irvin was Director of Admissions and Financial Aid at the Sidwell Friends School for 15 years. She has served on the faculty of the National Association of Independent Schools Workshop for Admissions Officers, held membership on numerous local and national boards and committees, including the Secondary School Admission Test Board (SSATB). In 1988, she received the SSATB's prestigious Bretnall Award for her exemplary contributions to independent school admission. A brochure is available that describes the types of services, including a telephone consultation for those unable to travel to Washington. (see ad at back of book)

LEARNING TO LEARN....................(703) 922-5783

6028 Knights Ridge Way
Alexandria, VA 22310

Contact: Betty Brandon-Monroe, MA

Utilizing an individualized approach, full educational services for pre-school-adult are offered and include tutorials in all academic subjects, reading writing and study skills. Each program combines cognitive and personal aspects of learning, builds on strengths to overcome weaknesses, and incorporates personal expectations.

Diagnostic testing: WISC-R. WAIS-R, McCarthy, Independent school admissions testing and placement recommendations. SAT prep, College prep, Gifted programs, computerized learning, remediation of LD. Special attention to behavioral problems and emotional factors involved with learning.

In home tutors are available in all neighborhoods upon request. Flexible summer tutoring schedules are offered. Tutoring in office/home /school. Consultation with professional and schools. Liaison to school/ work/ business.

PATRICIA S. LEMER....................(301) 654-0944

6701 Fairfax Road
Chevy Chase, MD 20815

Educational Diagnostician: Patricia S. Lemer, M.Ed.

Patricia S. Lemer is an Educational Diagnostician who evaluates a child's aptitudes and achievement, and makes specific recommendations for instruction. Using a developmental, multi-disciplinary approach, she helps parents identify remediation most appropriate for a child experiencing academic difficulty. She also assists in locating appropriate educational alternatives if a school change is indicated.

As a consultant to many area independent schools, where she also does admissions testing, Ms. Lemer is familiar with the needs of students from nursery age through high school.
As a parent-child advocate, she also works with families who need assistance in obtaining special education services from their public schools.

MATH CENTER.....................(202) 244- 6853
Also known as the Hypatia Math Center

3311 Macomb Street N.W.
Washington, D. C. 20008-3329

Director : Mrs. Persis Joan Herold, M. Ed.

The Math Center follows recommendations by the National Council of Teachers of Mathematics, offering remedial tutoring; diagnostic testing' methods classes for teachers, tutors, and other interested adults;

classes in recreational math; and a group tutoring program for middle school students for six weeks during the summer.

Year-round tutoring is available by tutors trained at the Math Center. Our emphasis is on the use of manipulative materials for concept development, and games and other activities for practice and drill. Individual in-depth testing is required for remedial students from fourth grade up in order to ensure that tutors provide appropriate instruction.

BERNICE W. MUNSEY, Ed.D....................(703) 276-8228

3623 N. 37th Street
Arlington, VA 22207

Director: Bernice W.Munsey, Ed. D.   Associate: Wanda M. Juraschek, B.A.

Educational Counseling: Day School - Boarding School - College

Assisting individual students and their families with their educational decision by identifying appropriate educational options, admissions requirements, and application processes.

Educational Testing : Intelligence, Achievement, Gifted, Learning Disability, Admission, Myers-Briggs.

License: Licensed Professional Counselor; National Certified Counselor.
Education: B.A. Wellesley College; M.A. Hood College; Ed.D. Virginia Tech

Memberships: Independent Educational Consultants Association, National Association of College Admissions Counselors, Secondary School Admission Test Board, Association for the Gifted; American Counseling Association; Association for Psychological Type; Orton Dyslexia Society; Learning Disabilities Association of America; American Speech/Hearing/Language Association.

Relevant experience: First Educational Counselor, U. S. Dept. of State Family Liaison Office; founder and first president, Learning Disabilities Association of Virginia; secretary/board member, Learning Disabilities Association of America.

THE NORTHERN VIRGINIA FAMILY DAY CARE ASSOCIATION..........(703) 455-5214

P.O. Box 3712
Merrifield, VA 22116

The Northern Virginia Family Day Care Association has been serving the interests of its members since 1976. It supports 16 area chapters with over 450 total members. NVFDCA advocates safe day care home environments, developmentally appropriate activities, and positive provider-child interaction to give children the opportunity for future success.

PAUL K. PENNIMAN.......................(202) 364-4263

3522 Davenport Street, N. W.
Washington, D.C. 20008

Mathematics Tutor : Paul K. Penniman

Paul K. Penniman is a mathematics tutor who has fifteen years of experience in mathematics instruction primarily at the secondary school level. A former chairman of the mathematics department at the Edmund Burke School, he is familiar with all kinds of mathematics curriculum and all kinds of styles of teaching and learning mathematics. His tutoring experience ranges from the severely disabled to the highly able, from elementary students to college students and adults. He is the author of the forthcoming Beyond Innumeracy: How to Solve the Problem in the Math Classroom.

Mr. Penniman received his B.A. in mathematical sciences and his B.A, in psychology from Johns Hopkins University in 1978. He is a member of the National Council of Teachers of Mathematics and the Independent Schools Mathematical Association of Washington. In 1983, he helped found the Computer Association of Independent Schools.

RESOURCES FOR CHILDREN....................(202) 544-5222

124 12th Street, S.E.
Washington, D.C. 20003

Director: Susan Dranitzke, M.Ed., M.S.W.

Services: Educational Counseling for parents and children, problem solving for children with social, emotional, or learning difficulties; school or grade placement consultations for students in independent or public schools, D.C., MD., and VA.; ages served: nursery, elementary, high school, day or boarding, special education; parenting education groups.

Biography: B.A. Sarah Lawrence College, M. Ed. University of Maryland; M.S.W. at Catholic University. Licensed Clinical Social Worker. Twenty years experience as an educator and counselor. Directed Resources For Children since 1980. Previously Special Education Counselor, Dominion Day School, teacher at Yale Child Study Center and Capitol Hill Day School. Past President (1984) of Parents Council of Greater Washington.

RIDLEY & FILL, SPEECH & LANGUAGE ASSOCIATES, Chartered.....(301) 652-8997

4909 Hampden Lane, Suite 1
Bethesda, MD 20814

Ridley & Fill, is a group practice of speech-language pathologists. Services are provided to children and adults of all ages, and include diagnostic evaluation of speech-language problems, individual and group therapy, as well as other services.

Ridley & Fill's Summer Language Camp is a unique program incorporating language therapy and a regular day camp in one setting.

Ridley & Fill is known for its innovative approach to treatment of difficult problems such as classroom intervention with the language-learning disabled, and use of ultrasound in treatment of articulation disorders.

Ridley & Fill has affiliations with a number of private schools (such as Georgetown Day School, Sidwell Friends School, The Lowell School, Kingsbury Day School and National Children's Research Center) as well as with professionals in other disciplines.

A.B. ROCKPORT INSTITUTE..................................(301) 279-2383 (703)448-4440
FOR CAREER CHOICE & EDUCATIONAL DIRECTION

10124 Lakewood Drive
Rockville, MD 20850 (mailing address)

1485 Chain Bridge Road, Suite 302
McLean, VA 22101

Director: Nicholas Ayars Lore

Aptitude & Personality Testing as an aid to making educational decisions:

According to recent surveys, more than half of intelligent professionals feel they may have made a less than ideal career choice. As parents, we hope this will not happen to our own children. Yet, the process of selecting a college and choosing a major is, for many families, essentially the same as it was a generation ago.

For most young people, it is best to make a choice of general career direction by the time a college major is selected. The ideal time to begin an in-depth exploration of possible careers is between the ages of 15 and 17. Success and satisfaction in one's career depends to a great degree on a close fit between a person's natural talents, aptitudes, personality characteristics and the nature of their work. Families with a clear sense of these areas of strength make much better decisions throughout the educational years.

Since 1981, Rockport has offered career testing programs that measure these important traits. We can help you assure the most rewarding future for your son or daughter.

LAURA SOLOMON, Ed. S.......................(301) 495-0046

1109 Spring Street, Suite 706
Silver Spring, MD 20910

Special Education Consultant

Dr. Solomon has been working with children and families for twenty years. She specializes in school placement and diagnostic evaluation for children birth through high school, development of individual education plans (IEPS) , and consultation to parents and schools in the areas of social-emotional development, behavior management, curricular modifications, and instructional strategies.

SPECIFIC DIAGNOSTIC STUDIES, INC....(301) 468-6616

11600 Nebel Street, Suite 130
Rockville, MD. 20852

Director: Lynn O'Brien, M. Ed.

Specific Diagnostics is a full educational service for pre-school through adult; testing, admission testing for 18 area schools, tutoring, study skills, S.A.T. Prep. Founded in 1973 for the learning disabled, growth has expanded to assisting the under- achieving, different learning style-student. The nationally recognized S.O.S. Strengthening of Skills, study skills program teaches strategies in: listening, note taking, memory, time management, and test taking. SOS is given in the Rockville office throughout the school year as well as at numerous independent schools during the summer.

Specific Diagnostics has an experienced staff of 50 qualified educators and psychologists to meet the academic needs of all students.

RUTH B. SPODAK, Ph.D.....................(301) 770-7507

6119 Executive Boulevard
Rockville, MD 20852

Ruth Spodak is a licensed psychologist specializing in Learning Disabilities. She performs comprehensive psycho-educational evaluations for children and adults, to define their strengths and weaknesses, and determine if learning disabilities and/or attentional problems are interfering with their ability to achieve their potential. Full recommendations and consultation services are provided to coordinate academic modifications, therapeutic intervention, and school changes as needed.

Counseling is also provided for individuals and families to help in understanding and addressing learning disabilities within the family. Particular specialization with Gifted/Learning Disabled individuals.

WILLIAM R. STIXRUD, Ph. D., AND ASSOCIATES...................(301) 565-0534

1109 Spring Street, Suite 706
Silver Spring, MD. 20910

William R. Stixrud, Ph. D. and Associates is a group of experienced professionals dedicated to offering the finest in educational testing and tutoring of students with learning disabilities. Our tutoring objective is to help students become active, independent learners. We teach strategies to promote the development of specific skills, thus enhancing school performance. When appropriate, content from the classroom is used to enable students to successfully meet academic demands. Our students are taught to generalize strategies to new academic and real-life situations.

Our tutors have expertise in a variety of methods, including the Stevenson Language Skills Program, the Orton-Gillingham method and the University of Kansas Learning Strategies. Tutoring services include: reading, written language, math, study and organizational skills, cognitive strategy training and word processing skill. Tutoring is available at the client's home , school or our Silver Spring office.

FRANCES TURNER LTD. ....(301) 299- 2012

11137 Hurdle Hill Drive
Potomac, MD 20854

Director: Frances Turner, M. Ed., Educational Consultant

Services: Frances Turner offers experienced, personalized, educational consulting services built around the philosophy that the student be thoroughly involved in the process and the primary focus of the school selection decision. She provides educational guidance to parents seeking advice about appropriate schools that meet the academic, emotional and social needs of their children in grades Pre-K through High school in public/private day or boarding schools. Educational services provide consultations with parents and schools, screening for readiness, achievement testing, presentations to parent groups, classroom observations and specific recommendations about suitable schools procedures for admissions.

Biography Frances Turner has a Masters Degree in Education and Reading and has dedicated over 20 years to educating young people in public and private schools in New York and Maryland. She was former Assistant Head/Director of Admissions, Dean of Students and Reading Specialist at McLean School, Potomac, Maryland for 10 years. Frances has served on AIMS admissions workshops and been guest speaker for numerous school/parent organizations. She is currently a member of the Advisory Board of the Bender-Dosik Parenting Center.

WAKE, KENDALL, GREENE, SPRINGER, ISENMAN & ASSOCIATES......(202) 686-7699

5247 Wisconsin Avenue N. W., Suite 3A
Washington, D. C. 20015

Wake, Kendall, Greene, Springer, Isenman, & Associates provides a full range of educational and psychological services to individuals and schools throughout the Washington Metropolitan area. These include assessment, counseling, and school consultation for clients ranging from pre-school age to adult. All services are individualized to meet specific needs and are performed by licensed psychologists and experienced educational diagnosticians.

INDEX

INDEX KEY For SCHOOLS

+...........Extended Day or Day Care

*...........Ungraded

b...........Boarding

&...........LD/ED

x...........Grades to be added

N.W. Washington, D.C.

N.W. Washington, D. C. (continued)

	Name	Address	Grades	Sex	Page
+	Nat'l Presbyterian	Nebraska Ave.	N-6	C	109
+	Nationhouse Watoto	Park Road	N-12	C	109
+	Nativity Catholic Academy	Georgia Ave.	N-8	C	110
	Oakcrest	Yuma St	7-12	G	115
+	Our Lady of Victory	Whitehaven Pkwy.	N-8	C	120
+	Owl Schools	16th Street	N-6	C	121
	Parkmont	16th Street	6-12*	C	122
+	Rock Creek Intern'l School	California St.	N-3x	C	129
+	Roots Activity	N. Capitol St	N-8	C	129
+	Sacred Heart	Park Road	N-8	C	130
+b	St.Albans	Wisc. & Mass Ave.	4-12	B	130
+	St. Ann's Academy	Wisconsin Ave	K-8	C	132
+	St. Augustine	V Street	N-8	C	134
+	St. Gabriel's	Webster St.	K-8	C	137
	St. John's College H.S.	Military Rd.	7-12	C	138
+	St. Patrick's Episcopal	Whitehaven Pkwy.	N-6	C	143
+	Sheridan	36th Street	K-8	C	149
	Sidwell Friends (Mid/Upper)	Wisconsin Ave	5-12	C	150
	Washington Academy	Connecticut Ave.	9-PG	C	162
	Wash. Ethical Society	16th Street.	9-12	C	163
+	Wash. International	Macomb St.	N-12	C	164

N.E. Washington, D. C.

	Archbishop Carroll	Harewood Rd.	9-12	C	6
	Holy Name	West Virginia Ave.	N-8	C	81
+	Jewels of Ann	Bunker Hill Rd.	N-6	C	86
+	Nannie Helen Burroughs	50th Street	N-6	C	107
	St. Anselm's Abbey	S. Dakota Ave.	6-12	B	133
+	St. Anthony	12th & Lawrence	K-8	C	134
+	St. Benedict the Moor	21st. Street	K-8	C	135
+	St. Francis de Sales	Rhode Island Ave.	K-8	C	136

S.E. Washington, D.C.

	Name	Address	Grades	Sex	Page
+	Assumption School	High View Place	N-8	C	9
+	Capitol Hill Day	S. Carolina Ave.	N-8	C	27
+	Dupont Park School	Alabama Ave.	N-10	C	41
+	Holy Comforter	E. Capitol St	N-8	C	80
+	Little People's Paradise	15th Street	N-6	C	95
+	Naylor Road School	Naylor Rd	N-6	C	110
+	Our Lady of Perpetual Help	V Street	K-4	C	119
		Morris Rd.	5-8	C	119
+&	Our Lady Queen of Peace	Ely Place	N-8	C	120
+	St. Francis Xavier	O Street	K-8	C	137
+	St. Peter's Interparish School	3d Street	N-8	C	144
+	St. Thomas Moor	4th Street	N-8	C	146
+	Sr. Clara Muhammed	M. Luth. King Jr.Ave.	N-8x	C	151

Montgomery County, Maryland

	Name	Address	Grades	Sex	Page
	Acad. of the Holy Cross	Kensington	9-12	G	1
+	Barnesville School	Barnesville	N-6	C	10
+	Barrie Day School	Silver Spring	N-12	C	10
+&	Broschart School	Rockville	K-12	C	20
	Bullis School	Potomac	4-PG	C	21
+	Butler School	Germantown	N-6	C	23
+	Calvary Lutheran	Silver Spring	K-6	C	24
	Chas. E. Smith Jewish Day	Rockville	K-12	C	27
+&	Chelsea School	Silver Spring	1-12	C	29
+	Children's Learning Center	Rockville	N-5	C	32
+	Christ Episcopal	Rockville	N-8	C	33
	Concord Hill	Chevy Chase	N-3	C	36
	Connelly School,Holy Child	Potomac	6-12	G	38
	Ets Chaiyim	Rockville	N-8	C	46
+	Evergreen Montess	Kensington	N-6*	C	47
	Forcey Christian	Silver Spring	N-6	C	52
	French International	Bethesda	N-13	C	55
&	Frost School	Rockville	7-12	C	56

Montgomery County, Maryland (continued)

	Name	Address	Grades	Sex	Page
+	Gaithersburg Int'l Montess.	Gaithersburg	N-1*	C	57
b	Georgetown Prep.	N. Bethesda	9-12	B	59
	German School	Potomac	K-13	C	61
	Good Counsel H.S.	Wheaton	9-12	C	64
+	Grace Episcopal Day	Silver Spring	N-K	C	66
		Kensington	1-6	C	66
	Green Acres	Rockville	N-8	C	68
+	Hadley Acres	Gaithersburg	K-8	C	70
+	Harbor School	Bethesda	N-2	C	71
+	Hebrew Academy	Silver Spring	N-12	C	72
+	Hebrew Day Institute	Rockville	N-6	C	73
+	Hebrew Day/Mtgy County	Silver Spring	K-6	C	73
	The Heights	Potomac	3-12	B	74
+	Hellenic American Acad.	Bethesda	N-5	C	74
+	Holton Arms	Bethesda	3-12	G	79
+	Holy Cross Elementary	Garret Park	K-8	C	80
+	Holy Redeemer	Kensington	K-8	C	81
+	John N. Andrews	Takoma Park	N-8	C	87
	Landon	Bethesda	3-12	B	90
+	Lone Oak Montessori	Bethesda	N-5*	C	96
+	Maharishi School	Wheaton	N-8	C	98
+	Manor Montessori	Potomac/Rockville	N-3*	C	99
+	Mater Amoris	Ashton	N-6*	C	100
	Mater Dei	Bethesda	1-8	B	101
&	McLean School	Potomac	K-9	C	102
+	Montrose Christian	Rockville	K-12	C	106
	Muslim Community School	Potomac	N-9	C	106
+	Newport Preparatory	Kensington	N-12	C	112
+	Norwood	Bethesda	K-6	C	113
+	Oneness Family School	Chevy Chase	N-6	C	118
	Primary Day	Bethesda	N-2	C	125
	Puritan Christian	Laytonsville	N-12	C	126
	St. Andrew's Episcopal	Bethesda	6-12	C	131
+	St. Bartholomew's	Bethesda	K-8	C	134

Montgomery County, Maryland (continued)

	Name	Address	Grades	Sex	Page
	St. Francis Episcopal	Potomac	N-2	C	136
+	St. John's Episcopal	Olney	K-8	C	138
+	St. Peter School	Olney	K-8	C	144
b	Sandy Spring Friends	Sandy Spring	N-12	C	147
+	Sidwell Friends (Lower)	Bethesda	K-4	C	150
+	Sligo Adventist	Takoma Park	N-8	C	151
+	Spencerville Jr. Acad	Silver Spring	K-10	C	152
	Stone Ridge	Bethesda	N-12	G	153
&	Takoma Academy	Takoma Park	9-12	C	156
	Thornton Friends	Silver Spring	9-PG*	C	158
+	Washington Christian	Silver Spring	N-8	C	162
+	Washington Episcopal	Bethesda	N-6	C	163
+	Wash. McLaughlin Christ.	Takoma Park	N-8	C	165
	Washington Waldorf	Bethesda	N-12	C	165
+	Winchester School	Silver Spring	N-1	C	168
+	Woods Academy	Bethesda	N-8	C	170
b	Yeshiva High	Silver Spring	7-12	B/G	171

Prince Georges County, Maryland

+	Ascension Lutheran	Landover Hills	N-7	C	8
+	Beddow School	Ft. Washington	N-8*	C	12
+	Beltsville Adventist	Beltsville	K-8	C	12
	Berwyn Baptist	College Park	N-6	C	13
+	Bethel Bible Christian	Camp Springs	N-8	C	13
	Bishop McNamara	Forestville	9-12	C	16
	Canterbury School	Accokeek	7-12	C	25
+	Capitol Christian	Upper Marlboro	K-12	C	26
	Christian Family Montessori	Mt. Rainier	N-6*	C	35
+	Clinton Christian	Upper Marlboro	N-12	C	35
+	Concordia Lutheran	Hyattsville	N-8	C	37
+	Cornerstone Christian Acad	Bowie	N-12	C	39
	DeMatha High	Hyattsville	9-12	B	40

Prince Georges County, Maryland(continued)

	Name	Address	Grades	Sex	Page
	Divine Peace Lutheran	Largo	1-8	C	41
	Elizabeth Seton	Bladensburg	9-12	G	44
+	First Baptist School	Laurel	N-6	C	50
+	Freedom Christian	Forestville	N-12	C	55
+	Friends Community School	College Park	K-6	C	56
+&	Grace Brethern	Clinton	N-12	C	65
		and Temple Hills	1-5	C	65
	Grace Christian	Bowie	K-8	C	65
+&	Henson Valley	Temple Hills	N-6*	C	75
+	Holy Family	Hillcrest Heights	N-8	C	80
+	Holy Trinity Episcopal	Bowie	K-6	C	82
+	Hope Christian Acad.	College Park	N-6	C	83
+	Independent Baptist	Clinton	K-12	C	84
+	Julia Brown Montessori	Laurel	N-3	C	87
+	Lanham Christian	Lanham	K-12	C	92
	Laurel Baptist	Laurel	K-12	C	92
+	Montessori Children's	Bowie	N-8*	C	103
+	Nat'l Christian Acad.	Ft. Washington	N-12	C	108
+	New City Montessori	Hyattsville	N-5*	C	111
+	New Hope Acad.	Landover Hills	N-8	C	111
+	Our Lady of Sorrows	Takoma Park	N-8	C	120
+	Paint Branch Montessori	Adelphi	N-6*	C	122
	Potomac Heights Christian	Indian Head	N-8*	C	124
+	Queen Anne	Upper Marlboro	7-12	C	126
+	Riverdale Baptist	Upper Marlboro	N-12	C	128
+	St. Joseph's	Beltsville	K-8	C	140
+	St. Mary's Star of Sea	Accokeek	K-8	C	143
	St. Vincent Palloti	Laurel	9-12	C	147
	Silver Spring Christian	Hyattsville	9-12	C	150
&	Summit School	Upper Marlboro	1-8	C	155
	Wash. New Church School	Mitchellville	K-10	C	165
+	Willowbrook Montessori	Hyattsville	N-4*	C	167

Anne Arundel & Howard Counties, Maryland

	Name	Address	Grades	Sex	Page
+	Aleph-Bet Jewish Day	Annapolis	K-5	C	3
+&	Annapolis Area Christian	Annapolis	K-12	C	4
+	Antioch Christian	Arnold	N-12	C	5
	Archbishop Spalding	Severn	9-12	C	7
	Arnold Christian Acad.	Arnold	N-6	C	8
+	Atholton Adventist	Columbia	N-8	C	9
+	Bethel Christian Acad.	Savage	N-8x	C	13
+	Book of Life Academy	Annapolis	N-l2	C	18
+	Calvary Baptist	Glen Burnie	N-12	C	23
+	Chesapeake Academy	Arnold	N-5	C	31
+	Chesapeake Montessori	Annapolis	N-6*	C	31
	Gibson Island School	Pasadena	K-5	C	62
	Glenelg School	Glenelg	K-12	C	62
+	Granite Baptist Church	Glen Burnie	K-12	C	67
&	Harbour School	Annapolis	N-12	C	71
+&	Indian Creek	Crownsville	N-8	C	85
+	Key School	Annapolis	N-12	C	88
	Lake Shore Christian	Pasadena	N-10	C	90
+	Love of Learning Montessori	Columbia	N-6*	C	96
	Martin Barr Adventist	Gambrills	K-8	C	100
+	Montess. Int. Children's House	Annapolis	N-4*	C	104
+	Odenton Christian	Odenton	N-10	C	117
	Old Mill Christian Acad.	Millersville	N-12	C	118
+	Open Door Christian	Hanover	N-7	C	119
+	St. Andrews Elementary	Edgewater	N-5	C	131
	St. John Evangelist	Severna Park	K-8	C	140
	St. Martin's Evangelical	Annapolis	N-6	C	142
+	St. Mary's School	Annapolis	K-l2	C	143
	Severn School	Severna Park	6-12	C	148
	Tree of Life Christian Acad.	Glen Burnie	K-12	C	159

Frederick & Hagerstown, Maryland

	Name	Address	Grades	Sex	Page
+	Banner School	Frederick	K-8	C	9
+	Broadfording Christ.	Hagerstown	N-12	C	19

Frederick & Hagerstown, Maryland (continued)

	Name	Address	Grades	Sex	Page
b	Frederick Acad. Visit.	Frederick	N-8	G	54
+	Frederick Christian	Frederick	N-12	C	54
+	Frederick Adventist	Frederick	K-8	C	54
	Grace Academy	Hagerstown	K-12	C	64
+	Heritage Academy	Hagerstown	N-12	C	75
+b	Highland View	Hagerstown	9-12	C	77
	New Life Christian	Frederick	K-12	C	111
b	St. James School	St. James	8-12	C	137
	St. John's Literary	Frederick	9-12	C	139
	St. Maria Goretti	Hagerstown	9-12	C	141
	Truth for Youth	Hagerstown	K-8	C	160
	Walkersville Christian	Frederick	K-12	C	161

Alexandria, Virginia

	Name	Address	Grades	Sex	Page
+&	Alex. Country Day	Russell Rd.	K-8	C	4
+	Aquinas Montessori	Mt. Vernon Hwy.	N-6*	C	6
&	Bishop Ireton	Cambridge Rd.	9-12	C	15
+	Brentwood Academy	Nalls Rd.	N-3	C	18
+	Browne Academy	Telegraph Rd.	N-8	C	20
+	Burgundy Farm	Burgundy Rd.	N-8	C	22
+	Calvary Road Christian	Beulah St.	N-8	C	24
	Chesapeake Ability	Industrial Dr.	K-12*	C	30
+	Christian Center	Franconia Rd.	N-6	C	34
&	Different Drum	Telegraph Rd.	9-12*	C	41
+	Elfland School	Glenwood Dr.	N-1	C	43
+	Engleside Christian	Highland Ln.	K-12	C	45
b	Episcopal High	N. Quaker Ln.	9-12	C	45
+	Gesher Jewish Day	Valley Drive	K-6	C	61
+	Grace Episcopal	Russell Rd.	N-5	C	66
+&	Heritage Academy	May Blvd.	N-6	C	76
+	Immanuel Lutheran	Bellaire Rd.	K-6	C	84
	Islamic Saudi Academy	Richmond Highway	K-12	C	85
&	Leary School	Lincolnia Road	1-PG*	C	92
+	Montessori of Alex.	Florence Lane	N-6*	C	104

Alexandria, Virginia (continued)

Fairfax and Prince William Counties, Virginia

Fairfax and Prince William Counties, Virginia (continued)

	Name	Address	Grades	Sex	Page
+	Sudley Montessori	Manassas	N-3*	C	155
+&	Sydenstricker	Springfield	N-2	C	156
+	Talent House	Fairfax	N-6	C	157
	Tara/Reston Christian	Reston	N-12	C	157
+	Town & Country Vienna	Vienna	N-3	C	159
	Trinity Christian	Fairfax	1-8	C	159
+	Vienna Jr. Academy	Vienna	K-9	C	160
	Way of Faith Christian	Fairfax	N-12	C	166
	Westminster School	Annandale	K-8	C	167
+	Woodbridge Christian	Woodbridge	K-11	C	169
+	Word of Life Academy	Springfield	N-12	C	171

Arlington & Falls Church, Virginia

&	Bishop Denis O'Connell	Arlington	9-12	C	15
+	Cloverlawn Academy	Arlington	N-6	C	36
+	Congressional School	Falls Church	N-8	C	38
+	Early Years Montessori	Falls Church	N-3*	C	42
+	Falls Church Chldrn's House	Falls Church	N-2*	C	49
	Grace Lutheran	Falls Church	K-8	C	67
	Juniper Lane	Falls Church	N-3	C	87
	Montess. Sch. Holmes Run	Falls Church	N-6*	C	105
	Our Savior Lutheran	Arlington	K-8	C	121
	Rivendell School	Arlington	K-8	C	128
+	Teresa Home	Arlington	N-5	C	157

Loudoun and Fauquier Counties, Virginia

+&	Faith Christian	Sterling	K-8	C	49
b	Foxcroft	Middleburg	9-PG	G	53
+	Highland School	Warrenton	K-8	C	76
	Hill School	Middleburg	K-8	C	78
	Leesburg Christian	Leesburg	N-12	C	93
+&	Loudoun Country Day	Leesburg	N-8	C	96
	Notre Dame	Middleburg	9-12	C	114
b	Wakefield Country Day	Marshal	N-12	C	160

Other Area Schools

Index to Educational Specialists

NOTES